TURNING POINTS IN
SOCIAL SECURITY

Turning Points in Social Security

From "Cruel Hoax" to
"Sacred Entitlement"

SHERYL R. TYNES

STANFORD UNIVERSITY PRESS
Stanford, California   1996

Stanford University Press
Stanford, California
© 1996 by the Board of Trustees of the
Leland Stanford Junior University
Printed in the United States of America

CIP data appear at the end of the book

Stanford University Press publications are distributed
exclusively by Stanford University Press within the
United States, Canada, Mexico, and Central America;
they are distributed exclusively by Cambridge
University Press throughout the rest of the world.

To my Grandmother, Verne F. Milette

and

her grandchildren's children

Acknowledgments

Writing a book is a journey in many senses. It is an adventure with its share of disappointment and ecstasy; like most journeys, it is preferable to share the burdens and joys. Various colleagues, friends, and family members provided me with intellectual and emotional sustenance and camaraderie along the way. I would especially like to thank the following individuals.

The journey began with writing a dissertation, and therefore my dissertation committee requires thanks, if not first-born children. I thank Doug McAdam and Neil Fligstein for their high standards and expert lead on much of the journey. They spent countless hours with me—many of our deliberations were the most inspirational and intellectually invigorating exchanges I experienced as a student. They are my heroes and friends. My sincerest appreciation and respect also go to Courtney Cleland, Travis Hirschi, and Jim Shockey for their support and encouragement. This group allowed my work to move forward, offering just the right combination of support and constructive criticism. Beverly Armstrong was there for the duration, and her worth to all who know her is incalculable.

In doing the research, countless archivists and librarians deserve special credit. They provided the road maps in collecting the data and tracing the legislation, and without their assistance, it is likely that I would still be trying to figure out a systematic way to do my work. Mary E. Rephlo, Archivist, Legislative Archives Division of the National Archives, shared her expertise above and beyond the call of duty, as did Thomas Connors of the George Meany Memorial Archives of the AFL-CIO. Helen Laney, the Librarian of the National Association of Manufacturers, was generous and helpful with the material held in the NAM library. Anne Harvey and Angela R. Taylor of the American Association of Retired Persons provided helpful information regarding AARP. At the Social Security Administration, Jan Olson, Orlo R. Nichols, and Barbara A. Lingg provided useful data, requiring much of their time and energy.

Several other individuals deserve special mention. Meredith McGuire provided research money when it was much needed, as well as countless hours of encouragement and advice, and John Donahue has strengthened my persistence by being a stable and energetic role model. Joane Nagel, Theda Skocpol, and Joey Sprague provided votes of confidence and tremendously insightful comments on this work. Finally, friends and family continue to sustain me, enabling me to excel while retaining a sense of humor that comes from healthy priorities. I give my love and thanks to my parents, Bob and LaVerne; to my husband, Gary; to my brother Gene; and to my friends Hank, Kelly, and Teri. For my son Grayam, daughter Tess, and nieces Sadie and Heidi, I hope this work serves in some small way to make the world a more secure, just, and safe place as they grow up. The book is dedicated to these children and to my grandmother, for their wisdom and joie de vivre.

S.R.T.

Contents

Figures and Tables

Figures

Tables

TURNING POINTS IN
SOCIAL SECURITY

CHAPTER ONE

Introduction: From Socialist Menace to Sacred Entitlement and Beyond

DURING THE DEPTHS OF the Great Depression, with the official unemployment rate at 25 percent, imagine the boldness of proposing a new tax on both employers and employees to fund a compulsory federal old-age insurance program. Yet this was what the Roosevelt administration did in the 1930s in proposing a tax on payroll (one-half to be paid by the employer and one-half to be paid by the employee). Representative Charles Eaton, a Republican from New Jersey, warned of the precedent such a tax would set—a model for "sovietizing" the distinctive American values of self-reliance and personal initiative. In his opinion, these were embodied best in American industry (CR 1935: 5583). There were Democrats who agreed. Representative John J. O'Connor (D-New York), envisioned a future including old-age insurance as one where we would have the "spectacle of sons and daughters giving up supporting their parents and wanting the Federal Government to support them. We of the great State of New York take care of our deserving aged people, but we do not deceive and delude them" (CR 1935: 5461).

Despite the early controversy, today this tax is one of those least questioned by the American public. Its widespread acceptance is remarkable, especially considering the magnitude of the tax for the average worker. Similarly, there was concern initially over the "Big Brother" potential of Social Security numbers, yet these numbers are widely used today as identification numbers without the least public notice.

It is clear that attitudes have come a long way. Although Social

Security now seems relatively sacrosanct, it was not born that way in 1935, nor did it even represent the same things to Americans then as it came to later. Most early proponents of the program did not intend for it to become the cornerstone of an individual's retirement income, but as old-age insurance benefits grew in relation to other retirement income over the decades, Americans have had to be constantly reminded of the *supplemental* nature of old-age insurance.

These reminders were necessitated not only because of a lapse of collective memory but also because of people's increased expectations based on changes in the program over the years. Figure 1 shows how the amount of preretirement income replaced by old-age insurance benefits of an average worker (i.e., the "replacement rate") has changed dramatically over time. When old-age insurance benefits were first paid in 1940, typical beneficiaries received 27 percent of their preretirement income in old-age insurance benefits. This replacement rate fell to a historic low of 16 percent in 1949, and climbed to a high of 54 percent in 1981. Between 1981 and 1985, the replacement rate fell to 41 percent. These changes are important because they represent a "change in the deal," or a change in the nature of this social contract between generations. These changes represent altered thinking regarding the minimum level of provision for our retirement years that should be covered by society-wide old-age insurance benefits.

None of this is to imply that there was universal opposition to Social Security in the 1930s, or universal acceptance at the close of the twentieth century. Edward D. Berkowitz addresses the "development of the welfare state from conflict to consensus and back again" (1991: xvii). Indeed, during the 1980s it was nearly impossible to listen to a newscast or read a newspaper or magazine that did not address the "crisis" in Social Security and the variety of proposals to deal with this crisis. But there was considerable diversity of opinion: some commentators declared that Social Security was a total failure, others said it was a partial success, and still others argued that it represented an overwhelming victory (Oriol 1987). Some described Social Security as an unsound intergenerational chain letter; at the other extreme, some analysts considered it the best U.S. example of community and mutual support. When study-

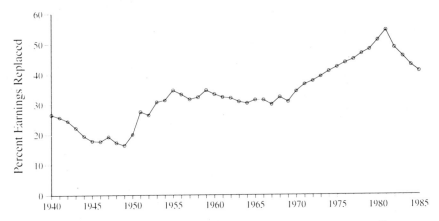

Fig. 1. Percent of earnings replaced by old-age insurance, 1940–1985. (Source: Orlo R. Nichols, SSA)

ing policymaking in the 1980s, however, one could not help noting that old-age insurance seemed relatively inviolable. Even the Great Communicator himself, President Ronald Reagan, was rebuffed when he suggested relatively modest changes in the program.

Despite the range of evaluations, Social Security is clearly the most far-reaching and enduring antipoverty program in U.S. history. In 1959, according to the U.S. Census Bureau, 35 percent of the elderly lived in poverty; today only 12 percent do, compared with 14.2 percent of the population overall (DeParle 1993). When initiated in 1935, Social Security was a noteworthy experiment in sociopolitical policy formation, and its endurance, inviolability, and taken-for-granted nature are evidence of its success. The research in this volume analyzes key historical turning points in order to understand the various forces that led to the endurance of the program.

Over the years, there have been significant and numerous threats to the Social Security program. Even after the major hurdle of passing the legislation was overcome, there were no appropriations for staff, equipment, or supplies. Later, the Supreme Court agreed to review the constitutionality of mandatory participation in a federally administered old-age insurance program. In the first years of the program, some employers were "noncompliant" in registering workers. World War II deflected attention away from domestic programs, and the communist-scare rhetoric of the 1950s and later meant that some Americans advocated increased military spending instead of expanding Social Security. During the 1970s, when the expected trade-off between unemployment and inflation failed to materialize, the resulting "stagflation" (rising unemployment coupled with higher prices), dealt a double blow to the trust funds.

In spite of these challenges, old-age insurance expanded in terms of both workers covered and benefits offered. Social Security bureaucrats borrowed typewriters and personnel in order to launch the new program in 1935. During the 1936 presidential campaign, Roosevelt's Republican opponent, Alf Landon, lambasted Social Security as " 'unjust, unworkable, stupidly drafted and wastefully financed . . . a cruel hoax' " (McNutt 1940; see also Schlesinger 1960: 613–14). Significantly, Roosevelt won 61 percent of the popular vote in 1936, and many interpreted this as a mandate for Social Security. The constitutional threat to the program was weathered when the Supreme Court declared old-age insurance constitutional in 1937. After about 1940, employer noncompliance was minimal, and American public opinion remained solidly in support of the program. Benefits and coverage were greatly expanded, and even after the crisis in the late 1970s and early 1980s, some pronounced the trust funds as fiscally healthier than in a long while (see Weaver 1990 and the sources she cites). Today Social Security is often called an "entitlement," and indeed, most of us would feel the detrimental effects of a collapsed system, either personally or because of elderly grandparents or parents who depend solely or partly on Social Security benefits.

Considering this political history of Social Security, who or what determined the shape, direction, and endurance of these turning points over time? This book is concerned with several key questions:

1.What were the important legislative turning points in the political history of Social Security legislation?

2.What individuals or organizations were active in the social or political debates surrounding these turning points?

3.Why were some of these actors more successful than others in influencing policy outcomes, and what are the opportunities or constraints these organizations faced?

A second major concern is the often contradictory interpretations of the development of Social Security and the role of the state. Building upon prior analyses of policymaking dynamics, my interpretation knits together the key insights from major theories into a more dynamic explanation of the development of Social Security. It acknowledges the economic, political, and cultural context but also takes into account the importance of specific organizational and social movement actors in shaping the historical institutionalization of Social Security. This theoretical framework allows for complexity and feedback in the political process, and helps to account for the groups that influence change over time.

This focus on the entire history of Social Security allows us to determine which factors are evident across time and which are period-specific. In addition to broad historical material, I analyze the roles of specific organizations: the Social Security Administration, business and industrial associations such as the U.S. Chamber of Commerce and the National Association of Manufacturers, elderly advocate groups such as the American Association of Retired Persons and the National Council of Senior Citizens, and labor unions, including the AFL-CIO. These organizations actively altered the political and economic landscape. The account of key turning points and organizational actors leads to a multicausal model that draws widely from the literature in sociology, organizational theory, social movements, political science, history, and economics.

In the remainder of this introductory chapter, I review some of the earlier literature regarding Social Security, and propose an alternative model that systematically utilizes organizational variables to study key turning points in old-age insurance legislation. Following this discussion, I present the five time periods that emerged—the time periods that frame the organization of the remainder of the book.

What Forces Shape Policymaking?

A decade ago, the United States seemed mired in warnings of the "crisis" in Social Security. Knowing that this crisis did not occur over night, I wondered what had led to the predicament of the 1980s. This question led me to study the organizations that animated the political history of Social Security from the 1930s through the 1990s. Although I did not begin with an organizational framework in mind, I gradually came to realize that organizational actors, in the broadest senses of those words, were central.

Initially, I consulted a wide variety of secondary sources, many of which helped shape this volume. Martha Derthick's *Policymaking for Social Security* (1979) is probably the best known and deservedly acclaimed work on social insurance in the United States. This work by a political scientist demonstrates that administrative leaders of social insurance in the 1930s were fundamentally in sympathy with the lower classes. My own research corroborates this point, but Derthick's focus is on policymakers and their choices, independent of social conditions (1979: 12). As comprehensive and systematic as her analysis is, it does not recognize the importance of the larger social context in which policy choices and changes were made. Derthick relies heavily on official memoirs and oral histories conducted in the 1960s (Cates 1983: 151–52), which are inevitably tinged by policymakers' reconstructions using retrospective accounts. Also, whereas Derthick organizes her analysis according to the specific actors ("Program Executives," "Congress," "Political Executives," etc.), I have chosen to allow the fascinating story of Social Security to unfold in a chronological analysis.

Other important works that I build on include Edward D. Berkowitz's *America's Welfare State: From Roosevelt to Reagan* (1991). Berkowitz presents three relatively short case studies of old-age insurance, welfare, and health insurance. He focuses mostly on the policymaking process, as viewed from within bureaucracies, and less on actors outside the administrations (such as business or labor). By contrast, my account of old-age insurance policymaking focuses on a wide variety of actors both inside and outside state bureaucracies, and it addresses only old-age insurance in greater detail. The analysis presented here differs from Jerry R. Cates's *In-*

suring Inequality: Administrative Leadership in Social Security, 1935–54 (1983) and Jill Quadagno's *The Transformation of Old Age Security: Class and Politics in the American Welfare State* (1988) in that it is more far-reaching historically (they end with 1954 and the 1970s, respectively). Both these works make useful conflict analyses, emphasizing the power of elite actors in policymaking to reproduce the capitalist system and its inequalities.

Derthick presents a sympathetic perspective of administrative leadership; Cates comes to a diametrically opposite conclusion: administrators' "goal achievement, organization-as-tool view is the appropriate interpretation of administrative leadership's role in producing social security's antipoor bias" (1983: 136). Cates says: "*Social insurance* is a fluid concept, a social and political construction. It means largely what we want it to mean; those with strategic placement and command of powerful organizational resources have been able to exert great influence over our perception of the concept" (1983: 155). I would agree, but I would also emphasize that there are powerful organizational actors *outside* the administrative leadership that have influenced the shape of current-day policies. Similarly, Quadagno concludes that welfare programs are "not unique features of advanced capitalist nations but have always served to regulate the labor supply. . . . The social organization of production determines the nature and form of relief programs" (1988: 6).

Rather than a monocausal perspective (e.g., capital always benefits or wins, or bureaucrats or administrators uniformly get their way), the organizational focus that I offer is a dynamic explanation that allows for changing political fortunes and alignments. It is at once more detailed and broader than previous works—more detailed in the analysis of specific legislative turning points, and broader in its focus on the entire history of these shifts. Different historical periods present organizations with different opportunities for and constraints on action. Persistence favors organizations with resources when new opportunities for action arise. Unlike some writers on the subject, I am convinced that social movements can make a difference, that capital does not always win, and that administrators do not have total control over the shape and direction of policymaking. No single element explains all these legislative turning points, and in interpreting the dynamism and complexity of the political process we must take full account of this richness.

I define legislative turning points as changes of three sorts: (1) extensions of programs or benefits that included entire new categories of workers (as in 1950, when Social Security benefits were extended to regularly employed farm and domestic workers); (2) changes in either the earnings base or the contribution rate used to calculate the total Social Security tax to be paid; and (3) changes in the amount of benefits paid under existing programs. With these major turning points in mind, I set out to focus on these legislative changes in old-age insurance to determine which social forces have continued to dominate policymaking.

There are three major programs of Social Security: unemployment insurance, public assistance (for the blind, needy elderly, and orphaned), and old-age insurance. The first two programs are needs-based; old-age insurance is allocated regardless of need. For two reasons, I decided to address primarily the old-age insurance section of Social Security. (I do not cover in depth the unemployment or means-tested sections of Social Security legislation.) First, I realized that the volume of government documents on old-age insurance alone was enormous if I intended to analyze the entire history of the program. Second, although there are links between the means-tested programs and non-means-tested, there are also inherent contradictions in combining or comparing means-tested social welfare with across-the-board social insurance for retirement (Ferrara 1980). These two types of social welfare legislation differ greatly in the mechanisms that are used to determine who gets money and the philosophy behind the measures, and also in the organizations involved in policy change.

Using government documents, including the *Congressional Record*, Senate Finance Committee and House Ways and Means Committee hearing reports, and Social Security Administration records, I read transcripts of proceedings related to each legislative turning point. I was determined to let the record speak for itself, believing that, ideally, methodological frameworks constrain our interpretive freedom. Essentially, I employed an inductive methodology.

The U.S. Government is the world's largest publisher, and government documents provide a rich source of primary materials for the social-historical researcher. Committee hearings, especially, often contain data gathered by opposing sides to bolster their arguments. Letters to Congress, petitions from individuals and organizations, and other documents entered in the *Congressional Record* provide both engaging reading and an important context for the periods under study.

Despite this wealth of information in government documents, after this work was completed I was uncertain whether or not I had fully understood what actually lay behind the legislative shifts. Various groups and individuals registered their official opinions in these documents, but I wanted to understand what considerations had weighed most heavily in their thinking. Clearly, I needed more specific information, both from recognized political leaders and from lesser-known agents of change.

The next phase of the project centered on archival research in the National Archives, as well as archival records of the AFL-CIO, and the National Association of Manufacturers (NAM). These records are a gold mine of information, and, not incidentally, a source of endless amusement, revealing not only of the state of the times but also of historical trivia. Studying the records of the 1956 disability insurance amendments to Social Security in the National Archives, I found records boxes filled with balsa wood postcards, lavished with feathers, bells, and beads, expressing support for the amendments. Apparently, groups representing these people had organized a massive mail-in campaign. There are dusty boxes full of memos, letters, and reports, from Franklin D. Roosevelt, Arthur J. Altmeyer, key congressional leaders, bipartisan commissions on Social Security, and so on, some of them primary sources, and some important smoking guns.

In all this mass of information, I noted specific organizations or social movements and leaders that were key players. These became the basis of a systematic analysis of groups that supported or opposed changes in old-age insurance legislation. Only in this last phase did I develop my theoretical framework, which, by emphasizing the organizational dynamics that influence policymaking, became more than a strictly historical account. This volume does, I think, add detail and richness to the story of Social Security, while employing a unique theoretical framework that underscores the forces behind the political history of old-age insurance. Past research on the subject of what forces control policymaking has followed four general models: pluralist, instrumentalist, structuralist, and state-centered. The pluralist model views the state primarily as an arena in which competing interests negotiate and compromise over specific pieces of legislation. The instrumentalist model regards the state as an instrument of capital, with business dominating social policy. The structuralist model argues that the state does not adopt policies favoring economic elites because these groups push them but rather adopts such policies to ensure its material resources and legitimacy. State-centered models argue that the state has potential autonomy that depends on its organizational structure and resources, which are not necessarily synonymous with the imperatives of capitalism. Together, these four approaches form a continuum, in which the state's role ranges from relatively passive to relatively active. Aside from fodder for academic discourse, is there anything at stake in these debates? If "what is past, is prologue," then contemporary observers should take care to understand the historical political process with regard to our social provisions for old age.

PLURALIST MODELS

Pluralists emphasize a democratic process in which most interests have the *potential* to be represented in policy debates, with compromise occurring over final outcomes; there is no single center of power, but rather multiple centers. Polyarchy helps to tame power, secure the consent of all, and settle conflicts peacefully (Dahl 1989). Pluralism focuses on the ability of various groups to organize and coalesce around issues that interest or directly involve them. Robert Dahl, for example, would not argue that all groups have equal access to resources, but he does argue that in any democratic political process, almost every interested group has access to some political resources.

Pluralists further argue that there is no single set of all-powerful leaders who agree fully on their major goals, or have enough power to achieve their goals; frequent cleavages among and between those in power are sufficient to negate or dilute tendencies toward polarization. Dahl, noting how easy it is to exaggerate the importance of pressure groups such as the NAM, the Chamber of Commerce, and the industry associations, points out that such groups are inhibited from united action by the diversity of the views and interests among their members (1967: 414–15). Thus, policymaking requires a coalition of different sets of leaders who may have divergent goals. Pluralists view the state as primarily a neutral arbiter in the debates over legislation.

Pluralism illuminates certain features of Social Security policymaking. Almost all official accounts emanating from the Social Security Administration argue that changes in Social Security legislation reflect processes of negotiation and compromise involving competing interests. Indeed, when members are appointed to advisory councils or special commissions, official documents record which members represent the "public," "business," or "labor." According to these accounts of Social Security legislation, outcomes have generally been accepted by most—and this, pluralists argue, is one of the main strengths of democracy. Emphasis on the process of and various stages in hammering out legislation helps us to understand long-term dynamics. Dahl is also accurate in stating that powerful interests do not always agree on the appropriate policy position. Finally, it is useful to take into account that there are a number of important actors in the legislative process, and that legislation is a process of negotiation among these actors.

The perspective employed here however differs in two central ways from a pluralist account. First, pluralist frameworks suffer from the relatively abstract level of theorizing regarding "the state." The state in the U.S. case includes the President, Congress, and the Social Security Administration (SSA), which often have quite different interests. Second, the state is not the neutral arbiter as pluralism suggests. Viewing the state as a neutral arena results in an image of policy as an outcome of *other* organizations' actions, but in fact the state bureaucracy can also act as an *architect* of policy. Social Security has altered the way Americans think about caring for the elderly, and the program created a huge new bureaucracy that gradually became an important actor shaping its own destiny.

More critically, my perspective diverges sharply from a pluralist account in its differentiation between the ideal and the real, a difference of which pluralists are very conscious (Dahl 1989). Organizational actors *do* differ in their access to accurate information regarding political decisions, their ability to mobilize resources, and their access to powerful decision makers. The early Social Security Board, for instance, had more access to Roosevelt than did the Townsendites, and in the creation of Social Security there was a relatively small number of elite groups represented in congressional debates. Disincentives to organize include costs such as time, money, and lost opportunity in pursuit of other goals. Certainly, taxpaying workers would seem to be a logical interest group with regard to the Social Security payroll tax, but the sheer size and diversity of workers' groups has meant that, until recently, their interests have not had real representation.

I am particularly skeptical of the pluralist notion that interests are usually embodied in individuals or organizations. Social structures can limit organizational action, because not all groups are equally capable of organizing themselves. For example, some observers explain the low political participation rate of the lower and working classes as a reflection of their apathy or alienation, without taking into consideration that this low participation may be a rational response to their perceptions of reality (Wilson 1973: 14). In contrast to a pluralist view of organizations, I suggest that interests are often socially constructed and situationally specific. For these reasons we must not assume that the ways in which individuals or organizations define their interests or policy objectives are constants. Conflict perspectives provide some answers to the question of how interests get shaped.

CONFLICT MODELS

Two conflict theories are useful for explaining the emergence and persistence of social welfare legislation. Instrumentalists argue that capitalists are central players in the expansion of the welfare state. I would suggest that the average American would name business and industry last in a list of those supporting the initiation and expansion of Social Security; thus an instrumentalist account is seductive in its counterintuitive nature.

Instrumentalists argue that capital dominates in the economic and political arena, and uses the state as a tool or instrument to further its interests (Domhoff 1990; Useem 1984; O'Connor 1973; Piven and Cloward 1971). These authors suggest that capitalists use social welfare legislation, and thus, by extension, the state, to regulate and legitimate existing economic relations. In this vein, Michael Useem (1984) argues that the upper class is unified through common experience and intermarriage, and G. William Domhoff notes the incredible degree of overlap between the capitalist-based class and the political and military power elite. More importantly, these authors argue that these economic or business interests dominate policymaking in a variety of direct and indirect ways. For example, with regard to Social Security legislation, Frances Fox Piven and Richard A. Cloward (1971) argue that relief arrangements are initiated or expanded in times of disorder, whereas in times of political stability they are abolished or restricted. Similarly, James O'Connor (1973) writes of the "fiscal crisis of the state," which results from monopoly capital foisting social welfare costs onto the state, and will lead eventually to the demise of the state. The state, in other words, has been used as a tool to maintain or increase monopoly capital's profits. The welfare state absorbs the social costs of the monopoly sector's production (because of its reliance on technology and mechanization, hence less labor-intensive production). The welfare state also serves to create more jobs, thereby further supporting the capitalist system. The monopoly sector socializes the costs of production but not the profits; hence, the state's demise is inevitable. O'Connor's thesis, like pluralist accounts, has little room for independent action by the state.

The instrumentalist's approach, though useful, has serious limitations. It does not clearly identify the mechanism by which capital's interests get translated into actual policies, and it grants big business and industry too much in the way of rationality and foresight. It also understates the very real divisions among elites brought about primarily through economic competition. State actors are not always the handmaidens of capital, and capitalists do not necessarily "set the goals" for state policymakers (Amenta and Parikh 1991: 128).

The second conflict framework utilized to address policymaking is a structuralist account. Structuralists are leading critics of instrumentalist models, arguing that focusing only on the revealed preferences of economic elites ignores the structural foundations of capitalism, the process of capital accumulation, and the class struggle (Block 1977; Gold, Lo, and Wright 1975). Structuralists do not see business elites as the primary *cause* of political change, but as *symptomatic* of the underlying processes of capitalist development. They argue that the state can, and does, adopt policies that are at odds with the expressed preferences of economic elites. Under this framework, given that the state's main task is to promote the centralization and concentration of capital (Poulantzas 1978), the state asserts power to ensure the long-term survival of the capitalist system. Economic elites, on the other hand, are less likely to focus on the long term, and will tend to promote policies that serve their short-term interests. When does the state go against the wishes of capital? According to structuralists, the state is relatively autonomous in times of crisis or dissension; it is the unifying factor in the power bloc.

Jill Quadagno's work is a structuralist account of Social Security policymaking. She notes that changes in the social organization of production serve to regulate the labor supply (1988: 6), and that these considerations are central in explaining social welfare policies in the United States. Writing about the Social Security Administration, Quadagno argues that the agenda of program bureaucrats was circumscribed by the political economy of Southern congressional representatives. She posits that the economic division of labor patterns the organization of the state, and economic dimensions of political structures are critical to understanding policy outcomes.

Quadagno also asserts that as early as 1929, the National Industrial Conference Board suggested the establishment of a central pension fund, under the jurisdiction of the federal government, and she goes on to argue that there has been inadequate recognition of the degree to which employers accepted Social Security legislation. She is critical of the concept of the "relative autonomy of the state": "A conception of an autonomous state, mediating between class factions, vastly oversimplifies the policy-making process. Either capital or labor may initiate and attain independent agendas, to which the state must respond, and these private sector events set limits on or even determine the possibilities for state action" (1988: 177). Quadagno believes that the concept of "the state" is too abstract, for there are numerous state actors, often holding contradictory positions. Indeed, I would argue that other important concepts necessary for an analysis of Social Security policy—conceptions of "capital," "labor," and "elderly advocate groups"—are also too abstract. Like the notion of "the state," these theoretical constructs, too, should be broken down into their constituent organizational actors in order to avoid contradictory conclusions based on more abstract theoretical categories.

The limitations of structuralist accounts are most evident in their economically deterministic postulate, which says that the political superstructure (including the state) is essentially built upon economic foundations (Block 1987; Burawoy 1990). My model emphasizes multiple causes, but I would also argue that business and industry are not the only parts of society that have economic interests. State bureaucratic actors, and organizations representing the elderly, labor, and other groups also have economic or material interests. Labor unions, individual states, the elderly, students, the disabled, and the poor have all developed certain economic interests associated with Social Security.

The central contributions of conflict theories are the focus on economic interests and the macroeconomic context. It is of course true that elites play a role in policymaking, and the broader economic environment has a dramatic effect on Social Security legislation. The direct effects of unemployment and inflation on the trust funds are evident, and certainly the economic climate influences the tenor of the debates. However, both instrumentalist and structuralist accounts presume that the capitalist class, and organizations that represent this class, take strategic action in a conscious, rational manner; conflict approaches are in this sense consistent with other analyses that assume conscious, forward-looking behavior (Pfeffer 1982: 163). My organizational model does not accord such omniscience either to elite groups or to state actors.

James Q. Wilson's comment on pluralist and conflict models sums up the weaknesses of the two approaches. He says it is an error to assume "either that every social interest has one or more organizations representing it (the pluralist fallacy) or that every organization represents the underlying objective interests or social condition of its members (the Marxian fallacy). . . . Max Weber understood this fully: the emergence of an association or even of spontaneous social action out of a common class situation is not to be taken for granted but is something to be explained" (1973: 14). We may say that pluralist models focus on how aggregates of individuals or interests come to have political power (a sort of bottom-up perspective), and that conflict models focus on how social structures limit political power (a top-down perspective). The model that I follow here combines these two approaches by emphasizing organizational actors as the unit of analysis.

STATE-CENTERED MODELS

State-centered models offer much potential for understanding both the constraints and the opportunities provided by state structures, as well as the sometimes powerful impact of organizations, events, and individuals outside the political mainstream. Partly as a response to the limitations of conflict theories, state-centered explanations insist on the state's potential autonomy, which depends on the state's administrative or organizational structure and the resources it commands, and not necessarily on the demands of capitalism. State-centered theoretical frameworks generally use Weber's definition of the state as the political organization that claims a monopoly on the means of coercion within a certain geographical unit.

For example, Theda Skocpol (1984) rejects the view that the state is merely the handmaiden of capital; rather, the state can have relative autonomy from the economically and politically dominant classes, and indeed sometimes goes against the wishes of powerful groups. As proof, she cites instances of hostility between the state and the dominant classes, and she argues that the initiation of Social Security in the 1930s was a crisis that unhinged dominant economic interests, thereby calling for a strong, unifying state. Although the NAM, for example, did not believe that industry should have to pay taxes for the social security of employees, the state went against its wishes. Skocpol emphasizes the role of social policies and administrative arrangements developed in the individual states before 1935, which shaped the eventual form of the original Social Security legislation. State-centered theorists recognize that the state is not always autonomous or unified, and that social pressure from outside the state can have an impact on policymaking (Evans, Rueschemeyer, and Skocpol 1985). Further, state capacities and interests are historically variable.

Recognizing the relative autonomy of the state is essential because the state may be an important actor in policy debates. An interpretation of political change, such as the development of old-age insurance, should retain the idea that various state actors can actively shape legislation, and that state bureaucracies, and other actors representing the state, often act back upon their environment.

The model presented here also addresses specific actors in organizational and social movements that have been active in Social Security policymaking. Instead of overly abstract analyses of "the state," "capitalists," and "labor," we compare the smaller elements in kind—"apples to apples"—as a way of furthering our understanding of these dynamics (Esping-Andersen 1990; Evans, Rueschemeyer, and Skocpol 1985). Thus, different actors or organizations within the state may have interests that oppose each other. The state, far from being a single actor, is made up of individuals and organizations that sometimes compete with each other and often disagree. Presidents complain that Congress won't support them, and congressionally approved packages are vetoed by Presidents. In the early years of the Social Security program, there were important differences between what Roosevelt, the early Social Security Board, and Congress could accomplish. Any autonomy was primarily exercised by Roosevelt, and far less by the Social Security Board and Congress. Dahl makes a convincing point: "Because no one can long remain a Congressman or a Senator if he cannot win an election, all often pay some attention, most of them pay a great deal of attention, and some give paramount attention, to calculating the effects their actions are likely to have on the way their constituents will vote in the next election" (1967: 130). Conversely, program bureaucrats are generally less preoccupied with election politics and, given their typically longer tenure, are more apt to focus on longer-term outcomes. In order to study political change, we need to differentiate elected officials and bureaucratic roles, presidential and congressional positions, and political outsiders and political insiders. Only by looking at the role of specific organizations can we understand how these actors come to have interests that sometimes oppose other interests in the public or private arena (Salisbury et al. 1987: 1230). Middle-level theories have the dual benefits of specificity and the recognition of causal complexity in political processes.

In grappling with the diverging conclusions about Social Security policymaking of conflict and state-centered models, one must allow for the differing time periods analyzed. For example, much of Theda Skocpol's work focuses on the Civil War period through the initial Social Security legislation that was initiated during the Great Depression, an extremely tumultuous period in American history. By 1933, official unemployment had reached 24.9 percent, and Roosevelt and the Congress perceived this as a major threat to capitalism. As the Depression worsened and the unemployed grew more vocal and restless, it became clear that unemployment could no longer be blamed on the fate or fault of individuals; it was redefined by many as a collective disaster that demanded structural changes. Many even questioned the legitimacy of the economy and the whole political system. Communists agitated in breadlines, flophouses, among loiterers at factory gates, and at the intake sections of relief offices. The sheer magnitude of unemployment was devastating to the economy, and in response the public issued a mandate for swift decisive action through their relatively widespread participation in radical movements. Roosevelt and members of Congress viewed the retirement provisions of old-age insurance as one way of easing unemployment and the resulting economic stagnation. It would be a slow process, but given time, massive numbers of workers could move out of the labor force and become consumers rather than producers. The creation of Social Security in the context of the Great Depression was, therefore, atypical of most political change, which often affects some entrenched component of the state.

James O'Connor (1973) and Jill Quadagno (1988) focus primarily on the 1950s in their analyses. From a broad historical perspective, the prosperity of the 1950s was also atypical, coming as it did following the tremendous changes of World War II. The infusion of payroll taxes during the war, when employment for the war effort was high, had overflowed the Social Security trust funds, and many urged expansion of coverage and benefits. To focus solely on business and industry's position during this period is to misrepresent the broader support for Social Security that existed during this time.

These different time periods are part of the reason for the conflicting conclusions regarding power in the political process. One has to recognize that the forces that brought about the beginning of Social Security and shaped its early development are not necessarily the same as those that ensured its long-term survival. Social Security became an entrenched institution by creating a community of diverse interests—a clientele that would not look favorably on cuts in the program. Successful bureaucracies become entrenched and institutionalized through the normal activities of the political process. An analysis focused on organizations over time allows us to note the changing alignment of organizational interests, hence the changing relationships between organizational actors over time. By tracing the historical evolution of old-age insurance, we can better distinguish between patterns and idiosyncracies, and perhaps even predict the most likely future occurrences.

Social Security: An Organizational and Institutional Framework

Organizations are of great scholarly and practical significance. Organizations are particularly important for interpreting Social Security policymaking for several reasons. First, the emergence of Social Security coincided with America's "search for order" that began at the turn of the century. The preeminence of the bureaucratic organizational form grew out of the regulative needs of the new urban-industrial life (Wiebe 1967). In addition to this bureaucratization and rational organization of government activities, there was the corresponding development of special interest group politics operating at the national level. Interest groups are key players in twentieth-century politics.

Second, as a result of the above developments, the turn of the century witnessed a plethora of research and theory regarding organizations. Alexis de Tocqueville was impressed upon his visit to America in 1831–32 with the preponderance of associations. " 'Whenever at the head of some new undertaking you see the government in France," he observed, "or a man of rank in England, in the United States you will be sure to find an association' " (1951: 106). Although there is some research on political organizations (Wilson 1973), much contemporary organizational literature focuses explicitly on private organizations (e.g., businesses). Political organizations are very important, as a different kind of organization, and we need more research in this area (Brunsson 1985: 186). In studying concrete political organizations, we must avoid beginning with grand theoretical abstractions; rather, such studies need "analytical induction and historically grounded comparisons" (Evans, Rueschemeyer, and Skocpol 1985: 348). We must also guard against a monolithic conception of these groups (Esping-Andersen 1990; Korpi 1983).

A final reason for focusing explicitly on organizational dynamics is that most of us spend the greater part of our lives working within or dealing with large organizations. A fuller understanding of these dynamics can lead to more self-reflection, and therefore to more effective and efficient methods for achieving what is desired, whether privately or politically. Effective political change requires individuals to pool their resources and coordinate their actions (Lindblom 1980: 100; Knoke 1988: 311). Individuals, regardless of their charisma or power, need others to enact social, political, economic, or ideological change.

The definition of organizations used here is broad: organizations are composed of groups of people who consciously coordinate their activities to achieve some end (Mayhew 1986: 17). Social movements, formal associations, state bureaucracies, advisory councils, and bipartisan commissions all constitute important organizational actors. The model presented here focuses on the effects of larger social structures on organizations, and how organizations in turn act upon these social structures. In other words, the sociopolitical environment is simultaneously an opportunity, a constraint, and an outcome; it is both cause and effect. As Charles E. Lindblom notes:

A policy-making system itself has a great effect on the very aspirations, opinions, and attitudes to which policy responds. It does not operate as a kind of machine into which people feed their wants or needs and out of which come policy decisions to satisfy them. The machine itself manufactures wants or needs. Molding the aspirations of citizens, it brings some issues to the agenda and discards others, puts some policies but not others before citizens or policy makers for choice and forms the opinions that will decide these choices. (1980: 114–15)

Thus, preexisting pension and relief arrangements in the late 1920s and the early 1930s, along with changes in the political and economic environment—the decline of patronage politics, the stock market crash, declining investment and production, and unemployment—set the stage for Social Security policymaking in the 1930s. Theda Skocpol and Edwin Amenta (1986: 149) use the term policy feedbacks to explain these dynamics. "Once instituted, social policies in turn reshape the organization of the state itself and affect the goals and alliances of social groups involved in ongoing political struggle. Thus the Social Security Act of 1935 strongly affected subsequent possibilities for bureaucratic activism, as well as alliances and cleavages in postwar American social politics" (Weir, Orloff, and Skocpol 1988: 25). Important analytical stages of the policymaking process include setting the agenda; specifying alternatives; choosing among alternatives by congressional vote, presidential decision, and other agents; implementation of the decision; and later outcomes (Kingdon 1984: 3).

The model presented here emphasizes the importance of combinations of political factors rather than single origins of policy events, as well as interactive effects between the broader sociopolitical environment and organizations (e.g., outcomes at "time one" can be causes at "time two"). Because it is a model that moves beyond "single-factor hypotheses" (Skocpol and Amenta 1986: 152), it embodies several sociological variables: organizational persistence, interests and incentives, coalition formation, timing and time, and ideology. Although I discuss these variables separately, individually they represent only one thread in a more general fabric.

ORGANIZATIONAL PERSISTENCE

Organizational observers often assume that organizational survival is a central concern of organizational leaders, but survival alone is an insufficient criterion for understanding political change. Political power often stems from what I shall call *organizational persistence*. In this case, organizational persistence refers both to the prevalence of various lobbying groups in promoting Social Security legislation and to the institutionalization of Social Security itself. Organizations that survive and are active in political debates over the long term have positive effects on actors within those organizations, as well as on outsiders' perceptions of the organization's political power.

Much like the very tenuous early years of a privately owned business, the beginning years of political organizations are often crucial for mere survival. Thus, the process of institutionalization is a variable, not a given. Merely passing legislation is not enough to assume the survival of a program; institutionalization also requires following through with appropriations and later supporting amendments. Organizational persistence over the long term may in part reflect the level of resources that the organization is able to command, but constituencies of support are also created by conferring benefits. When old-age insurance benefits were first paid in 1940, not only was a new community of interests involved (beneficiaries), but those who were excluded, having less generous alternative pension arrangements, or none at all, rallied around the idea of expanded coverage.

Further, the NAM and the U.S. Chamber of Commerce were two politically powerful and persistent organizations relevant to the debates surrounding Social Security. These two organizations are very active in legislative debates that concern them, and they frequently testify in opposition to other significant groups; often, their opinions prevail (Wilson 1973: 311). At the outset, the NAM opposed Social Security legislation, but once it was evident that the laws would be passed, NAM played a role in shaping the final legislation in the 1930s.

In much the same way, persistence affected the coverage of farm and domestic workers; the original plan provided them old-age insurance, but pressures placed on Congress by politically entrenched Southern congressmen cut them out of the final legislation. The Southerners were opposed to the idea of federal control that might weaken local autonomy, and they also feared that federal monies would lessen the economic dependence of blacks in an economy based on sharecropping and tenant farming (Quadagno 1985). Thus, we must pay attention to the *dynamic processes* of legislative histories, for it is quite evident that the passage of initial legislation is not always the same as follow-through and implementation; it is in the *implementation* of policies and later legislative tinkering that organizational persistence and the economic resources of powerful, entrenched organizations pay off. Certain things happen outside the control of organizations, but powerful groups, organized to articulate their interests when the time is right, can alter the initial legislation by their persistence. Powerful organizations have the resources required to maintain a presence in the legislative debates.

Persistence, resources, and coordination give certain groups the edge over social movement leaders who, though they may be able to arouse short-term passions, are unable to sustain interest in their programs or policies. Typically, these movements dissipate or are suppressed (Higley, Burton, and Field 1990: 421–22). Robert H. Salisbury writes: "It is characteristic of movements that many of the formal organizations within them have brief and highly volatile lives, and a large share of the sympathetically inclined individuals takes part only sporadically, if at all. Consequently, even though a movement may be very large in sympathy, it is typically uncertain in its mobilizable strength" (1984: 67).

Especially for social movements involving the poor, sustaining political power over the long term can be very difficult; by and large, they can only make sporadic challenges (Gamson 1975; Tilly 1975). Owing to the restraints of economy, social status, and psychological orientation, working-class groups do not typically organize on a sustained basis. The working class has to worry about matters of daily survival, and their lower levels of education and occupational prestige mean that their sense of political efficacy (as well as outsiders' perceptions of their political clout and aggressiveness) are weakened (Wilson 1973). The lower classes do, of course, sometimes benefit from Social Security policymaking, at times as a result of their protests. The cards may be stacked against them in terms of sustaining political organizations, but other groups may also claim to speak on their behalf when political opportunities are available (Wilson 1973: 85).

Especially during crisis periods, hypothetical thinking is required of organizational actors, and "organizational interests" become harder to define. Though organizations with greater economic resources may be able in normal times to sustain pressure in legislative debates, this advantage is lessened during crisis periods, when disruptions in the status quo mean that social movements and relatively radical ideas usually have the greater audience. Finally, policy outcomes do not always favor elite groups; there are instances when the "interests of elites" are misrepresented or there are unintended outcomes.

Despite these idiosyncratic occurrences, a key variable for this analysis is organizational persistence. Nelson W. Polsby observes, "Innovation in American politics is not always the work of a day, and the pursuit of successful innovation is consequently often not a task for those who need quick gratification" (1984: 173–74). Short-lived social movements or occasional public outcries do not generally make for effective policymaking; moreover, when the general public does register discontent, it tends not to demand specific legislative remedies, and it does not oversee the legislative process over time (Polsby 1984: 169; Burstein 1985: 68). It is in the writing and implementation of specific legislation that organizational persistence secures organizational goals.

INTERESTS AND INCENTIVES

Interests and incentives are important variables in analyzing political organizations. Before we can ask, "Whose interests are served?" we must understand how interests come to be defined. Neil Fligstein and Doug McAdam point out that political processes construct interests: "In stable worlds, it will be relatively easy to identify interests because they will be highly related to the actor's position. . . . In situations where there is objective crisis . . . skilled strategic actors will be able to innovate new interests" (n.d.: 36). Interests are thus variable and not necessarily inherent.

Because transformations of interest occur for a variety of reasons, we must take into account the dynamic aspect of interests: political mobilization, for example, often occurs *after* changes in the larger political environment. One study of elderly advocate groups found that many of these groups were formed after major legislation was passed that benefited them, so they were not one of the causes of its passage (Walker 1983). In other words, the organizational actors who constitute the state are usually not neutral arbiters of externally generated interests; rather, on many issues, government organizations seek to promote their own unique agendas (Laumann and Knoke 1987: 382).

Further, since business, industrial, and labor organizations vary enormously in size and structure, they have a wide variety of economic and political interests that sometimes conflict with those of other members within their own group. This diversity makes associations of individual enterprises more unpredictable in how they represent the "best" interests of members. Also, groups that are more or less similar may take different organizational positions on legislation because of differences in perceptions of what constitutes the best interests of the organization. Particularly in times of crisis, organizational actors may respond very unpredictably; at other times, perceptions of interests tend to coalesce and remain consistent from year to year, not only for individuals and organizations but also across coalitions of organizations.

Obviously, part of the interpretation of interests depends on the leadership within organizations, and the persons at the top of the organizational hierarchy are the ones who usually articulate interests. According to Salisbury (1984: 67), "It is not member interests as such that are crucial, but the judgments of organizational leaders about the needs of the institution as a continuing organization." In interpreting such organizational interests it is thus more important to analyze the personality attributes of the leaders rather than those of persons lower in the hierarchy. For persons at the middle or lower levels, specific role demands will explain more of their behavior than any personality-related dimensions (Wilson 1989: 209).

Interests can also be transformed through the political process itself. Both Jean-Jacques Rousseau and John Stuart Mill noted that conceptions of self-interest are often altered by participation in public affairs (Salisbury 1978: 19). As Salisbury points out, "In a complex political world it is often unclear who has won. The political process continues: alignments, coalitions, and changing tides of fortune. So, too, do our notions of what it is we want and seek" (1978: 34). Former Secretary of State George Schultz attributed the difficulty of managing public organizations to such changing definitions of interest: "'It's never over.' Nothing is ever settled; debates over what many agencies should do and how they should do it are continuous, and so the maintenance of support for the agency is a never-ending, time-consuming process of negotiating and then renegotiating a set of agreements with stakeholders who are always changing their minds" (in Wilson 1989: 197). The whole matter of the relationship between organizations and interests is one that should be explored rather than assumed as given.

We must also pay attention to the incentives to organize. Mancur Olson, Jr. (1965) has discussed the importance of selective incentives and the free-rider problem for organizations. He and other authors argue that political organizations are not generally organized to apply pressure in debates over public policy but rather organize around the desire for particular incentives or material benefits that they cannot otherwise get (Olson 1965; Wilson 1973; Salisbury 1984). The AARP has mastered the art of providing selective incentives to their members, and they are a political powerhouse with regard to Social Security policymaking.

Incentives to organize are strongest in the name of opposition—mostly to oppose some perceived threat—rather than to advance some new idea (Kingdon 1984: 208; Pfeffer and Salancik 1978). Organizational membership tends to be larger when there is something to fight. For example, around the turn of the century, labor unions organized more strikes and businesses formed antistrike and antiunion leagues. Many of these began as local organizations; later on, business leaders recognized that they could be more effective by joining together to form state and then national associations. These were the beginnings of the U.S. Chamber of Commerce (Quadagno 1988). A study of the NAM found that membership fluctuations coincided with changes in labor union membership. The NAM met each challenge by labor unions with increased membership (Gable 1953). In this way, threat begets organization (Wilson 1973), and threats are a more powerful incentive to organize than the mere opportunity to advance an issue in a positive way. Even within the three branches of government, veto powers and opposition politics are more common than active and positive propositions (Lindblom 1980: 84). Polsby, writing about the passage of bills in the legislative process, notes that "most of the dispersed powers in the process are essentially negative: legislation can be stalled or defeated in so many different ways by so many different people" (1986: 158).

Incentives to organize are also influenced by the relative numbers of potential beneficiaries and potential contributors; the size of interest groups can be inversely related to political strength (Becker 1983). When a relatively small group (compared with the remainder of the population) lobbies for economic benefits, the costs are widely distributed and benefits are focused. Smaller groups are also easier to organize, further contributing to their advantage in political debates. By contrast, larger groups, relative to the remainder of the population, require heavier economic burdens for smaller payoffs. The early years of Social Security were characterized by relatively large benefits to the elderly for relatively low costs to each individual taxpaying worker. This balance resulted in little opposition to increases in Social Security. The later years of the program have been characterized by a demographic and economic tipping point, at which costs have risen rapidly and a smaller number of workers have had to bear this heavier burden. Thus, various conflicting groups are now vying for power.

Undeniably, so far as economic incentives to form or be active in political organizations are concerned, employer organizations have certain built-in advantages. They do not have to overcome the resistance of workers (as workers do with businesses), and their greater financial resources can reduce the costs of individual membership. Not the least advantage is that in any particular industry, there are fewer firms than workers, so that the collective will is easier to muster and to maintain (Wilson 1973: 143–44). This is not to say that large corporations have complete power and control. As Edward O. Laumann and David Knoke note: "Organizational resources are finite, even for the largest corporations, and the system's persistence over indefinite time means that the political game will never be finished. Every organization must limit its involvement, husband its resources, and play for limited gains" (1987: 386–87). One way to combat the problem of limited organizational resources is to form coalitions with other organizations, to pool resources and coordinate the mutual effort.

COALITION FORMATION

Coalition formation is central in political life, and the emergence of "cross-class coalitions" can greatly affect the growth of welfare states (Orloff 1988: 42). Coalitions can be linkages between or among individuals, classes, and organizations. They are temporary, instrumental, sometimes symbolic aggregations of these social groups, but they are crucial vehicles in social and political change. They may involve odd bedfellows. The very existence of coalitions shows the problematic nature of abstract theoretical categories like the state, capital, and labor. For example, the coalition supporting the original Social Security Act of 1935 included some business organizations, but perhaps surprisingly, not all representatives of labor unions. One cannot generalize about such coalitions as if they were monolithic or continuous entities.

Coalition formation has numerous benefits. In the political arena, timely and accurate information is essential to operating effectively; knowledge and information are indeed power (Laumann and Knoke 1987: 13). Wilson calls timely and precise information "the prime currency of politics" and notes that there are expectations of reciprocity in sharing information. Furthermore, if a political actor works alone when dealing with an important issue, there is always the risk of having incomplete information and perhaps unknowingly antagonizing prospective allies (Wilson 1973: 279).

Coalitions provide information about the activities of the organizations, and they create channels of communication; they are an important first step in obtaining the commitment of other important actors in the environment. They can also legitimate the focal organization (Pfeffer and Salancik 1978: 145). Social networks matter, so much so that leadership can be conceptualized as centrality in the communications network (Polsby 1986: 110).

This sharing of information eliminates a degree of uncertainty and makes outcomes somewhat more predictable (Pfeffer and Salancik 1978: 146).

TIMING AND TIME AS POLITICAL AND ORGANIZATIONAL FACTORS

The impact of timing and time further illustrates the interrelationships between the broader economic and political environment and organizations. "Even typically 'unrelated' events may be linked by sharing a historical moment . . . that defines them as competing for the scarce attention of diverse actors" (Laumann and Knoke 1987: 40). Both the nature and the number of other events on a policy agenda, many of them unforeseen, can influence otherwise unrelated policies. This horizontal dimension is what I will refer to as *timing*; I refer to the vertical dimension as *time* (Laumann and Knoke 1987).

Various scholars have noted the existence of windows of opportunity for policy innovation—as a result of the alignment of change-promoting factors, or the convergence of actors, alternatives, and widespread support. Timing is especially important as a climate of receptivity that allows ideas to take hold (Burstein 1985). John W. Kingdon says, "The critical thing to understand is not where the seed comes from, but what makes the soil fertile" (1984: 81). This climate is fostered by: "(1) the interests of groups in society, (2) the intellectual convictions of experts and policymakers, and (3) comparative knowledge, usually carried in the heads of experts or subject-matter specialists, knowledge of the ways in which problems have been previously handled elsewhere" (Polsby 1984: 166).

Skocpol (1992) has traced the influence during the 1930s of various models and proposals for pension plans that had worked in the individual states or in other countries. The political success of the new Social Security program centered around launching a trial balloon that finally worked. Trial balloons can be political speeches or tentative moves of an organization toward new agenda items, and if they are successful, they can redefine social problems and answers. Polsby observes: "There is very little new under the sun. A great many newly enacted policies have been 'in the air' for quite a while. In the heat of a presidential campaign or when a newly in-augurated President wants a 'new' program, desk drawers fly open all over Washington. Pet schemes are fished out, dusted off, and tried out on the new political leaders. There is often a hiatus of years—sometimes decades—between the first proposal of a policy innovation and its appearance as a presidential 'initiative,' much less a law" (1986: 86). Nonetheless, the timing of a trial balloon is all-important. A window of opportunity may open, but if a solu-tion is not readily available, the window may close. Conversely, a proposal may exist, but the political conditions may not be ripe for it to be promoted (Kingdon 1984: 216). Organizational theo-rists call this organizational phenomenon a "garbage can" model of decision making. These models "assume that problems, solu-tions, decision makers, and choice opportunities are independent, exogenous streams flowing through a system" (March and Olsen 1989: 12). Problems, agendas, and alternatives are separate streams that may converge if the opportunity comes; the garbage can image implies a throwing together of problems and solutions in an often helter-skelter mishmash.

Once a new organization or innovation is launched, timing con-tinues to be important. Outcomes can later become causes. Much like a fork in the road, the choice of certain options at one point in time forecloses alternative routes. The early years of an organi-zation therefore greatly determine its ongoing structure. Paul A. David (1985: 335) suggests a path-dependent model in which "his-torical accidents" or choices made early in the process are crucial. He traces the way in which the development of the typewriter key-board, determined the eventual "lock-in" of the QWERTY sequence. A keyboard arrangement that placed on the home row the se-quence DHIATENSOR (the ten letters that appear in over 70 percent of the words in the English language) allowed for typing speeds 20 to 40 percent faster, but it was abandoned in favor of QWERTY because the industry expected that form to become the standard. The timing, or earlier debut, of the less-efficient QWERTY keyboard became the main reason for its success.

In an excellent example of the interrelationships between tim-ing, coalition formation, and policy outcomes, Gosta Esping-Andersen conducted a detailed longitudinal analysis of the development of the Swedish and Danish welfare states (1978, 1985). He shows that over time, policy choices made by parties in power are crucial to understanding later policy development: events at "time one" consolidated or undermined electoral coalitions, and these coalitions were the very ones that political parties at "time two" depended upon.

The vertical dimension of time in regard to old-age insurance includes issues of uncertainty, short-term versus long-term orientations, and time as it relates specifically to social insurance plans. First, uncertainty and organizational stress generally occur when models for problem-solving are nonexistent (Derthick 1990). One way to eliminate uncertainty and an extended search for solutions is for organizational actors to consider only a limited number of decision alternatives (Cyert and March 1963: 83). Another way in which organizations attempt to avoid or manage uncertainty is to focus on short-term events and evade judgments on the long term (Pfeffer and Salancik 1978: 282; Cyert and March 1963: 118–20). This strategy often leads to incremental change.

These issues are especially relevant for understanding political organizations. National politics are biased toward decisions that can be made quickly, and toward problems that seem to be acute, not chronic. Quoting Polsby: "When a crisis occurs, leaders must act. The pressures of time and events, the multiple competing demands on our national government, mean that, unavoidably, policy-makers are less systematic, less orderly in their decision-making than they would be if they could fully control their environments" (1986: 5–6). Second, there is a difference in the time perspective of various state actors. Elected officials, quite understandably, have a different attitude toward short-term and long-term decisions from that of bureaucratic officials. Members of Congress, concerned about getting reelected, often have goals quite different from those of people who have to worry about the actuarial balance in the Social Security trust funds. It is all too often the case that politicians treat large trust fund reserves as an incentive to increase benefits, ignoring the actuaries' emphasis on building up the reserves. During both the expansion and retrenchment phases of Social Security, election-year timing is central to our understanding of the turning points.

The argument that electoral-economic cycles influence Social Security policymaking is supported by evidence of election-year timing for Roosevelt in the 1930s (Wright 1974), and of Social Security benefit increases between 1950 and 1972 (Tufte 1978). That is, the more popular expansionary legislation of the 1950s and 1960s took place, almost without exception, every election year. In 1977 and 1983, Congress avoided inflicting the pain of retrenchments, with little offsetting benefit, during election years.

Tenure also affects organizational actors' time orientation. Bureaucrats and congressional representatives tend to think in terms of careers, whereas Presidents now have no more than eight years. This difference affects the way in which politicians focus their energies:

> The President is intent on the problem of the moment, which is to pass high-priority items in his program. He asks his congressional allies to spend power in behalf of this goal. The congressperson, who has to worry about the possibility of a future transfer to a desirable committee or a private bill that he or she thinks may mean political life or death at some future time, is naturally inclined to hoard power or to invest it so as to increase their future stock of resources. (Polsby 1986: 194)

Finally, time is an important dimension of any social insurance program. Lester Thurow (personal communication) notes that in providing old-age insurance pensions, all societies have faced what he calls the "first generation gift" and the "last generation problem." The first beneficiaries generally receive much more in benefits than they contributed, and the "last generation" must be concerned with who will pay for their benefits. For these reasons, Social Security has been likened to an intergenerational chain letter, with the built-in potential to be a zero-sum political hot potato. In the early years, benefits could be increased without any noticeable impact on the taxpaying workers; today, the rate of the Social Security payroll tax and the level of benefits for the retired are important bones of contention.

IDEOLOGY

While economic factors are certainly important when analyzing Social Security policymaking, other noneconomic sets of beliefs are also central. Human beings act in both instrumental and expressive ways; therefore, the final concept employed throughout this analysis is ideology. As used here, it refers to sets of beliefs and ideas in our culture that relate to the role of social insurance programs. Ideology influences the Social Security bureaucracy, and the bureaucracy also influences ideology. Ideas regarding the family, demographics (fertility and immigration), unemployment, and equity and adequacy in the provision of social insurance are central ideological considerations. Indeed, these are not independent sets of beliefs—they are interconnected. For example, if old-age insurance benefits are inadequate, then family dynamics can be affected in that someone has to care for the aged, disabled, or needy. There is a great deal of power symbolized in defining and processing the terms of any debate. Some examples of how ideologies are shaped illustrate this power.

The recruitment process of social organizations themselves can reinforce or alter ideologies (Brunsson 1985: 16; Wilson 1989: 64). Early staffing of the Social Security Board (later known as the Social Security Administration), involved careful screening of candidates, only those known to support Roosevelt's vision of "social security" were employed. This is not to say that players *other* than Roosevelt's hand-picked lieutenants were incapable of influencing Social Security policymaking. Kingdon (1984: 208–9) distinguishes between visible participants who affect the agenda and hidden participants who affect the alternatives. External to the Social Security bureaucracy, various social movements played a key role in defining the issues in the early debates.

Social movements are noninstitutionalized political expression, and though tactics can vary from more reformist to more revolutionary, these actors *can* influence ideology. Social movement theorists discuss a dynamic called radical flank effects, which refers to situations where more radical actors serve to shift the terms of the debate toward a more extreme direction than would occur without their involvement. This dynamic can have spin-off effects whereby policies, such as Social Security, formerly considered radical, gain new support in the more heated political context. Powerful political actors look to these social movements for reasonable coalition partners that speak for the movement (Haines 1984), but the presence of more radical members serves to realign the terms of the debate.

In general, however, it is organizational persistence that prevails. Over the longer term, regular participants in the political process are more likely to help frame the issue or set the agenda. Political outsiders will generally have more difficulty in getting their definitions of the problem accepted as valid (Laumann and Knoke 1987: 315).

Three important shifts in the ideological climate surrounding Social Security legislation have occurred during its history. First, with extremely high unemployment during the Great Depression, unemployment was ideologically redefined by many as a collective social problem rather than as a problem of personal inadequacies. Second, the relative emphasis on the equity versus adequacy of old-age insurance benefits has varied greatly over time. During the early and later years, equity was the focus; during the middle years, adequacy was the catchword. This shift is related to the success of many elderly advocate groups in defining these benefits as "earned." Yet the debates over "adequacy" reflect the elasticity of the concept of "earned" benefits. The ability of the AARP and other elderly groups to reinforce the idea of "earned" benefits (despite the fact that many beneficiaries in the early years drew out far more in benefits than they ever paid in) reflects their power to define the ideological agenda.

The third ideological shift involves society's ideas about old-age insurance as a contract or a form of community. During most of the early years, Americans supported old-age insurance as a way of fostering goodwill within society. Old-age insurance monies stimulated the economy, helped the elderly to enjoy a more dignified retirement, and created jobs for younger and middle-aged workers. After the amendments of 1972, however, the economic context became more zero-sum (one person's gain was another's loss), and the notion of old-age insurance as a contract became prevalent. Elderly advocate groups maintained that old-age insurance represented an intergenerational contract, and groups of tax-paying workers united in opposition to higher and higher Social Security payroll tax rates. Ideology clearly plays an important role in framing policymaking.

The theoretical framework advocated here adds clarity and precision to the debates over political power and decision making, by considering organizational actors representing *all* levels—elites, the middle class, the working class, and the lower class. This model is not monocausal or deterministic in focus. It *does* say that, in the longer term, political outcomes will favor those groups with the most economic and political resources; however, such is not *always* the case. Windows of opportunity open mostly during times of economic or political turmoil, and it is at these points that organizations can reorient political debates. The social context that permits organizational actors to make a difference depends on their political placement in relation to other allies, and on the political resources of a wide variety of state actors. These alignments necessarily change over time. In general, representatives of more reformist social movements are chosen by political actors to signify the opposition. This serves to temper more radical political change.

Five periods in the history of old-age insurance emerged, and the chronology of these legislative turning points shapes the organization of the remainder of this volume. Table 1 shows key turning points in Social Security since its inception. There were seventeen amendments studied. For each of these amendments, Table 2 shows the earnings base, contribution rate, and average monthly benefit that corresponds to the amendments. Chapter 2 covers the

TABLE 1

Legislative Turning Points in Social Security, 1935–1985

Year	Effect
1935	Established system of federal old-age benefits covering workers in commerce and industry. Benefits to be payable beginning in 1942 to qualified persons aged 65 and over. Payroll tax of 1 percent each on employers and employees, payable on wage base of $3,000 was to be imposed on January 1, 1937, and was scheduled to rise in steps to 3 percent by 1949.
1939	Authorized supplemental benefits for dependents of retired workers and for surviving dependents in case of death. Starting date for monthly benefits was moved to 1940. Tax rate increase to 1.5 percent, originally scheduled to occur in 1940, was postponed to 1943.
1943	Continued the tax rate at 1 percent until 1945 and authorized the use of general revenues to cover any financial deficit in Social Security.

TABLE 1

Continued

Year	Effect
1950	Extended compulsory coverage to nonfarm self-employed (except for certain professional groups), and to regularly employed domestic and farm workers. Authorized optional coverage for employees of state and local governments and nonprofit organizations. Benefits increased by 77 percent, wage base raised to $3,600 in 1951, and tax rate allowed to rise to 1.5 percent. Authorization to use general revenues repealed.
1952	Benefits increased by 12.5 percent.
1954	Compulsory coverage extended to self-employed farmers, categories of farm workers not covered in 1950 amendments, and miscellaneous self-employed professional groups. Voluntary coverage extended to ministers and members of religious orders. Wage base raised to $4,200 in 1955, and benefits increased by 13 percent. Provisions for "disability freeze" to protect workers from loss or impairment of benefit rights during periods of total disability. Increased tax rates for the 1970s.
1956	Disability insurance benefits added, payable at age 50. Women permitted to retire at age 62 with reduced benefits. Coverage extended to lawyers, dentists, veterinarians, and optometrists. Tax rate increased by 0.25 percent to finance disability benefits.
1958	Increased benefits by 7 percent and raised wage base to $4,800. Benefits added for dependents of disability insurance beneficiaries, and eligibility standard for disability insurance was liberalized. Tax rate increased to 2.5 percent for 1959.
1961	Permitted men to retire at 62 with reduced benefits. Miscellaneous liberalizations, such as increase in widows' benefits. Tax rate increased to 3.125 percent for 1962.
1965	Hospital insurance (Medicare) became law. Benefits increased 7 percent. Tax rate increased to 4.2 percent and wage base to $6,600 for 1966. Coverage extended to doctors.
1968	Benefits increased by 13 percent, wage base raised to $7,800.
1969	Benefits increased by 15 percent.
1971	Benefits increased by 10 percent, wage base raised to $9,000.
1972	Benefits increased by 20 percent, indexed to CPI, to be effective January 1975. Wage base raised to $10,800 for 1973. Tax rate for 1973 raised to 5.85 percent.
1973	Benefits increased by 11 percent. Automatic adjustments rescheduled to begin June 1975. Wage base raised to $13,200.
1977	Passed to meet unexpected deficit. Tax rate increase scheduled for 1978 unchanged, but increase to 6.13 percent in 1979 scheduled, along with higher tax rates for later. Wage base increases in excess of expected automatic adjustments.
1983	Extended compulsory coverage to federal civilian workers and nonprofit employees. Prohibited state and local governments from terminating coverage. Delayed payment of COLAs, accelerated payroll tax increases, and revised tax treatment of benefits. Raised full benefit eligibility age gradually from 65 to 67. Authorized interfund borrowing among three trust funds and maximized trust fund investment income.

TABLE 2
Financing and Average Monthly Benefit of Old-age, Survivors, Disability, and Hospital Insurance

Act[a]	Years[b]	Earnings base	Contribution rate[c] (pct.)	Average monthly benefit under OASDHI[d]
1935–47	1937–49	$ 3,000	1.000	$ 93.07
1939	1939–49	3,000	1.000	
1950	1951–53	3,600	1.500	164.84
	1954	3,600	2.000	
1952	1953	3,600	2.000	
1954	1955–56	4,200	2.000	207.84
1956	1957–58	4,200	2.250	
1958	1959	4,800	2.500	214.75
	1960–61	4,800	3.000	
1960	1961	4,800	3.000	
1961	1962	4,800	3.125	236.88
	1963–65	4,800	3.625	
1965	1966	6,600	4.200	247.63
	1967	6,600	4.400	
1968	1968	7,800	4.400	236.53
	1969	7,800	4.800	
1969	1970	7,800	4.800	250.33
	1971	7,800	5.200	
1971	1972	9,000	5.200	302.24
1972	1973	10,800	5.850	359.01
1973	1974	13,200	5.850	338.25
	1975	14,100	5.850	
	1976	15,300	5.850	
	1977	16,500	5.850	
	1978	17,700	6.050	
1977	1979	22,900	6.130	367.57
	1980	25,900	6.130	
	1981	29,700	6.650	
1983	1982	32,400	6.700	
	1983	35,700	6.700	
	1984	37,800	7.000[e]	
	1985	39,600	7.050	
	1986	f	7.150	
	1987	f	7.150	
	1988	f	7.510	
	1989	f	7.510	
	1990	f	7.650	

SOURCES: "History of the Provisions of Old-Age, Survivors, Disability, and Health Insurance, 1935–1981," U.S. Department of Health and Human Services, Social Security Administration, Publication No. 11-11515, January 1982, p. 19. Average monthly benefits under OASDHI in 1981 dollars from Social Security Bulletin, Annual Statistical Supplement, 1981, p. 70. Post-1982 statistics on earnings base and contribution rate taken from various sources.

[a]Year act legislated.

[b]Year act effective.

[c]Employer and employee each contribute equal percentage.

[d]Old-age, survivors, disability, and hospital insurance benefits in 1981 dollars.

[e]Employee pays 6.7 percent. Employee's additional 0.3 percent is supplied from general revenues.

f Will be adjusted by federal law to reflect increasing income levels.

pre-1935 period and events leading to the passage of the Social Security Act in 1935. Especially for a new bureaucracy, the early years are the crucial years. Many laws establishing new programs are passed without the necessary appropriations to fund the program. Programs instituted in one presidential administration may not be continued in another administration. According to Robert Dahl, "Nothing is harder to create than a new institution, nothing harder to destroy than an established one" (1967: 378).

Chapter 3 covers the origins phase of 1935–49. Although the 1935 Act and the 1939 amendments were the only major pieces of Social Security legislation passed during this fifteen-year period, these years were a crucial time for the fledgling bureaucracy. Chapter 4 highlights the events of the glory days of the program from 1950 to 1969, when the program grew enormously. Changes during these years gave broader coverage and higher benefits and added new programs for disability and hospital insurance. As the ground rules or status quo shifted, new ways of doing business emerged for all groups involved. Once these interests became invested in maintaining or expanding the benefits they derived from Social Security, incremental changes were common. The cash benefits program created a clientele that lobbied for extended benefits, and those not yet included lobbied for extended coverage. The public came to rely on Social Security income; so much so, that in the 1980s there were reminders that Social Security was never intended to replace all income lost through retirement.

Chapter 5 deals with what may be considered the tipping point of the program, a change that occurred from 1970 through 1976. The 1972 amendments were the last in a long line of major benefit increases; after 1972, amendments took the form of programmatic retrenchments. The 1972 amendments linked Social Security benefits to the Consumer Price Index. Chapter 6 covers the period from 1977 to 1990, a time of general retrenchment and public disillusionment with the program. The crisis in the trust funds and entrenchment of the bureaucracy meant less power and authority for the Social Security Administration. Social Security had evolved into a more tightly coupled, zero-sum system.

The framework of these chapters will give the reader a brief sketch of the economic and political environment characteristic of each of these periods. Through this framework, I show how factors both external and internal to the bureaucracy created a context that was primed for the various legislative turning points. Next, I discuss the nature of proposed changes, delineating supporters and opponents, as well as the legislative outcomes. Finally, I reiterate how organizational dynamics illuminate many of the political and social outcomes. Chapter 7 concludes with some thoughts on the future of the program, based on the organizational dynamics presented in the preceding chapters.

CHAPTER TWO

Ground Zero: The Early Years

> I remember that on election day in 1932 there was a strange
> unrest in America. There was murmuring in the marketplace.
> Mortgages were being foreclosed and people were losing their
> homes and farms. Those who had jobs were being dismissed
> because there was no business, and the factories were idle.
> There were long breadlines; thousands were hungry and cold.
> The citizens of the United States were afraid.
>
> —A mid-western homemaker, quoted in Ashworth 1936: 41

ONE OF THE MOST interesting aspects of studying legislative
policymaking is analyzing the early debates on original legislation.
Social Security is no exception. Perhaps this is why this early period
is also the area where by far the most work has already been done.
The key piece of legislation during this time period was the Social
Security Act of 1935, which instituted both federally administered
old-age insurance and state-administered unemployment compensation. This chapter covers events that led to the passage of the
1935 legislation.

The reason for discussing the pre-1935 period as distinct from
later developments lies in the "ground zero" nature of the early
debates, when the program was still controversial and alternatives
were more evident. Policymakers grappled with the changing interests, problems, and capacities of a patchwork of state-level old-age
pension plans, federal emergency relief, and local poor relief (Katz
1986; Orloff 1988). Old-age insurance, as contemporary observers
know it, was not entrenched bureaucratically or in the minds of
American taxpayers in the 1930s. Indeed, contemporary observers
of the Social Security program tend to forget just how controversial the early payroll tax was—a new tax that was proposed during
the worst economic crisis this nation has ever known. It would not
be until the legislation of the 1950s that we would witness frequent
expansions of the program.

In my discussion of the pre-1935 years, I begin with the important events and shifting ideologies in order to show the economic and political landscape of the period. I then discuss important organizations or individuals who either supported or opposed

Social Security in its early form, as well as the organizational dynamics at work.

The Economic and Political Context

Americans pride themselves on their individualism, but as early as 1831 Alexis de Tocqueville recognized that it was not individualism as such but "voluntary association" that was "the real key to social action and organization in the United States" (in Lubove 1986: 1). Before the New Deal, social insurance or relief was a combination of public and private ventures. Michael B. Katz observes, "The precise configuration of relief arrangements varied from state to state, indeed from county to county, but almost everywhere complex funding and administrative arrangements blurred the boundary between public and private" (1986: 46). In the 1920s there were numerous relief programs, including poorhouses, individual families and private charities, voluntary philanthropic associations, and a patchwork of state or local public assistance, but the private sector was much preferred, as Roy Lubove explains:

> The crucial consideration in allocating relief and rehabilitation responsibilities to the private sector was its presumed superiority in safeguarding against pauperization. For one thing, the poor could not interpret private assistance as a right; they had no statutory claim whatever. Similarly, the private sector would prove less susceptible to political pressures for liberalization of economic benefits. Most important, the private sector was better equipped to exert those moral and religious influences which would prevent economic assistance from degenerating into a mechanical dole and source of pauperization. (1986: 186)

Despite this preference, programs of economic relief in the United States were administered both publicly and privately, as were the old-age pensions that had evolved. There was a massive Civil War pensions system in the late 1800s and early 1900s. At the turn of the century, 95 percent of Civil War veterans were receiving Civil War pensions, and by 1910, over one-third of all men in the north, and one-quarter of all men in the United States were covered under this system (Skocpol 1992).

Some private employers, in an effort to "scientifically manage" their labor force, had developed private pension plans in the late

1800s. Pensions became part of the bureaucratizing mechanism, the archetype of the calculable organization being bureaucracy, not democracy (Lipset, Trow, and Coleman 1956). In the early 1930s, of all the workers covered by employer pension plans, 80 percent worked for railroads, public utilities, and metal industries (Lubove 1986: 128). These employers were the larger and more bureaucratic sectors of business, industry, and finance, and they wanted a more efficient way of dealing with older workers. Company pension plans offered an easy, objective way to retire older workers, and pensions replaced the old, informal personnel practice of providing for loyal older workers who were in need. The employer could fulfill this moral obligation in a consistent, predetermined manner. What had formerly been decided on an individual, case-by-case basis could now be dealt with bureaucratically. In addition, some employers perceived that pension plans afforded an efficient, fair method for retiring older, more highly paid workers, and replacing them with young workers who were full of energy and had the most up-to-date training. A further incentive for employers to develop their own pension plans was the attraction of creating a pool of money that they could invest and earn interest on, and on which no taxes would be levied. Some of the business opposition to the original Social Security Act stemmed from the existence of these private pension plans.

There were numerous limitations to most of these early twentieth-century plans, however. Theda Skocpol points out that the United States could have moved to a genuine old-age insurance policy for working men after the Civil War veterans died, but the middle class viewed these pensions as a dangerous precedent of government largesse; their resistance was a major obstacle to broadening the provision of social insurance (Skocpol 1992). Employer-provided pension plans, though more favorably viewed, could be withdrawn, and many were. Of the 418 employer pension plans in existence in 1929 at the time of the Wall Street crash, 45 had been abandoned by 1932 (Slichter 1949: 9). By 1932, only 15 percent of all U.S. workers were potentially covered under these plans, and a mere 5 percent of the needy aged received pensions (W. Graebner 1980: 133). Perhaps most importantly, the majority of employer pension plans implied a moral rather than legal obligation on the employer's part. These plans usually had no provisions for accrued liabilities, and some specifically stated that pensions would be reduced in case of insufficient funds (Lubove 1986: 128).

Labor unions were especially critical of these corporate retirement plans, charging that employers used the pensions as a means of manipulating their employees. The American Federation of Labor contended that private pension programs were conducive to discriminatory practices, and they were eager to shift control of pensions from the private corporations to the "more neutral hands of state and national governments" (W. Graebner 1980: 51). The unions' objections were based on various grounds. First, a pension that a company could grant or withhold at its own discretion could prove an effective weapon in combating union organization in the first place. Second, concentration on future pension benefits, traded for present wage increases, was a poor bargain if the company collapsed or discontinued the plan. Third, unions appealed more strongly to younger workers, who were generally more concerned with wage and hour concessions. Fourth, the unions cited cases of workers going on strike and losing their pension rights, and instances where employers called pensioners back to work during strikes. Finally, these pensions were not portable, so workers were bound to a single employer to retain their pensions.

The Great Depression wreaked economic, political, and ideological havoc with the above-mentioned arrangements. The stock market crash of 1929 and the ensuing Depression brought economic ruin unlike that of any period in American history. In 1933, one out of every four persons was officially listed as unemployed (see Fig. 2). The traditional ideological emphasis on hard work, thrift, and individual initiative suddenly rang hollow to the masses of unemployed. Such massive unemployment meant that the unemployed began to blame the system, rather than themselves as individuals.

The Communist Party in the United States seized increasing attention, and in 1932, for the first time in U.S. history, a Communist Party candidate ran for President and captured 102,785 votes (USBC 1975: 1073). Communist Party membership, though still relatively small, increased during the Depression. Nelson W. Polsby, writing about presidential powers, notes:

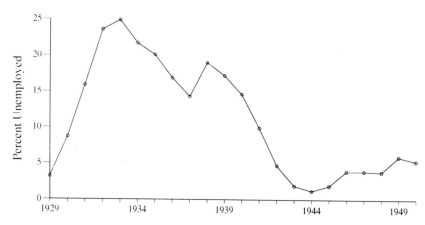

Fig. 2. Civilian unemployed rate, 1929–1950. (Source: Historical Statistics of the U.S.)

There are occasional periods of severe domestic difficulty in which presidential proposals find ready acceptance in Congress. One such period was the famous first 100 days of Franklin Roosevelt's first term of office, when the presidential honeymoon coincided with the depths of a depression. . . . An impressive volume of legislation was enacted during this period, some of it remarkably innovative, but it would be wrong to suggest, as it sometimes is, that the 100 days were merely a demonstration of presidential mastery over Congress. Rather, both Congress and the President responded in much the same way to the urgency of external events. (1986: 208–9)

For business and industry, high unemployment meant lack of spending power on the part of the general public, with a depressant effect on sales and profits. Given the economic context—a booming economy in the 1920s followed by the economic collapse in the 1930s—historically unprecedented departures from private voluntary efforts were forthcoming. It was clear that existing relief and pension programs could not deal with the magnitude of problems associated with massive dependency.

One of the chief reasons for the passage of the original Social Security Act was high unemployment (Gratton 1986). Both the unemployment compensation and the old-age insurance components of Social Security legislation (these were separate titles of the 1935 act) were designed to deal with the problem of unemployment.

Old-age insurance was looked upon as a way of retiring massive numbers of older workers and ultimately transforming them from producers to consumers. But the range of possible solutions to these problems was relatively wide, and it is this factor that makes the form of the 1935 act important. In this political shake-up, Social Security emerged as one of the most significant and enduring of the New Deal reforms. It represented a major shift in emphasis from personal initiative and hard work to provision of a measure of security for all citizens.

In 1934, Roosevelt established the cabinet-level Committee on Economic Security (CES), led by the Secretary of Labor (Frances Perlkins), and including the Secretary of the Treasury, the Attorney General, the Secretary of Agriculture, and the Federal Emergency Relief Administrator. Roosevelt instructed the CES to make a comprehensive study of the conditions that lead to destitution and dependency, and to recommend appropriate measures that would provide protection against the causes of insecurity.

The CES studied the issues, and in addition to the realization that the states could not be expected to be responsible for the enormous relief measures that were required, it was also recognized that the profit motive of business and industry might not ensure the best old-age insurance coverage possible. After noting the shortcomings of private or state-administered pension plans, and the success of foreign nations with national old-age insurance plans, the CES's beliefs were strengthened in the wisdom of federal control.

Roosevelt's enthusiastic support of the Social Security Act of 1935 ensured its success. Roosevelt was enormously popular—he won 57 percent of the popular vote in 1932, and 61 percent in 1936 (USBC 1975: 1073)—and Social Security was a top priority for him; Democrats interpreted attacks on Social Security as attacks on Roosevelt. Moreover, Roosevelt's political astuteness made him successful in his maneuvers to secure the passage of his preferred version of Social Security legislation. Part of his success relates to the concept of coalition formation. Amid the economic and political disarray, previously entrenched interests were momentarily distracted or dislodged. For example, in the early discussions of Social Security, Roosevelt appointed an Advisory Council on Social Security. In order to make it seem that all interests were represented in these early debates, Roosevelt was careful to include representatives of business and industry, labor, and the public (USNA, "Chairman's Files-011-011.1"). In truth, however, this coalition was carefully stacked to include only those representatives of the various interests known to be favorable to the proposed system. Industrial and business groups known to be opposed to Social Security — such as the National Association of Manufacturers and the U.S. Chamber of Commerce — were simply not asked to participate. A letter dated August 16, 1934, from Arthur J. Altmeyer (then Second Assistant Secretary to Secretary of Labor Frances Perkins) to Mary Dewson, vice chair of the Democratic National Committee, reveals how the selection was stacked:

There is an Advisory Council to be appointed to assist the President's Committee [CES]. This Advisory Council will be to some extent representative of the various interests affected but should consist of persons who are in full sympathy with the objectives of the program. Miss Perkins would like to have you serve on this Advisory Council. In any event she wants your recommendations as to persons whom you think should serve. If you will only think of persons as much like yourself as possible you will know the type of person that Miss Perkins has in mind. She is particularly anxious to have people who will be able to stimulate and shape public opinion in their respective communities. (USNA, "Altmeyer-011")

Thus, existing dissension within groups known generically as "business and industry," "labor," and "the public" was used to Social Security's advantage by Roosevelt and other proponents of social insurance, through their choosing a coalition of representatives known to be sympathetic to Roosevelt's contributory program. In other words, members of the Advisory Council were to be selected first as individuals sympathetic to the cause, and only secondarily because of their affiliation with a particular business, industry, finance, or labor group. Newspaper accounts noted only that representatives of "business and industry," "labor," and the "public" served on the council.

The idea of the "relative autonomy of the state" is evident here. It is also clear that the state is not one unified force. According to Skocpol, during periods of crisis, the pressure for change from below as a result of class struggle is so great that the state should act relatively quickly, with less regard for capital's position (1980: 178). Charles and Mary Beard described the support for Roosevelt:

Despite minor dissents and controversies over details, the country as a whole rallied enthusiastically to the support of President Roosevelt during the spring and summer of 1933. Companionship in misery and fear almost turned politics into a love feast. Powerful business leaders cooperated with the administration in a spirit of cheerful compliance contrasting sharply with the hostility which they had displayed toward Bryanism, Progressivism and the New Freedom. It seemed that the concussions of the crisis had shaken their assurance in themselves and their system. The old program of "letting nature takes its course" had lost its glitter. . . . In the spring and summer of 1933 the Lords of Creation were distraught and for the moment had no rallying point save the Chief Executive of the nation. (1939: 244–45)

Clearly, there was a mandate from the public for change in the 1930s, but the nature of the change envisioned varied according to the source. What we see in the early years is a continuum of autonomy within the state. (Similarly, the autonomy of various state actors is also historically variable.) President Roosevelt had more autonomy than did others in his administration, and early administrative supporters had more autonomy than did congressional representatives. From 1933 to 1936, Congress was more liberal than Roosevelt, and it was quite ready to pass noncontributory pension legislation in the election year of 1934. Roosevelt held Congress back by appointing the Committee on Economic Security, which delayed legislation, and then he pressed the more fiscally conservative contributory program upon Congress.

Roosevelt's CES and the Advisory Council, however, were not the only groups working on proposals to deal with the economic hardships brought on by the Depression. Wallace Sayre, writing in 1936, spoke of the "political ground-swell," which he attributed to massive unrest with the existing sociopolitical order. One of the most popular competitors of Social Security was the Townsend Old-Age Revolving Pension Plan. Francis E. Townsend was a retired physician from Los Angeles who circulated a petition to Congress in 1933 proposing a "revolving" pension, which would be financed by a tax to be paid each time a transaction was made in the process of production or marketing. Critics, many of them supporters of Social Security, labeled the tax pyramiding and argued that the economic costs would be enormous. The Townsend Plan promised everybody over the age of 65 benefits of $200 per month. In order to stimulate the economy, pensioners would have to prove that they had spent the entire $200 in any particular month in order to get the following month's pension. Again, critics argued that the administrative costs of collecting and monitoring such documentation would be excessive. Nevertheless, the Townsend movement was large and well organized; by 1935, Townsend claimed 3.5 million paid supporters, and 7,000 Townsend Clubs had been organized (Weaver 1982: 70). Twenty million people signed petitions asking Congress to pass the Townsend Plan (*CR* 1935: 5456). Although Townsend later lost much of his popularity after he refused to answer questions posed by a congressional committee and was declared in contempt of Congress (and then pardoned by President Roosevelt), the Townsend movement survived into the 1980s (Gollin 1981: 109). Both the amount of the monthly pension and the flat nature (everyone would receive the same amount regardless of need) meant that it was considered much more radical than the CES proposals.

Another competitor to Social Security was Senator Huey Long's Share-Our-Wealth campaign. This grandiose scheme, an attempt to follow through on Roosevelt's 1932 campaign promise to give the American people an opportunity to "share in the redistribution of wealth" (*CR* 1935: 9908), proposed a federal tax of 100 percent on annual incomes in excess of $5 million and/or property valued at more than $50 million. The revenues were to be distributed by giving everyone a homestead, car, radio, and washing machine. Persons over the age of 60 who had annual incomes of less than $1,000 and property valued at less than $10,000 would receive monthly pensions of $30 (Weaver 1982: 70).

The Kingfish hired a flamboyant, thirty-year-old Disciples of Christ preacher named Gerald L. K. Smith. Smith, who later became the doyen of America's white supremacists, toured the towns and hamlets of the Delta South with his master's message. "Let's pull down these huge piles of gold until there shall be a real job. . . . Not a little old sow-belly, black-eyed pea job but a real spending money, beefsteak and gravy, Chevrolet, Ford in the garage, new suit, Thomas Jefferson, Jesus Christ, red, white, and blue job for every man!" . . . Within eighteen months there were 27,431 Share Our Wealth clubs, with a total membership of 4.7 million. (Gollin 1981: 110)

Still another competitor of Social Security was the National Union for Social Justice, founded by the charismatic radio priest of Detroit, Father Charles Coughlin. This was the first mass pressure movement of American Catholics. Reverend Coughlin advocated "a silver-backed currency . . . nationalizing industry, and . . . saving the working man from 'the vested interests'" (Gollin 1981: 109). Like Townsend, Coughlin had millions of supporters, but the movement collapsed after a barrage of anti-Semitic rhetoric forced his religious superiors to order him off the air.

Various other relatively small, esoteric, and radical groups presented other radical alternatives. The Utopians proposed planned production, three-hour work days, and retirement at age 45. Other alternatives were Upton Sinclair's socialistic EPIC (End Poverty in California, later renamed End Poverty in Civilization); the conservative American Liberty League, whose primary intention was to detach the more conservative Democrats from their support of President Roosevelt; and the Southern Committee to Uphold the Constitution, which had a program and purpose very similar to those of the American Liberty League but was based in Georgia and Texas. The role of these advocate groups, in retrospect, was one of shifting the ideological agenda. All these social movements provided a radical alternative to the Social Security program. Most of them promised benefit amounts greatly in excess of original Social Security benefits (about $14 per month). The social movements literature notes that "radical flank effects" of this sort do force some reaction from legislators, albeit less radical solutions. Both Frances Perkins (1946) and Edwin Witte (1962) testify to the importance of the Townsend movement on their strategies for securing the passage of the Social Security Act in 1935. Carolyn L. Weaver, noting the effect, says:

The success of the Townsend movement may well have been more apparent than real, for a great deal of the literature on the movement was written by affiliates of the CES and other social insurance advocates. The incentive was strong to overstate the popularity of radical plans so as to pose false alternatives to the economic security bill. Indeed, the immediate effect of both the Townsend and Long movements was to smooth the way for the Social Security Act, which by contrast could only appear moderate. (1982: 71)

Indeed, compared with the social movements of Townsend, Long, and Coughlin, the old-age insurance program that was eventually instituted was not radical at all. As Alan Brinkley (1982) pointed out, and Robert Sherrill underscored in a review of Brinkley's book, it is one of the "funnier ironies of history . . . that Roosevelt owes his liberal sainthood to having been goaded by ideological roughnecks like Long and Coughlin into advocating reforms he was basically rather cool to. They manipulated the Great Manipulator. Roosevelt was not grateful. He and the big business community agreed on many things, but nothing brought them into such enthusiastic agreement as their distaste for Long and Coughlin" (Sherrill 1982: 13).

Support for Social Security

Having portrayed these more radical alternatives as possible solutions, the supporters of Roosevelt's program then had to discredit their value in relation to their preferred version of Social Security. It was relatively easy to discredit the high benefit amounts, such as the $200 per month promised by the Townsend Plan, by citing actuarial estimates on the costs to workers of such large monthly benefits. Social Security advocates had always emphasized the need for a balance between the taxpaying worker and the beneficiary. Also, the notion of a flat pension plan was inconsistent with America's meritocratic ideology. The Social Security program that emerged linked the amount of wages earned and the amount of benefits to be paid out and fitted well with the long-standing American ideology of fairness.

As the popularity of these various programs attested, the public, many of them in dire economic straits, registered their dissatisfaction with existing conditions, and petitions to Congress did not go unheeded. The *Congressional Record* reveals that Congress felt compelled to do something about the economic hardships brought on by the Depression and the very high unemployment rates. Indeed, one finds a great deal of testimony to the effect that the whole capitalist economy was in danger of collapse. A statement by House Ways and Means Chairman Robert L. Doughton (D-North Carolina) exemplified this concern: "The existence of such a large relief problem, the presence of insecurity on such a vast scale is a serious threat to our economic order. . . . The fact that several of these proposals have attracted a wide-spread following implies a threat to our existing institutions which should not be regarded lightly" (*CR* 1935: 5468). Speaking about the Townsend revolving pension plan, Representative George Burnham (R-California) reported that he had received "numerous petitions bearing the names of thousands of my constituents who are vitally interested in the plan and demand its consideration" (*CR* 1935: 5583). (Townsend's great popularity in California may have persuaded a Republican representative from that state to demand the consideration of Social Security.) Representative James Mott (R-Oregon) asked, "Is this body, the duly constituted representatives of the people and the law-making authority of the people, going to deny completely these petitions of the people?" (*CR* 1935: 5457) Representative Richard Duncan (D-Missouri) also reported that the "letters we get from the old folks in our districts are pitiful. They believe honestly in their hearts that they are going to get $200 a month or $100 a month" (*CR* 1935: 5547). Representative Byron Scott (D-California) believed in providing adequate coverage and criticized some of his fellow legislators:

Most of us have sort of grown up with certain fundamental concepts and convictions. When we were learning them they were perhaps correct. In the meantime, however, so much has happened, and things have changed so in the past few years that many people are left in a confused state of mind. . . . Very few people [used to believe in] unemployment insurance or old-age pensions. Rugged individualism was the accepted theory. . . . Our technological development has tended to throw men out of employment, but at the same time it is tending to increase the national income, the wealth that is produced each year. . . . The funny part about it is that we were so willing to move clear up to the twentieth century as far as our technological development is concerned, but when somebody comes along with an invention in the social field we turn it down because our minds cannot grasp a new idea. (*CR* 1935: 5547–48)

Opponents of Social Security used the long-standing argument that social insurance of any sort would encourage idleness. Chairman Doughton disagreed: "Quite the contrary. The worker's right to benefits is conditioned upon his previous employment, and social insurance will do nothing to break down the sacred American tradition of self-reliance and initiative. . . . It must be recognized that the aged person in need of public assistance is in a different class from the ordinary relief case. There is no question of returning him to society as a wage earner. His time of gainful employment has passed" (*CR* 1935: 5468–69). Many supporters of Social Security emphasized this same concern with efficiency and economic usefulness. Mott stated, "Those who are able to do the work required by modern industry are those who are physically able and who have not reached the age limit of their economic usefulness in and to industry" (*CR* 1935: 5568). Mott was a supporter of Social Security as long as the worker would be required to "retire from competition and to spend his pension money." This logic was very similar to that employed under the Townsend Plan.

It was also argued that the burden of providing for the elderly was depressing the initiative of younger workers. Senator Robert F. Wagner (D-New York) stated, "The incentive to the retirement of superannuated workers will improve efficiency standards, will make new places for the strong and eager, and will increase the productivity of the young by removing from their shoulders the uneven burden of caring for the old" (*CR* 1935: 9286). Again, it is important to reiterate that a major concern was the creation of new jobs. Representative Reuben Wood (D-Missouri) emphasized a key consideration in all retirement policies, citing the case of the Railroad Men's Retirement Act: "If it should go into effect, it is estimated that in the first year it will take out of service approximately 250,000 railroad men, placing them on a pension or annuity. That would naturally make openings for 250,000 younger men" (*CR* 1935: 5560).

Pleas for assistance and support for a federal Social Security plan also came from state and local governments, many of whom could not remedy these problems with existing local monies. A resolution was sent to Congress from the Board of Supervisors of San Diego County in California, urging Congress to pass the Social Security legislation. Fred Block and his colleagues write: "The massive unemployment of the Great Depression stimulated a wave of protests demanding 'bread or wages.' Local government authorities, their revenues depleted by the economic collapse, were both stymied in responding to these demands and fearful of resisting them. To cope with their dilemma, they lobbied in an increasingly alarmist spirit for federal emergency relief measures, until then unprecedented in the United States" (1987: 9).

The American Federation of Labor backed Labor Secretary Perkins in support of Social Security legislation. Not only was the Social Security Board originally housed in the Department of Labor building, but also labor unions wanted the Social Security Board to be administratively supervised by the Department of Labor (USNA, "AFL-1940"). The support of the AFL was not merely ideological. The Depression and high unemployment had virtually emptied the coffers of union pension plans, strike funds, and unemployment monies. The 1934 Proceedings of the AFL's annual meeting reveal this concern: "Even the most powerful unions of skilled workers, despite their herculean efforts to protect their members against these industrial hazards, find their treasuries depleted and themselves impotent to cope with these problems" (AFLA 1934: 207). The AFL anxiously looked forward to the economic relief provided by the new Social Security legislation. An instrumentalist analysis largely overlooks other forms of socialization of domestic security costs; the fact that local and state governments, and labor unions as well, sought economic relief from the federal government shows that other groups besides monopoly capital had economic interests in the expansion of the welfare state.

Some union officials even believed that their pensioners could be transferred en masse to the government system. In a letter dated June 5, 1936, from Arthur J. Altmeyer to Frank Morrison, secretary-treasurer of AFL, Altmeyer was skeptical of the idea: these plans, he wrote, "can be carried on without regard to the Social Security Act or can be modified so that the total benefits under the private system and under the Social Security Act combined are equal to what is now provided under the private system alone. However, the liability now existing in the case of persons already pensioned under private pension plans could not be transferred to the government system" (USNA, "AFL-1940").

The AFL's support of Social Security legislation was, therefore, not unqualified. The president of the AFL, William Green, agreed that labor should share the burden of old age insurance "because everyone gets old" (USNA, "AFL-1940"). He favored a tax on payroll to be paid by the employer and employee, and suggested that funds should be pooled in the various states rather than in company reserves. But Green did not agree that labor should pay any portion of the unemployment insurance tax. After all, he argued, it was the employers who laid workers off.

Both the AFL and the more radical subcommittee called the Committee of Industrial Organizations (which later split from the AFL unions and was renamed the Congress of Industrial Organizations) vehemently opposed the Townsend Plan. They called the proposed $200 per month pensions "unrealistic" (USNA, "American Federation of Labor"). Green clearly stated the reasons for this opposition in a letter to state and local union affiliates:

As responsible representatives of the interests of wage earners, the American Federation of Labor and its affiliated unions . . . approved unanimously a report of the Executive Council against too great of an extravagance in one phase of the Social Security program at the expense of tax increases on workers and failure to provide simultaneously for other pressing needs such as more adequate compensation for employment [the AFL during the early 1930s was lobbying for minimum-wage laws], provision for temporary and permanent disability, and health insurance. (USNA, "American Federation of Labor")

But security for workers also was perceived by some as security for business and industrial interests. Time and again the *Congressional Record* shows concern with the stabilization of the two. One arm of the Department of Commerce under the Roosevelt administration, the early Business Advisory Council, articulated these ideas. Although the Business Advisory Council was not an independently formed group of business representatives, it and other groups in favor of the Social Security Act consistently spoke of how the reduced purchasing power of the people causes "in itself recurrent industrial depression which arises out of the failure of consumption to keep pace with production" (*CR* 1935: 5572–73).

Opposition to Social Security

Despite a great deal of support for Social Security in the 1930s, the program was very controversial, especially in the Congress, in the early years (unlike the relative complacency and acceptance of the 1950s and 1960s). Support and opposition took strict party lines: roughly 30 percent of the Republicans voted "nay" on the first proposals, while fewer than 30 percent of the Democrats voted against them. (In the final House and Senate votes, however, only 14 Democrats and 23 Republicans voted against the act; USNA, "011-011.1".)

Early congressional opposition to the act emanated primarily from Roosevelt's diehard opponents among the Republicans. Their arguments followed the usual Republican objections: too many standards, too much federal domination, and high tax rates. They argued that the government could not and should not bear the burden. Representative Charles Eaton (R-New Jersey) declared: "I think we stand today in this country at the crossroads of a great decision which transcends all parties, all sections, and all interests; and this decision is whether we are going to choose American organized industry as the instrument for the solution of these tremendous, far-reaching problems, or whether we are going to resort to some modified form of Russianism and attempt to solve these problems by government." The New Deal was an un-American institution, he said, and "the ultimate aim of the New Deal is to place all American industry, business, and individual liberties under the control of Government here in Washington." Eaton emphasized the importance of this sort of view for politicians: "If you take the industrialists out and stand them before the wall and destroy them, what is going to happen to the politicians?" (*CR* 1935: 5581–82).

A contingent of powerful Democrats from the South, many of them senior members in charge of committees, also opposed Social Security on the grounds of federal intrusion. From the 1860s until the election of 1932, the Republicans had dominated most of the country outside the South, and since most of the Democrats in Congress were Southerners, they succeeded to committee chairmanships when the balance of power shifted to the Democrats. They were well entrenched in their home states, often running unopposed in general elections, and they stood to lose a great deal in their constituencies if they supported Roosevelt's Social Security programs. They argued that the Southern tenant farm–based economy would be undermined if federal dollars were pumped in. Indeed, when Social Security was enacted in 1935, agricultural and domestic workers were excluded; of course many such workers were blacks living in the South. Quadagno (1985) argues that the influence of the Southern Democrats is a central factor in explaining our bifurcated Social Security system—unemployment relief that is state-administered (granting states' rights and local autonomy), set apart from the federally administered system of old-age insurance.

There was also opposition from business and industrial organizations. From the moment the Social Security Act was proposed, some representatives of business and industry expressed fear that the program would restrict their freedom of movement, both in terms of preexisting corporate pension plans and in terms of excessive government regulation. Senator William H. King (D-Utah) received a telegram to that effect from the officers of Endicott Johnson Corporation: "For many years our company has assured its 19,000 workers protection similar to that provided in the pending Social Security program, and because of this we strongly urge that Federal legislation permit States to enact legislation allowing financially responsible employers to set up separate company reserves. If this opportunity is afforded New York State, we believe we can convince our legislature that such separate reserves are necessary to protect us as payer of high wages against low-paying employers in other States" (*CR* 1935: 1824). Clearly, the statement implied, pension reserves created capital for corporations, and protected their competitive positions within their respective industries. Representative John Taber (R-New York), who opposed the Social Security bill, had a similar objection: "Many industries have already set up old-age retirement propositions for their employees. Many industries are taking care of unemployment insurance themselves. No exemption is made for these people." When Taber was asked which industries provided unemployment relief, he could name only one, and that was American Telephone and Telegraph (*CR* 1935: 5545).

The objections from conservative business and industrial leaders mostly fell along the lines of protecting business. They feared the economic effects of high rates of labor turnover, and as William Graebner points out, "Decreased labor turnover was also conceived as a method of building conservative values into one's work force, an exercise that assumed special importance in the years immediately following World War I and in the late 1930s. Employers knew that a strike posed a whole range of different questions for older workers than for younger ones, and that their responses to those questions were more likely to be conservative" (1980: 36–37).

Other business and industry opposition stemmed from the notion of a payroll tax, half of which would be paid by the employer. Both the NAM and the U.S. Chamber of Commerce were totally opposed to any plan that would require them to contribute half the amount of the tax on wages. Skocpol points out that the NAM, "predominantly a spokesman for small and medium businesses was transformed during the early 1930s into an anti-New Deal vehicle dominated by big business" (1980: 168). A flier produced by the NAM and sent to thousands of industrialists throughout the United States in May 1935, a few months before the Social Security Act was passed on August 14, suggested that the "so-called social security [will] mean industrial in-security." The flier urged industry to "send your views on this bill at once to your senators" (USNA, "NAM"). Affiliates of the NAM did not think that industry should have to pay taxes "for the social security of its employees, and Alfred P. Sloan [president of NAM] announced that 'industry has every reason to be alarmed at the social, economic, and financial implications. . . . The dangers are manifest'" (Piven and Cloward 1971: 93). Silas Strawn, a former president of the U.S. Chamber of Commerce and the American Bar Association, condemned the act as "economically preposterous and legally indefensible" (ALC 1935: 130).

The opposition of the American Liberty League, strongly backed by General Motors and DuPont, emanated primarily from their perception that increased governmental intervention in the economy and the added burden of a new tax on payroll could have only ill effects. Representative Eaton wanted to give a chance once more to "American industry, American initiative, and American self-reliance to assert themselves. . . . [The New Deal] is simply one more step toward sovietizing our distinctive American institutions" (*CR* 1935: 5583).

There was also hostility toward Roosevelt's brain trust. Some members of Congress were concerned that industry was not being sufficiently reassured by the policies being developed by this group. The remarks of Republican Representative Harold Knutson (Minnesota) show the tenor of the hostility: "Not a man on the [Ways and Means] committee really understands this bill. It was drawn up by members of the 'brain trust,' many of whom, probably had never earned a dollar in their lives and they are not earning anything now—theorists, college professors, young whipper-snappers, some of them not dry behind the ears" (*CR* 1935: 5541). Representative Allen T. Treadway (R-Massachusetts), another business supporter, complained on April 12, 1934: "While this measure has been before Congress since the middle of January, and more than a thousand pages of testimony have been taken, I want to call attention to the fact that there was little testimony from persons of experience in business lines" (*CR* 1935: 5528).

The opposition of the two largest employer organizations, NAM and the U.S. Chamber of Commerce, may even have been somewhat muted owing to the influence of the Reconstruction Finance Corporation (RFC). Although the scope of the RFC was subsequently broadened, President Herbert Hoover had set it up in 1932 in hopes of bringing financial relief mainly to business. H. Parker Willis explained the plan in a 1934 article entitled "Business on the Dole":

This corporation was an institution whose mission it was to lend to hard-pressed banks and to certain classes of business enterprises, notably, as it turned out, railways and insurance corporations, the sums that were necessary to meet their current obligations. The RFC obtained the funds with which to carry out this work from the Treasury Department, while the Treasury (which already had a deficit in its own operations) obtained the necessary money by selling its bonds or notes to anyone who would buy them—largely to the banks. With the funds thus acquired, the hard-pressed railroads, banks, insurance companies and others paid off their creditors, in full or in part, as circumstances required. They now owed the government, which owed the community. (1934: 3)

In essence, some business and industrial leaders were concerned that if they spoke out too loudly against Social Security, the RFC would call their loans. Further, any vehement opposition on their part would appear as a blatant double standard: it's acceptable for the government to bail out business and industry, but not workers. Some of the potential opposition was thereby silenced.

Organizational Dynamics

In all this mélange of organizations for and against Social Security, all working in a period of grave unrest and uncertainty, one can discern the effects of organizational dynamics. Probably the central fact was the disarray of organizations representative of business and industry, and the selective coalition of the early Advisory Council. Although some business organizations were opposed to the original legislation in 1935, there were at the same time pockets of support even among business leaders. Two of these groups, the National Industrial Conference Board and the Business Advisory Council, fit well with a "corporate liberal" thesis, in that they represented progressive ideas on social welfare legislation. Indeed, James O'Connor (1972) uses the Business Advisory Council's support to bolster his argument.

Martha Derthick, too, has found evidence of business and industrial support:

While a large majority of businessmen initially opposed social insurance, fearing its costs and the effects on work attitudes and the economic system, there was also from the start a small number of prominent business executives who were prepared to argue the social necessity of it. Having a strong sense of social responsibility, such men were readily available for public service, and, having a need for business support, the Roosevelt administration and the Social Security Board were eager to engage them. . . . As coopted supporters of the program, these executives helped to counteract business opposition in the early days of strident opposition to the New Deal and eventually to win a measure of business acceptance for social insurance. . . . As ambivalence and internal division inhibited negative opposition, they also inhibited the formation of conservative alternatives to social insurance (1979: 134–35).

Derthick also shows how the insurance industry, though a potentially strong opponent of social insurance, was not at all united. Agents disagreed with management; eastern seaboard giants of the industry disagreed with the rest of the country; some argued that Social Security would destroy private insurance, while others argued that it could be used as a springboard, that is, to show the inadequacy of Social Security benefits and then sell private insurance to supplement them. As in the other sectors of business and industry, the more progressive members of the insurance industry prevailed. These companies had more staff resources and expertise, but more importantly, they were the ones to receive invitations from the Roosevelt administration to get involved in the formation of Social Security legislation (Derthick 1979: 136–42).

For the most part, the opposition from business came from large employers. Archival documents reveal that some, though not many, smaller employers, who did not have pension plans and had therefore few alternatives to offer, supported Social Security legislation from the start. As M. B. Folsom, the treasurer of Eastman Kodak, reported to the U.S. Chamber of Commerce, these companies were not in a financial position to provide the reserves necessary to set up their own pension plans (USNA, "USCC").

For organizational actors, both perceived interests and political power depend to a degree on the economic, political, and social environment. As noted earlier, political processes act to construct both rules and interests (Fligstein and McAdam, n.d.). In the turbulent environment of the 1930s, it was not easy for a wide variety of organizations to gain an understanding of, or agree upon, what their true interests were, and whether, in the Depression, those interests had changed. This disorganization of business, industrial, and insurance organizations, together with the perception of a major threat shared by members of Congress, gave Social Security supporters a window of opportunity to push their program. In this manner, power depends as much on the context as on the characteristics of the contenders (McAdam, personal communication).

Under Roosevelt, this politically adept group of politicians and civil servants gathered facts, garnered support, and guided legislation through the appropriate channels. Within this group known abstractly as "the state," there was politically effective coalition formation that has perhaps not existed since then. The President, key members of Congress, the Secretary of Labor, and other administrators were generally working toward the same goal. The careful selection of the original Advisory Council may have suggested that it represented all interested groups, but because it actually included only persons known to be favorable toward old-age insurance, as well as influential spokespersons in their communities, it had great control over the agenda. Who, then, limited the agenda and the debates? Obviously, the pluralist's notion of the state as a neutral arbiter cannot apply, for the state, far from soliciting the counsel of some important groups known to oppose the Social Security Act of 1935, simply left them out.

Another reflection of the nonneutral stance of state actors was the fear of some in business and industry of the RFC's calling their loans. Whether the danger was real or imagined matters little in terms of outcomes. This coalition formation also relates to the instrumentalist argument. Roosevelt and other state actors, in a number of ways, were able to use certain representatives of capital to further their interests—this certainly happened more often than the reverse. Not only did representatives of capital not seek out Roosevelt or other state actors, they did all they could, especially the NAM and the U.S. Chamber of Commerce, to stop Social Security legislation in the mid-1930s. This hardly fits in with the instrumentalist argument that it is primarily monopoly capital that acts to socialize the costs of an inefficient mode of production. Furthermore, not only were the NAM and the USCC opposed to Social Security in the early years, there were other "noncapital" organizations that *did* want to socialize the high costs of unemployment. Many AFL-affiliated unions had their own unemployment or pension funds before the Great Depression, and these were hard hit. Union coffers were quickly emptied. The AFL therefore actively sought to "socialize" its pension and unemployment costs through Social Security legislation.

This period provided a unique opportunity to social reformers and social insurance advocates. The relatively small group of reformers that had gathered some momentum around the turn of the century needed just such an event as the Depression to set the wheels of ideological and political change in motion. These groups could look not only to the past experience of the American system with relief and pension programs but also to various European models of social insurance. Organizational theorists' notion of mimicry lowering uncertainty is relevant. Processes of mimicry are important because they alleviate much of the risk and uncertainty present in major innovative change. The public-sector solution to the welfare program was evident in Germany, Belgium, Italy, France, and Denmark by the late 1800s. Social reformers and social workers in the United States had tested models of the welfare state in these nations, and they advocated these during the turn of the century (Weaver 1982). Similarly, others argued for an extension of the logic of Civil War pensions to male workers during the early twentieth century (Skocpol 1992). It would require the problems of the Great Depression, however, to initiate real changes.

The events preceding the Social Security Act of 1935 reveal that other organizational dynamics combined to make the program a reality. Popular protest movements put pressure on Congress to do something. Their concern with the collapse of the economy is apparent in congressional documents. Further, the ripple effect of high unemployment rates that had lowered consumption and reduced profits for most of business and industry gave Congress the chance to justify the program as alleviating unemployment while at the same time stimulating business. And after all, some representatives of business and industry supported Social Security; certainly, the radical alternatives to Social Security made the program more palatable by shifting the ideological agenda.

Nevertheless, the chaos engendered by the Great Depression did not in and of itself dictate the need for a Social Security program in the form it took. Though a broad number of solutions seemed possible, various key actors helped to limit the agenda. The Committee on Economic Security and President Roosevelt took an active part in shaping the programmatic outlines and molding public opinion. Roosevelt and his lieutenants, skilled strategic actors, were eventually successful in helping to define the range of alternatives considered with regard to Social Security.

The time perspective utilized by organizational actors is also illustrated during the early years. For example, many of the organizations representing business and industry reacted rather than acted. Especially for the organizational actors opposed to Social Security, the time perspective was considerably shortened, as is often the case in crises environments. There was far more unplanned adaptation than clearly mapped out strategy. The truncated time perspective and concept of limited rationality were much more evident during the early 1930s than the instrumentalist account allows for. The business and industrial organizations that opposed Social Security in the early years were uncertain of the effects of the program. For them, foresight and rationality were rarer than short-term perspective or limited rationality.

Many organizational actors have a short-term perspective and concentrate on the near future (Perrow 1986). They select from options that receive only as much attention as they deserve in the context of many important decisions that have to be made. Given that actors do not have complete and accurate information, and given that they only cursorily review their options, it is not surprising that the NAM and the U.S. Chamber of Commerce could not correctly predict how Social Security might ultimately serve them very well. It seems quite clear that, initially, some representatives of business and industry were made to swallow a pill they did not want. It was not a master-planned conspiracy, but rather an unplanned adaptation.

Eventually, as the next chapter shows, the organizations that represented more powerful groups responded in a way that was most beneficial for them. Their organizational persistence was a central difference between politically entrenched organizations and those representing more fleeting popular protest movements.

In turning to the events that occurred between 1935 and 1949, it is important to reiterate that it was not inevitable that Social Security would take the form it did, and it was not inevitable that it would survive.

CHAPTER THREE

The Push for Acceptance, 1935-1949

> Those taxes were never a problem of economics. They are
> politics all the way through. We put those payroll contribu-
> tions there so as to give the contributors a legal, moral, and
> political right to collect their pensions. . . . With those taxes
> in there, no damn politician can ever scrap my social security
> program.
>
> —Franklin D. Roosevelt, quoted in Schlesinger 1959: 308–10.

THE PASSAGE OF LEGISLATION, and persistence in following
through on legislative intent, requires monumental energy. Nelson
Polsby writes: "Most bills do not become laws; they are introduced,
referred to committees, and there languish and die. So even to
speak of a bill's actually becoming a law is to speak of an atypical
event" (1986: 138). Further, Congress will sometimes pass legislation but appropriate little or no money for the programs; in other
instances, what one Congress authorizes, the next Congress does
not wish to finance (Lindblom 1980: 67). Truly, the early years of
an organization are vital in determining both its longevity and its
structure. James Q. Wilson argues: "The formative years of a policymaking agency are of crucial importance in determining its behavior. As with people, so with organizations: Childhood experiences
affect adult conduct" (1989: 68).

Much like private businesses, the first days, months, or years of
an organization are a most critical period. This is especially true of
a new organizational form such as Social Security. Contemporary
observers of Social Security are inclined to forget just how controversial the early program was. The newly created state bureaucracy
was required to assign numbers to taxpaying workers, collect taxes
from employers, and submit a detailed budget without knowing
the costs of the new operation. The passage of the Social Security
Act in 1935 did not necessarily imply its long-term success; on the
contrary, the early years were shaky ones for the program. The
Townsendites were still a threat, Congress stalled on voting appro-

priations, firms did not always pay the new payroll tax, even the constitutionality of the plan was in some doubt. It was significant that all these issues were resolved in favor of the program. It was also significant that in all these cases, Congress and Social Security bureaucrats were forced to make concessions to powerful interests.

From 1935 to 1949, as political insiders and reformists, the early Social Security Board (SSB) was not an autonomous body set apart from powerful interest groups; rather, it chose accommodationist strategies to ensure the political success of the program. In doing so, it had to make compromises that scarred the program's economic integrity. Therefore, although the program endured politically, its trust funds were weakened for the long term. After Roosevelt was reelected in 1936, even staunch opponents began to mold the program to their interests. There was little point in further opposition, and the SSB appeared ready to work with these groups. Merely four years after passage of the original Act, the 1939 amendments weakened the link between contributions and benefits by granting benefits in case of death to the dependents and survivors of covered workers, and changing the starting date for benefit payments from 1942 to 1940.

These 1939 amendments, a major departure from the earnings-based features of the 1935 Act, were supported both by the SSB and by many representatives of business and industry, though for different reasons. Business and industry were not interested in socializing the costs of production but merely wanted to ensure that large pools of trust fund reserve money did not accumulate in the federal Treasury. This also explains why the 1939 amendments postponed the scheduled payroll tax increase (from 1 percent to 1.5 percent) until 1943 instead of 1940. The significance of the reserve will be discussed in depth.

Two other important reasons for the early success of the program will be discussed in this chapter. First, the type of personnel recruited were committed and zealous in their support of the program. Second, the close alliance between program administrators and Roosevelt meant that state bureaucrats had access to important information that outsiders, such as the Townsendites, did not have.

The Economic and Political Context

One year after the establishment of the Committee on Economic Security, the Social Security Act of 1935 was signed into law by President Roosevelt on August 14, 1935. It established a three-fold assault on problems brought on by the Depression. First, it established a state-administered system of unemployment compensation. Second, it initiated three federal-state needs-based grant programs: old-age assistance, aid to dependent children, and aid to the blind. And third, it instituted an old-age insurance plan for workers in commerce and industry that tied benefits to a person's work history, payable beginning in 1942 to qualified persons aged 65 and over. The payroll tax was imposed on January 1, 1937, at a rate of 1 percent each on employees and employers. This tax was payable on any wages under $3,000 per year and was originally scheduled to increase to 1.5 percent paid by both the employee and employer by 1939. Although full funding, as required of private insurers, was not mandated for Social Security in 1935, the original objectives of the program included provisions to accumulate a substantial reserve to make the program self-sustaining.

Under pressure from the White House, Congress agreed to postpone consideration of the Clark amendment, which would have answered the concerns of businesses with preexisting pension plans by exempting them from participation in the Social Security program. Roosevelt assigned a number of expert advisers to key senators to ensure the defeat of the Clark amendment, and he threatened to veto the entire Social Security package if the amendment passed (Weaver 1982: 91). Congress also defeated a provision for the sale of voluntary annuities by the federal government. The insurance lobby killed the voluntary annuities clause in the Senate. It would have allowed higher contributions than required by law, on a voluntary basis, and was intended to supplement Social Security. Organizations representing the insurance industry perceived it as a threat to their business, through the loss of relatively low-risk beneficiaries (USNA, "Insurance Industry-057.1").

To administer the program, a three-member Social Security Board was created by Title VII of the Act. Not more than two members of the SSB could be from the same political party, and they were selected by the President with the consent of the Senate. Significantly, the SSB was allowed to appoint attorneys and experts without regard to civil service laws. Because of this, they were able to choose carefully among the most avid supporters of social insurance.

Of the several threats to the program in the early years, the most serious was the question of its constitutionality. From 1935 until early 1936, seven of nine New Deal acts were declared unconstitutional (Weaver 1982: 108), and both Roosevelt and his supporters in Congress feared that the Supreme Court would not uphold the expansive federal regulation for compulsory old-age insurance embodied in the Social Security Act. For several preceding decades, the Court had subscribed to the notion that federal legislation should not interfere with areas of regulation thought to be the exclusive domain of the individual states (Lopez 1987). Many who opposed Social Security suggested that it was unconstitutional because the federal government can only tax to raise revenues for public purposes. The supposed unconstitutionality stemmed from the fact that Title VIII of the Social Security Act was "an enforced insurance premium for old-age annuities" (*CR* 1935: 5530).

Another difficulty faced by the early SSB was the continuing uncertainty and reluctance on the part of business and industry to support the program. The Business Advisory Council and National Association of Manufacturers vacillated in their support of the registration of workers. Both groups approved of a program to register efficiently all covered employees for Social Security taxation on April 30, 1936. On June 15, 1936, however, both groups withdrew their support on the advice of lawyers that this would preclude their legal rights to bring suit in connection with the constitutionality of paying taxes (USNA, "Business Advisory Council").

A concerted "employers' campaign" then began not only against the reelection of Roosevelt and other New Deal Democrats but also, in one last effort against Social Security (USNA, "Protest, Opposition, and Criticism"):

In early October a group of Detroit industrialists worked out a social-security campaign; and the Republican National Committee adopted it with enthusiasm.

The thesis was simple: the government was taking away the workers' money, and heaven alone knew whether the worker would ever get it back. (Nothing was said, of course, about employers' contributions.) In the last two weeks before election, placards began to go up in plants: YOU'RE SEN-TENCED TO A WEEKLY PAY REDUCTION FOR ALL YOUR WORKING LIFE. YOU'LL HAVE TO SERVE THE SENTENCE UNLESS YOU HELP REVERSE IT NOVEMBER 3. Workers opening their pay envelopes found a solicitous message:

> Effective January, 1937, we are compelled by a Roosevelt "New Deal" law to make a 1 per cent deduction from your wages and turn it over to the government. Finally, this may go as high as 4 per cent. You might get this money back . . . but only if Congress decides to make the appropriation for this purpose. There is NO guarantee. Decide be-fore November 3 — election day — whether or not you wish to take these chances.

. . . In St. Louis on the last Saturday, Landon asked how any administration could keep track of 26 million Americans. "Imagine the field opened for federal snooping. Are these 26 million going to be fingerprinted? Are their photographs going to be kept on file in a Washington office? Or are they going to have identification tags put around their necks?" (Schlesinger 1960: 635–36)

The Republican National Committee further charged that the pay-roll taxes constituted "a method whereby the government was collecting pennies from the poor to finance a wasteful govern-ment"; according to Arthur Altmeyer at the SSB, however, the campaign was a political boomerang — the public gave the Presi-dent and his supporters a tremendous vote of confidence (USNA, "Amendments 1937").

ROOSEVELT'S 1936 REELECTION

In his second inaugural address, on January 20, 1937, Roose-velt said, "The test of our progress is not whether we add more to the abundance of those who have much; it is whether we provide enough for those who have too little." Roosevelt had won 61 per-cent of the popular vote, while Landon gained only 37 percent. One cannot be sure what would have happened to the Social Secu-rity program if Roosevelt had been defeated, but his reelection certainly came at the right time to boost the program's odds for success. With the defeat of Landon, the Republican candidate who had lambasted Social Security, opponents of the program were gradually forced to admit that it was there to stay, at least in the short term.

Roosevelt interpreted his victory as a mandate for Social Security, and he responded to the possibility of the Supreme Court's declaring it unconstitutional with his famous Court reorganization plan. The Court's invalidation of many of Roosevelt's New Deal programs, including the National Industrial Recovery Act and the Agricultural Adjustment Act, had evoked strong disapproval not only from Roosevelt, his administration, many members of Congress, and dissenting justices, but also, it seemed, from a good measure of the public. Roosevelt was not about to let the Court similarly invalidate Social Security.

In a message to Congress on February 5, 1937, Roosevelt stated his case: "The Court . . . has improperly set itself up as a third House of the Congress—a superlegislature . . . reading into the Constitution words and implications which are not there, and which were never intended to be there" (in Lopez 1987: 9). Roosevelt proposed a bill whereby the President would be allowed to appoint one new justice for every justice aged 70 or older who had served on the federal bench for at least ten years. He stipulated that the total number of justices could not exceed fifteen. Since in 1937, six out of the nine Supreme Court justices were over age 70 and had served on the Court for more than ten years, Roosevelt could by means of carefully selected appointments get a Court that thought as he did. Depending on one's political point of view, this plan was called "packing" or "unpacking" the Court. To opponents of the New Deal, it was packing; Roosevelt Democrats saw it as unpacking, ridding the Court of stodgy thinkers and replacing them with justices who had new ideas and bold interpretations of the Constitution.

The Supreme Court's decision on the constitutionality of Social Security essentially depended on whether they decided to review the taxing and benefit titles of the Social Security Act together or separately. If reviewed together, it was clear that they provided a federal insurance program that was beyond congressional authority. If reviewed separately, they constituted a payroll tax on

employees, an "excise" tax on employers, and an earned benefit—
all within the purview of federal authority.

On May 24, 1937, writing for the majority, Justice Benjamin N.
Cardozo separately analyzed Titles VIII (taxes) and II (spending)
of the original Social Security Act. He wrote:

> Congress did not improvise a judgment when it found that the award of
> old age benefits would be conducive to the general welfare. The President's
> Committee on Economic Security made an investigation and report, aided
> by a research staff of Government officers and employees, and by an Advi-
> sory Council. . . . Extensive hearings followed. . . . More and more our
> population is becoming urban and industrial instead of rural and agri-
> cultural. The evidence is impressive that among industrial workers the
> younger men and women are preferred over the older. . . . With the loss
> of savings inevitable in periods of idleness, the fate of workers over 65,
> when thrown out of work, is little less than desperate. . . . The problem
> is plainly national in area and dimensions. Moreover, laws of the separate
> states cannot deal with it effectively. . . . Only a power that is national can
> serve the interests of all. (in Lopez 1987:11)

Through this decision, perhaps acknowledging Roosevelt's threat,
the Supreme Court reversed its own precedent, and in Helvering v.
Davis declared both the old-age insurance and unemployment provisions of the Social Security Act to be within the scope of federal
government regulation. In June of 1937, the Senate Judiciary Committee reported unfavorably on Roosevelt's Court reorganization
plan. The point was moot.

Support for Social Security

The dedication of the SSB administrators and staff was a crucial resource in the early years. Robert J. Myers, for many years
Chief Actuary of Social Security, noted, " 'Over the years, most of
the American staff engaged in program planning and policy development have had the philosophy—carried out with almost a
religious zeal—that what counts above all else is the expansion of
the program' " (in Derthick 1979: 24).

Although the SSB staff was ideologically committed to Social
Security, they wanted to avoid making Social Security a political
football. They were very cautious in promoting their position in

a nonpolitical manner. The reasons were clearly spelled out in a letter dated July 14, 1936, from Arthur J. Altmeyer, assistant to Secretary of Labor Frances Perkins, to Mary Dewson, chair of the Democratic National Committee. Altmeyer explained: "Our publicity policy so far has been to furnish explanatory data largely of a factual character rather than argumentative material. In so doing we have avoided any appearance of engaging in debate with critics, either political or otherwise. This policy, of course, is safer so far as avoiding criticism of partisan activity and we have also felt it has been safer so far as promoting the longtime program for social security" (USNA, "Democratic National Committee"). This information control was a tremendous source of strength for the SSB. In another letter, to Mary Dewson, dated September 2, 1936, Altmeyer said further: "We have tried to correct misapprehensions concerning the Social Security Act, regardless of whether these have arisen from partisan misstatements or genuine lack of understanding. However, we have tried to avoid the appearance of being on the defensive or of engaging in debate with critics. We have been told that is the most effective way to proceed" (USNA, "Democratic National Committee").

Another tactic designed to avoid any criticism of Social Security as a partisan program was an explicit policy of removing the SSB from actual congressional debates. The SSB's policy was to make recommendations to the House Ways and Means and Senate Finance committees (the two congressional committees that dealt with issues related to Social Security), and then to "let the Congressional Committees work them out from the Board's recommendations." In this manner, the SSB "let them fight it out up there" (USNA, "Report on Recommended Changes").

This philosophy was also evident in the resignation of the first chairman of the SSB, John G. Winant. Winant resigned in 1937, largely as a result of Landon's accusations against the Social Security program. Winant wanted to be free to defend the system in a more politically active way. Arthur J. Altmeyer was named chairman in 1937 and remained in this position until 1946.

Altmeyer was known as "Mr. Social Security," and to this day his leadership and influence are apparent. He enjoyed unflagging support from Roosevelt. He knew who Social Security's friends were, and he was at the forefront of the early efforts to expand and improve the Social Security Act. But state bureaucrats were required to be patient in instituting a full-fledged program, and Altmeyer's vision of Social Security was much grander than the plan instituted in 1935. In a 1937 address to the National Conference of Social Workers, Altmeyer noted, "Passing the laws is only, as it were, a 'curtain-raiser' in the evolution of such a program" (in Weaver 1982: 102).

Altmeyer's ability to deal with trying situations can be seen from his handling of early events. In addition to the threat of unconstitutionality, the new SSB also had to worry about funding. Congress had not voted appropriations, and consequently there was no central headquarters, and little in the way of personnel. During the first year of operation, Altmeyer, undeterred, borrowed typewriters, paper, envelopes, and even staff from other government departments (AFLA 1935). Once appropriations were made, Altmeyer carefully selected staff, from top administrators to regional field office directors, who were friends of the social insurance movement. There is an often-noted story about Altmeyer, kneeling down on the floor of his office, going through the array of hundreds of index cards containing the names of candidates for the regional offices. The advocates within the newly created SSB also began to conduct research and disseminate information to the public regarding the Social Security program. They cooperated with the Democratic Party and the AFL to defend and publicize the program.

Other events entrenched Social Security further. For example, after January 1937, when employees began paying Social Security taxes under the belief that they would receive old-age insurance, writers of the era acknowledged that "Any party that would attempt to wipe out this system would be committing political suicide" (Cardozo in Lopez 1987: 11). The close relationship between Roosevelt and SSB administrators, particularly Altmeyer, also helped in that it assured close coordination of political and administrative goals. With such coordination, and agreement on bottom-line issues and ideal dimensions of the new program, the public did not receive conflicting information. Often, when Roosevelt received a letter regarding Social Security, he would forward the letter to Altmeyer, with a note, "For preparation of reply for my signature." For example, William Green, president of the AFL, wrote to Roosevelt on June 22, 1937, requesting that a separate presidential commission be set up to study the experiences under the Social Security Act. In the reply Altmeyer prepared for Roosevelt, Altmeyer wrote: "I agree with you that this is a subject which requires careful and sustained attention. However, I am inclined to think that it would be possible to make the greatest progress in the study of the complex questions involved if the Social Security Board pursued the necessary studies and made the necessary contacts with the various interest groups, such as the American Federation of Labor, as its studies progressed" (USNA, "American Federation of Labor"). Roosevelt's reply to Green followed Altmeyer's wording exactly.

Another example of the close relationship between the two men concerned a December 15, 1938, memo from Altmeyer to Roosevelt in which Altmeyer highlighted recommendations for the maximum Social Security program desired. Altmeyer wanted to propose a maximum program so that any political compromises could be made from that point. Further, he did not want the President to be caught off guard regarding Social Security (USNA, "Report on Recommended Changes"). This relationship illustrated Roosevelt's intent to protect the program from excessive outsider meddling of any sort.

Altmeyer was also adept at assessing friend and foe. He received information from various sources regarding statements about Social Security made by various persons or organizations, and he was careful to thank his supporters. Altmeyer wrote John L. Lewis, chairman of the then separate Committee for Industrial Organization: "I have wanted to thank you personally for the statement you issued relative to the Social Security Act and particularly the commendation you extended to the Social Security Board organization. . . . Your statement helps tremendously in maintaining the morale of the workers in our organization who are trying to make the operation of the law a success" (USNA, "Altmeyer—011").

Altmeyer and other representatives of the SSB also began to persuade opponents that the Social Security program was in their best interest. A quote from Altmeyer illustrates his tactics:

In talking with business groups, in addition to stressing stability of purchasing power, etc., I have pointed out that payroll taxes afford a definite mathematical relationship between contributions and benefits so that the whole system may be kept within bounds. I contrast this with a system whereby benefits are paid out of the general treasury so that in the nature of things there can be no mathematical relationship, and, therefore, no top limit. I found it possible in this way to develop a line of thought that has never occurred to most employers and business men who think only of the immediate nuisance and financial disadvantage of payroll taxes. (USNA, "Protest, Opposition, and Criticism")

Indeed, the success of the SSB in the early years was due not only to its central location in the information network but also in great measure to its good judgment on which criticisms to respond to and which to ignore. The SSB was the clearinghouse for most information, and while other individuals or groups might take some interest in Social Security legislation, none had the SSB's access to information or devoted such time and energy to its promotion.

Gradually, both business and industry became supporters of Social Security. In part, the turn in attitude was due to lack of a unified opposition, the result of disagreements prior to the 1936 elections, in much the same way as disagreements had arisen between Green and Lewis and other labor leaders. As time went on, and the economic recovery that business and industry had anticipated was slow in coming, they had to accept the accommodations of the SSB bureaucrats. These bureaucrats wisely saw that it would be a good thing to ease the concerns expressed by various business, industrial, and labor organizations. It was clear that through payment of pensions, the spending pump would be primed. Thus the general tide of opposition gradually shifted toward a strategy of influencing the administration of the program and later amendments.

One way in which employers could cope with the new legislation was to pass their Social Security costs on—to the consumer in the form of higher prices, or to the worker in the form of lower wages, or to the government in the form of lobbying for tax breaks related to Social Security (such as excluding benefits from Social Security taxation, and later transferring increasing portions of wages and salaries into benefits packages). This was understood and acknowledged by most groups in the early period. At a February 4,

1937, meeting of the SSB, a discussion between Vincent Miles (SSB member) and R. R. Reagh, the government actuary, revealed this concern:

MILES: . . . the employers' tax is passed on to the consumer anyway.

REAGH: I don't see how you can possibly overcome that. That is true of every private pension system ever written, and it is true of the Civil Service Retirement plan. I don't see how you can escape that. (USNA, "Amendments—Discussion of Title II")

The fact that workers would have to bear the majority of the burden was understood almost from the outset. A 1938 master's thesis explained: "The taxes are levied so that most of the money comes from the largest group of contributors, the low-salaried workers and their employers. Business houses may be able to shift their share of the tax to consumers in the increased costs of goods, or to the workers in decreased salaries, or to the owners in decreased returns. . . . Ultimately, then, the employees as a group, both as workers and as consumers, will bear the major costs of the old-age benefits" (Dilley 1938: 26). Economist John Brittain has found in his work that, "given the level of productivity in a country, the presence of a payroll tax on employees tends to reduce the wage in dollars by roughly the amount of the tax" (1971: 125).

Other events reflected the gradual acceptance of Social Security by business groups. A member of the SSB who was invited to attend an April 30, 1936, meeting of the U.S. Chamber of Commerce reported: "The tone of the discussion about Social Security, on the whole, plus the fact that this meeting drew an attendance almost twice as large as the Chamber officials had expected, serves to indicate growing interest in the Social Security program on the part of business, and, I should say, less bitter antagonism and more sympathetic understanding" (USNA, "USCC").

The insurance industry further exemplifies this shift. A previously divided group, this industry began to agree that Social Security was beneficial for private insurance providers. Altmeyer and the SSB were fond of citing this industry's growing confidence in the program. Many insurance executives testified in favor of Social Security and argued that encouraging people to ensure their future through Social Security served to increase the public's awareness and interest in private plans. They made this point in a list of suggested responses to possible criticisms of the Social Security Act developed by the SSB, Social Security would not compete with private insurers:

> On the contrary, leading figures in the field of private insurance feel the act will be helpful to insurance . . . it is felt that the effect will be to popularize insurance, both on the part of individuals and on the part of concerns which will wish to provide additional old-age retirement coverage for their higher paid employees and executives, in addition to that provided under the Social Security Act. In a recent speech, a well-known official of a life insurance company recalled the opposition raised by private companies to the war risk insurance during the World War. Instead of its taking business away from private companies . . . private sales of insurance more than doubled because of the public consciousness of the insurance principle which was created. (USNA, "Protests, Opposition, and Criticism")

The benefit of Social Security to private insurers was that only certain groups were covered, and even then, at a minimum level, while the insurance companies could cater to the lower-risk, more highly paid workers. The fact that private insurers used Social Security as a risk-diffusing strategy was evident in a 1939 labor union newsletter: "Insurance companies now want social security records when they audit pay rolls and they don't want the business in some instances if they are not shown social security records" (USNA, "Amendments 1939").

Support from the business sector also came from the Business Advisory Council, as James O'Connor emphasizes: "Perhaps the most influential group in drawing up the Social Security Act of 1935 was the Business Advisory Council. This benchmark in the history of social insurance legislation was very much the product of corporate liberal planning" (1973: 139). It should be noted, however, that because the Business Advisory Council was part of the Department of Commerce, which was headed by a Roosevelt appointee, it was not necessarily representative of the general position of business before 1936. Further, it appears that any "representative" or "contrary" members were dropped. A 1936 Associated Press article reported: "Eighteen leaders in American business yesterday were named by Secretary Roper to be members of his business advisory council. They are to take the place of others who resigned or retired before Christmas. Causes of friction that almost disrupted the original council were believed eliminated. . . . The council became the center of controversy last year over charges and counter charges that friends and foes of the Administration were attempting to use it for their own propaganda purposes" (USNA, "Business Advisory Council Membership—1936"). Clearly, there are problems inherent in using such a group to illustrate corporate liberal planning. This council was in-house, divisive, and probably unrepresentative of the general opposition to the 1935 Social Security Act that emanated from business and industrial groups. It was set up to advise the SSB and to orchestrate consensus among business and industrial leaders regarding Social Security; it was not in any sense an independent representative of business opinion.

One of the issues that the Business Advisory Council dealt with after Roosevelt's reelection was garnering business support for registering workers. Altmeyer had asked the council for its recommendations about sending a questionnaire to the associations to determine whether they would cooperate in registering workers. A letter from Marion B. Folsom, chairman of the Business Advisory Council, dated May 5, 1936, noted:

[They] did not think it was good policy to put this question up to the associations as it might lead to a great deal of discussion and misunderstanding. The committee [recommends] that the Board could, in advance of any announcement of the plan, obtain the endorsement of a few important associations. If these endorsements could be made public soon after the announcement of the plan, it should be quite helpful in having the plan received properly by employers generally. The committee would suggest that larger employers be advised directly of the plan and that contacts not be confined to associations exclusively. (USNA, "BAC to Department of Commerce Board")

The Business Advisory Council also urged simplification in the administration of the program (e.g., keep the forms simple and the reports infrequent), incentives for the continuation of existing benefit plans, and exclusion from the definition of wages of sick pay, benefits, vacation, workmen's compensation, and contributions to stock and thrift plans. The council urged government to educate others in business and industry on how Social Security could be utilized to complement private plans, an indication of their greater access to insider information. They opposed higher contributions and the larger reserves that would result (USNA, "Amendments, 1938"). Fred Block and his colleagues, writing about support for Social Security, note:

> Once federal legislation seemed inevitable, at least some big-business leaders were willing to play a role in molding it. Some provisions of the Social Security bill originated in the work of a number of business-backed policy groups, including the Business Advisory Council of the Department of Commerce (headed by Gerald Swope of General Electric), Industrial Relations Counsellors (the consulting firm created and controlled by John D. Rockefeller, Jr.), and the American Association for Labor Legislation, which had been largely responsible for crafting the Wisconsin unemployment plan on which part of the act was modeled. Not surprisingly, a number of these "business statesmen" came from the retail sector, which had a stake in measures that promised to sustain mass purchasing power during economic downturns. A few leaders from such capital-intensive industries as oil also lent some support to the bill, since they did not depend on low-wage labor. (1987: 16–17)

Opposition to Social Security

However, not all went smoothly after Roosevelt's reelection, and those less enthusiastic about the program and the SSB continued to question their legitimacy. First, there was the problem of noncompliance. Top SSB administrators visited several regional offices and found the following types of noncompliance in 1937:

1) Use of questionnaires by employers which exceeded the requirements of the Social Security Board and the U.S. Treasury, requiring employees to return answers in reference to church, union membership, etc.

2) Deducting more than 1 percent from employees' pay in violation of the Act, especially in the field of hotels and restaurants.

3) Excess deductions to employees under the guise of defraying handling costs.

4) Refusal to hire persons without account numbers.

5) Making deductions from the pay of new employees but refusing to accept their account numbers.

6) Discharging employees on the pretext of increased costs due to Social Security taxes. (USNA, "Amendments through May 1937")

Labor unions accused employers of misusing the information received on the Social Security forms. Beginning very early, one of the major concerns of the labor unions was the confidentiality of the information that workers were required to submit to employers for Social Security purposes (USNA, "AFL-1940"). One plasterers' union reported that men over the age of 45 were not sent out on jobs because workmen's compensation premiums were higher for them than for younger workers. According to the union, employers were using the age information required for Social Security to discriminate against older workers (USNA, "Amendments 1939"). It was evident that many employers resisted and rejected the original Social Security Act. General acceptance of the program by business and industry was achieved only slowly.

Another important obstacle was the continuing threat of alternative programs, especially the Townsend Plan. The Townsend Plan continued to be very popular in the early 1940s. Furthermore, because the Social Security Act of 1935 called for the first pension payments to be made in 1942, many defenders of Social Security pushed vigorously to make the monthly benefit payments begin earlier. As early as February 5, 1936, Edwin Witte, professor of economics at the University of Wisconsin and executive director of the CES, in a confidential letter to Altmeyer, recommended speeding up first payments, prior to January 1, 1942. Witte believed this would induce a considerable number of old people to retire, leaving jobs open to a corresponding number of younger workers then unemployed. Also:

This amendment should considerably increase the popularity of the Social Security Act and help to check the support given to impossible old age pension schemes. Politically . . . [old-age insurance] as it stands is very weak because no one will get any benefits until 1942. . . . The proposed amendment will make a large number of workers eligible immediately for benefits. These will be distributed in practically every community in the country, and the fact that they will actually get money should serve very effectively to demonstrate that the Social Security Act does provide old age protection to a majority of the American people. (USNA, "Legislation Affecting SSA-OASI")

Witte acknowledged the added costs associated with his proposal, but he argued that since actuarial estimates were problematic anyway, the probable overall effect would probably be to advance the time when benefits would have to be paid in part from the general revenues. He felt that this time would be "in the distant future—1960 or thereabouts."

The original CES proposal called for the accumulation of a reserve in a trust fund, as opposed to putting the program on a pay-as-you-go basis. The SSB had initially also planned to accumulate substantial reserves for the Social Security program. It drew the analogy to the trust funds accumulated by private insurance companies to cover a portion of their outstanding obligations, with the reserve being an integral part of a sound scheme. But there was pressure from the Business Advisory Council, the NAM, and the U.S. Chamber of Commerce to freeze the tax rate at 1 percent (it was scheduled to increase to 1.5 percent in 1939), pressure from supporters to liberalize benefits (estimates were that average benefits would be only $14 per month), and pressure pay benefits sooner than 1942.

At first, Altmeyer urged others to consider increases in the benefit amounts first, and only after such consideration, to recommend how those benefits should be financed. He stressed the linkage between benefits and contributions. He argued that the only effect of freezing the tax rate and increasing benefits would be to "introduce in place of the present gradual and certain increase [in the payroll tax rates], abrupt and uncertain increases during the next few years" (USNA, "Pat Harrison"). Given that the insurance analogy was so closely adhered to in the early years (Cates 1983; USNA, "Amendments—Discussion of Title II"), this argument was not surprising.

By 1937, however, Social Security administrators were concerned that the five-year time lag between the collection of taxes and the payment of benefits was too long and that the best way to build confidence in the system was to begin paying higher benefits as early as possible to as many people as possible. Chairman Altmeyer also urged earlier payment of benefits and extension of coverage to all groups that desired it, as soon as was administratively feasible. Roosevelt at this time was only in favor of extension to wives, widows, and orphans—groups that were covered under the 1939 amendments (Cates 1983; USNA, "Amendments—Discussion of Title II"). Roosevelt later changed his mind and recommended broadening coverage of the Social Security Act to meet the threat of Townsendism and the Republican campaign for changes. Many of the groups that were excluded from the original legislation lobbied for coverage after 1936—for example, seamen, and employees of banks and religious and charitable organizations (USNA, "Amendments 1937").

Impetus for the move away from a trust fund was also prompted by Keynesian economics, popular during the late 1930s. John Maynard Keynes's *General Theory of Employment, Interest, and Money* (1936), which suggested that saving money was not conducive to economic improvement, was attractive to desperate politicians of the period. By 1937, even the SSB had abandoned the notion of a large reserve fund.

There were several ways to spend down the reserves, but the SSB shaped the legislative agenda with regard to this issue by limiting the information they presented to Congress. In a discussion between Altmeyer and J. Douglas Brown, consultant to the SSB, and professor of economics at Princeton University, Altmeyer asked Brown whether the board should recommend one way to pay larger benefits earlier, or whether they should submit various alternatives to Congress, indicating the implications of each:

BROWN: If you could take for granted that there would be a thorough discussion and understanding of what is involved in the two, then the proposal of alternatives might be wise, but I am afraid that the particular reasons for taking one alternative over the other by Congress might not be the basic philosophy, but might be certain other factors. . . . The precise way to do it is a pretty complicated one and I don't know whether the "people on the Hill" would understand the reasons one way or the other.

ALTMEYER: What you are trying to say is that the Social Security Board is really the linkage between the experts and the non-experts. We are trying to translate to the Congress the expertness as we understand it. (USNA, "Amendments—Discussion of Title II")

Unlike the SSB, congressional representatives did not have the time or the desire to consider all the actuarial details or pros and cons of the alternatives; in this sense the SSB was organizing and processing information for them. This gave state bureaucrats significant power to shape the political agenda. They had the opportunity to censor the information they gave to Congress. Overall, in 1938 Congress was more cautious than the SSB. An August 1938 memo from Altmeyer to the President relayed the information that Robert Doughton, chairman of the House Ways and Means Committee, and the Democratic members of that committee felt that "it would be dangerous to open up the question of Social Security in an election year" (USNA, "Amendments 1938").

Another potential stumbling block to the program occurred in the form of a 1937 Advisory Council. Historically, advisory councils have become a way to coopt the opposition (Derthick 1979: 89–90), but this was not the case in 1937. This advisory council, unlike others, was not welcomed by the SSB. It was appointed at the request of Senator Arthur Vandenberg (R-Michigan), a Social Security critic, and was greatly resented by the board and Altmeyer, who viewed it as unwanted outsider meddling. During the meeting of the Senate Committee on Finance when this advisory council was established, the SSB had reluctantly agreed because they felt they had no alternative (USNA, "Advisory Council through 1937"). A letter from Altmeyer to Representative Doughton (D-North Carolina), chairman of the House Committee on Ways and Means, explained: "The Social Security Board did not take the initiative in suggesting the creation of the Advisory Council on Social Security. . . . The Board was already following the practice of meeting with representative groups to discuss problems arising under the Social Security Act." A letter from Altmeyer to Senator Pat Harrison (D-Mississippi), chairman of the Senate Committee on Finance, reflected Altmeyer's concern: "I think it would be exceedingly unfortunate if we build up the Advisory Council into a sort of 'royal commission' which might assume too much authority and responsibility for the development of a program." One indication of Altmeyer's lack of enthusiasm for this council was the fact that the SSB did not meet with the council until October 1937, some eight months after it was created.

The SSB and its defenders relied on three political maneuvers to deal with these less uniformly sympathetic Advisory Council members. An interoffice memo from the Chief Actuary to Altmeyer, Mary Dewson, and others, dated November 8, 1937, explained that the first tactic was to discuss the important issues among a small circle of close confidants, slowly "educate" the other members of the group and encourage them to publicize any recommendations. Second, for the more vocal opponents of Social Security legislation, a radical flank tactic was adopted whereby defenders of the essential aspects of the legislation would vehemently criticize any compromise plan and present their own, more radical alternative (USNA, "Old-Age Insurance"). The purpose, of course, was to force the opposition to compromise with a more radical alternative, thus assuring that the original, more reformist, desires of the SSB were met. As an example, one of Altmeyer's first tasks was to submit various alternative plans for accomplishing the objectives of the Social Security Act. A letter from Professor Witte of the University of Wisconsin to Altmeyer reveals this political maneuver: "Your AC-1 plan might be an acceptable compromise provided the tax rates are not disturbed. Considering the fact that Congress in both houses is now so pronouncedly anti-Administration, however, I doubt whether it is advisable to propose this plan for Congressional action. . . . It is for this reason that I am still taking the position of being very critical of the plan. I want the anti-Administration men of the Council to be solidly committed to this plan before I reluctantly accept it as a compromise" (USNA, "Advisory Council 1938"). As a last resort for those who couldn't be convinced to support the administration and the SSB's position, they were allowed to "frame their program without further disclosure of the arguments which will be made against them" when their recommendations went to the congressional committees (USNA, "Advisory Council 1938").

Reserves were a major issue—as they still are. Was a reserve needed at all, and if so, how much was necessary to ensure that payments could be made without having such large amounts in reserve that it drained the economy? Conservative members of Congress spoke out against the reserve. Senator Vandenberg called the originally proposed $47 billion reserve "the most fantastic and the most indefensible objective imaginable. It is scarcely conceivable that rational men should propose such an unmanageable accumulation of funds in one place in a democracy" (in Weaver 1982: 111). The reserve was one of the major objections of business to Social Security after the passage of the 1935 legislation. The major objections to the reserve concept were that it would be a temptation to government extravagance; it would be a temptation to Congress and pressure groups; it would be impossible to find sound investments; any increase in savings might disturb the already precarious economy; and finally, it would freeze the national debt at $47 billion (USNA, "032.11").

The Business Advisory Council on Social Security opposed reserve funding and therefore argued for a reduction of the tax rates and an increase in benefits. In their opinion, the reserve was an "invitation to governmental extravagance and likely to result in increases in benefits which cannot be financed in the future" (USNA, "Amendments 1938"), and they were concerned about its deflationary effect, which would retard business and employment and further the despair of the Great Depression. At a meeting of the Business Advisory Council and the SSB on February 6, 1937, the members of the Business Advisory Council stated that benefits would probably have to be increased in the early years, because existing benefit amounts would be easily criticized as hideously low; instead, they advocated starting the benefits earlier and raising the amount to be received by beneficiaries (USNA, "Amendments—Discussion of Title II").

A U.S. Chamber of Commerce report also recommended a pay-as-you-go system: "It is very properly urged that there should be no dependence upon reserves calculated according to the actuarial principles necessarily used by private insurance companies, for the reason that such a procedure is wholly inconsistent with a government-operated, compulsory system of benefits, supported by taxation" (USNA, "Amendment of the Social Security Act"). The U.S. Chamber of Commerce therefore recommended postponing the scheduled tax increase from 1 percent to 1.5 percent on January 1, 1940. They also advocated a direct contribution from the federal government, a development that might be interpreted as in line with an instrumentalist argument if it were not for its timing. It was not until after the Chamber was certain that Social Security taxes would be collected that they attempted (unsuccessfully) to convince the federal Treasury to contribute to the trust fund. They did not seek out Social Security, but adapted to it after it was instituted.

The U.S. Chamber of Commerce also recommended paying

larger benefits earlier than was originally intended. Besides the disadvantages of a large reserve, they were also concerned with the interrelationship between old-age assistance and old-age insurance, feeling that the state-administered old-age assistance, with its higher monthly payments (approximately $30 per month), would make the welfare option of assistance more attractive than the incentive-based old-age insurance benefits amounts (approximately $14 per month under the 1935 provisions). Given their emphasis on a pay-as-you-go plan, they saw no need to delay paying benefits. The Chamber was careful to point out, however, that they opposed an overall increase in the costs of the program, any extension of benefits to new categories of workers, and any new provisions for temporary or permanent disability benefits.

The National Association of Manufacturers also instituted an internal committee to assess the impact of Social Security on their affiliated organizations, with the expectation that the committee would make recommendations regarding directions for future policymaking. A letter from William B. Warner, president of the NAM, to Averell Harriman, chairman of the Business Advisory Council, revealed a list of recommendations drawn up by NAM's Economic Security Committee, among them the following:

1. Limit to $3,000 the amount of taxable wages and salaries;

2. No benefits should be paid to persons directly engaged in strikes (i.e., unemployment compensation or pensions);

3. In order to place the rights of both members and non-members of labor unions on a level of equality, benefits should not be denied to any person for refusal to take union-organized employment;

4. Taxation of small employers as well as larger employers (most of the industries that NAM represented were larger);

5. The exclusion of benefits under the classification of taxable wages; and finally,

6. Opposition to the reserve. (USNA, "NAM")

In another letter from Warner to Harriman dated February 24, 1937, Warner reported that NAM's Economic Security Committee had reached this conclusion: "Except for building up a relatively small initial 'emergency' fund, there should be no accumulation of reserves under a nation-wide old age pension plan, (1) because such an accumulation is almost certain to lead to national waste and inflation, and (2) it would eventually be impossible for a government accumulating such tremendous reserves to validate its pension plan without taking over a substantial part of American industry" (USNA, "Amendments through May 1937"). Industry was concerned about the "socialistic" features of much of the New Deal legislation, and Social Security reserves were no exception. A further argument against the accumulation of a reserve was made by M. A. Linton of Provident Mutual Life Insurance Company of Philadelphia. "You are taking care of the aged and building for the future," Linton said; "You can't expect any generation to bear two burdens at once, so that is the real reason to get rid of the reserve plan" (USNA, "Amendments—Discussion of Title II").

But again, it is important to note that business and industry only slowly adapted to Social Security. Some business and financial leaders fought Social Security until benefits were paid in 1940. The author of an unpublished thesis in 1938 commented, "While it should be relatively simple to demonstrate to a businessman that an adequate security program would promote greater satisfaction and efficiency among his workers, and that it would nearly pay for itself out of the savings on charity and relief, there are few who actually take these factors into consideration" (Dilley 1938: 57).

Disagreement continued over such fundamental issues as benefit levels and extensions of coverage. On November 5, 1937, Benjamin J. Anderson, Jr., an economist with Chase National Bank, testifying during a meeting of the Advisory Council on Social Security, urged caution in extending benefits further than the allotment of the original legislation. He argued that even though the act was made as generous as seemed feasible in 1935, the fiscal situation had deteriorated since then; he cited an increase in the national debt, and urged a balanced budget. Financial institutions were obviously interested in protecting the Treasury (USNA, "Advisory Council Meeting of November 5–6, 1937").

Most of those opposing the provisions in the 1939 amendments to extend benefits to new groups of workers were, according to Edwin Witte, "smart enough to realize that increasing benefits is not the way to get lower taxes" (USNA, "Advisory Council 1938").

The Social Security Amendments of 1939

Forces opposing the 1939 amendments did not prevail. Thomas L. Stokes, in a May 12, 1939, article in the *Washington Daily News*, declared that the conservatives' "weakness in Congress is due to the constant pressure from constituents who want something offered by the New Deal. Congressmen must look to the saving of their own skins" (USNA, "011-011.1"). The Social Security amendments of 1939 added insurance protection for dependents of retired workers (aged wives, dependent children), and for widows and children of deceased beneficiaries (survivors). These amendments also moved up the date for payment of first benefits to 1940, instead of 1942; the tax rate increase to 1.5 percent, scheduled to occur in 1940 in the original act, was postponed to 1943, and subsequently, in later amendments, to 1950.

The 1939 amendments were a major concession to organizations representing business and industry. The freezing of the tax rate at 1 percent for the next eleven years meant that any reserve accumulation would be less than it would have been under the originally proposed increase to 1.5 percent. The larger benefit payments that were allocated were intended to provide more protection and to enhance purchasing power—again, a method of lowering reserves while stimulating consumption. Stokes, writing in the *Washington Daily News* in 1940, said that the beauty of the 1939 amendments was that they were "not a spending program in the usual sense, since the money already has been paid into the Treasury in earmarked taxes and therefore it would not represent 'deficit spending' nor affect the budget. The argument is that money collected in pay roll taxes would be thrown back into the stream of purchasing power and thus compensate for the withdrawals from purchasing power represented in the pay roll taxes" (USNA, "Altmeyer-011").

Furthermore, the amendments did not alter the concept of a trust fund (primarily as a concession to the SSB), and did create a Federal Old-Age and Survivor's Trust Fund for "safeguarding the insurance benefit funds" (USNA, "Doughton, Robert L."). However, the amount of the fund was cut from about $47 billion to less than $20 billion (Weaver 1982: 118). This meant that the program had shifted from a reserve-funded system to a pay-as-you-go system. In effect, the system that had started as an actuarially balanced program, in which any increase in benefits would require an increase in taxes, had become an intergenerational chain letter, with the latest beneficiaries at highest risk of losing their investment. Spending the trust fund reserves in this manner, only four years after passage of the original act, meant that the link between contributions and benefits was seriously weakened. This choice was both a blessing and a curse for the Social Security program. It was a blessing in the sense that similar programs could be initiated regardless of contributions; it was a curse in terms of long-term solvency. A 1940 *Business Week* article reported: "The present provisions regarding the investment of the moneys in the old age reserve account do not involve any misuse of these moneys or endanger the safety of these funds . . . the funds will continue to be invested in U.S. Government bonds—the safest investment in the whole world" (USNA, "LaFollette, Robert M.").

The most significant event during the decade of the 1940s, World War II, redirected Americans' attention from domestic problems and concerns to foreign affairs. Chairman Altmeyer, however, told the nation not to worry: "There will be no retreat for Social Security as the result of the defense program" (AFLA 1940). Aside from minor changes in Social Security, mostly dealing with postponing the tax rate increase, the 1940s were a time of settling in and assessing the progress made in the 1930s. Benefits were relatively low, and there were no increases. It was not a time of growth for the bureaucracy, nor a time of retrenchment. Although there was criticism from some that we should abandon our social experiments and divert all funds to national defense, others were convinced that it was only through *social* security that we could have *national* security (USNA, "AFL-1940"). In addition, because the war had created jobs and stimulated the economy, critics of the high costs of the program were rebuffed, if not preoccupied.

One important development during the 1940s had to do with labor unions and pensions. The AFL and CIO, determined to ensure security for families, worked for a "family wage" in collective bargaining agreements. However, during World War II, the War Labor Board mandated that wages could not increase because that would feed inflation. Workers dealt with this problem partly

TABLE 3
Republican Representation in Congress, 1935–1950

Year	Pct. House Republican	Pct. Senate Republican	Year	Pct. House Republican	Pct. Senate Republican
1935–36	26.2	28.1	1943–44	49.3	39.6
1937–38	23.6	20.8	1945–46	44.2	41.1
1939–40	39.2	28.1	1947–48	56.7	53.1
1941–42	38.4	31.2	1949–50	39.5	43.7

SOURCE: *Historical Statistics of the U.S.: Colonial Times to 1970*, Part 2, Washington, D.C.: U.S. Bureau of the Census, p. 1083.

by manipulating job titles, and also, of more lasting significance, unions began to fight for higher pensions, since they could not negotiate for higher wages. A mid-1940s political shift toward the right gave the Republicans political strength (see Table 3), and the Democrats still had the conservative "baggage of the South" (Quadagno 1987). This development, together with the 1937 split between the more reformist AFL unions and the more radical CIO unions, meant that a divided labor front was losing its drive to secure increased Social Security benefits. A 1948 ruling by the National Labor Relations Board stating that pensions were bargainable issues declared that from the unions' perspective, it was easier to push for private pensions than to fight for Social Security. This emphasis on private pension plans would have important implications for the developments of the 1950s.

One final substantive note is important. When the first benefits were paid in 1940, there were 159 taxpaying workers for every old-age insurance beneficiary (*Social Security Bulletin* 1971–85: 77), and 6.8 percent of the U.S. population was aged 65 or older (calculated from USBC 1975: 10). The dependency ratio of 159:1 was the result of several factors: relatively few Americans qualifying for benefits under the new program, a small proportion of the population being elderly, and large numbers of workers contributing to the trust funds. All these favorable factors would be reversed in later years, and major problems for the program would result.

Organizational Dynamics

Organizational persistence, interests and incentives, coalition formation, time and timing, and ideology are organizational dynamics that are evident during these early years. With regard to organizational persistence, as noted earlier in this chapter, the early Social Security program faced a number of challenges and threats to its longevity. It is noteworthy that all these issues were resolved in one way or another. Social Security was able to survive and persist, but the costs of the political compromises to the economic integrity of the program would later haunt the trust funds. As a political program and not an economic contract, the compromises made in the 1939 legislation dramatically shifted the balance between receipts and obligations. Those organizations that were able to persist throughout the legislative process had their concerns addressed by Congress. In this sense, organizations must remain forever vigilant, and vigilance requires enormous economic and political resources.

With regard to organizational interests, it is clear that groups sometimes referred to abstractly as "capital" and "labor" were internally divided on the precise definition of their "interests," even at the organizational level. In the tremendous economic and political turmoil, "interests" became even more difficult for organizations to define. Uncertainty means shifting realities and shifting perceptions for organizational actors. For example, there was a split within the U.S. Chamber of Commerce between big and medium or small businesses.

Historian Arthur M. Schlesinger Jr., describes the annual meeting of the U.S. Chamber of Commerce at the end of April 1935:

Not all businessmen were in all-out-opposition. The Chamber of Commerce meeting showed the existence of a deep rift between those who wanted at least to maintain diplomatic relations with the New Deal and those who insisted on war against it. The first class was made up to a degree of big businessmen, living in big cities, college-educated. . . . These men were less affected personally by New Deal measures than were small businessmen. A large corporation could absorb the impact. . . . Appreciating the importance of public relations, appreciating in some cases the problems of government, men of this sort were inclined to view Roosevelt's efforts, if not with positive sympathy, at least with the conviction that they could exert more influence from the inside than from the outside.

The second class consisted mostly of medium-sized and small business-men, largely from small towns, in the main less educated, less wealthy, and less sophisticated than the others. These men were directly hit by New Deal measures as the big men never were, in terms of status as well as of profits. They felt injured by political hostility and threatened by social change. They could not understand what in the world was going on in Washington. They were determined to dig in their heels and fight for the America they knew. The intransigents among the big businessmen played on their fears and provided them with leadership. . . . In this spirit, the Chamber . . . enthusiastically voted its opposition to the proposed two-year extension of NRA, to the social-security bill . . . and to all labor legislation.

A few big business leaders took care to dissociate themselves from this outburst. "As a member of the United States Chamber of Commerce," Thomas J. Watson of International Business Machines wrote the President the next day, "I deeply regret the sweeping criticisms of the Administration, but I am sure their action does not reflect the sentiment of businessmen in general." The Business Advisory Council—including among others, Watson, Henry I. Harriman, the outgoing president of the Chamber, Winthrop Aldrich of the Chase National Bank, Walter S. Gifford of American Telephone and Telegraph, W. Averell Harriman of Union Pacific, Myron Taylor of United States Steel, Gerard Swope of General Electric, and Robert E. Wood of Sears Roebuck—called at the White House and came out for the two-year extension of NRA and other administration measures. But this did not modify the public impression of an across-the-board repudiation of the New Deal by organized business. (1960: 271–72)

Similarly, labor unions were divided on the issue of what their "true" interests were with regard to Social Security legislation. Indeed, labor organizations were bitterly divided on a variety of issues during this time period. Differences in philosophies, hence strategies, led in 1937 to the ouster of CIO-affiliated unions from those affiliated with the AFL. John L. Lewis, the new president of the CIO, was impatient with the AFL policy of slow, deliberate growth. However, over time there were increasing rumors that there was Communist infiltration of CIO-affiliated unions.

Writing of the divisions within labor organizations during this period, James A. Wilson noted the following:

For the first thirty or forty years of its history, the American Federation of Labor (AFL) and most of its affiliated unions opposed, in the name of voluntarism, certain forms of government intervention in labor-management affairs or indeed in the economy generally, even when the proposed legislation was aimed at improving the welfare of workers (as with minimum-wage or maximum-hour laws or unemployment insurance). By contrast, the Congress of Industrial Organizations (CIO) and most of its affiliated unions favored from their inception sweeping legislative programs on behalf of workers. (1973: 121–22)

The CIO wanted a more generous program than Social Security, while the AFL was more conservative in its approach to old-age insurance. They were not one cohesive group, and this lessened their political efficacy. Further, both organizations were more concerned with unemployment and public works programs than they were with old-age insurance (Schlesinger 1960: 269).

The extensive discussion of speeding up Social Security benefit payments from 1942 to 1940 illustrates the use of incentives in organizations to gain loyalty and support from "members." Early payment was conceived at least partly to garner public support for Social Security, and supporters of this change also argued that payment of benefits in 1940 would prime the economic pump and reduce the reserve; this argument was used by the Social Security Board to try to convince those members of business and industrial organizations that were opposed to Social Security.

With regard to coalition formation, Roosevelt and Altmeyer were masterful at making alliances that divided their enemies. By giving increasing numbers of groups a political and financial stake in the system's success or survival, they helped to ensure the long-term viability of the program. Two examples of the importance of coalition formation are evident in the early years. At the broader political level, Roosevelt was particularly adept at coalition building. He brought together a broad-based national coalition of entrepreneurial business people who felt handicapped by Wall Street domination, intellectuals, Southerners, blacks, women, farmers, and workers. New industries in communications and electronics, for example, were much more in favor of the New Deal than was big business in general, particularly giants like General Electric, the Radio Corporation of America, the National Broadcasting

Company, the Columbia Broadcasting System, and International Business Machines. Joseph P. Kennedy, who invested in both new regions of the country and new industries, was in Roosevelt's corner. But Roosevelt did not draw upon the Democratic Party as such (i.e., the national committee, ward, or precinct), but instead relied on a coalition of diverse groups (Schlesinger 1960: 411–12). It is significant that John G. Winant, the first chairman of the Social Security Board was a Progressive, not a Democrat.

The second example of the importance of coalitions was the close relationship between Roosevelt and the early SSB. Roosevelt encouraged the use of the early SSB members as the sole expert witnesses in congressional testimony regarding Social Security. Congress did listen to alternative proposals, but the early supporters of Social Security were political insiders who knew what to say, when to say it, and whom to say it to. This unique close alliance within the polity, between Roosevelt and the early SSB, helped to fend off many of the early attacks made on Social Security. It was a crucial resource in this period of economic crisis and programmatic instability.

With regard to time and timing, there are relevant observations for these early years. With regard to the time perspective, it is clear that Roosevelt and SSB personnel had a long-term vision for the program. However, in the early, tenuous years, these political actors were forced to limit their time horizons and make compromises in the short term. Similarly, specific organizations representing business and industrial interests often exhibited shortened time spans. These organizational actors were split with regard to long-term interests, and more often exhibited limited rationality. Again, during the 1930s and 1940s, we see more reaction than action, more unplanned adaptation than clearly mapped out strategy. The concept of limited rationality (Perrow 1986) was much more evident in the 1930s and 1940s than was a rational, instrumental plan of action. We see the same dynamic for representatives of labor. The fact that accommodation to many of the organizational actors representing business and industry, in the early years, occurred at later stages of the political debates reflects the fact that there was only some "corporate liberal" planning.

Even after the original act was passed, various business and industrial groups perceived Social Security as a socialistic menace. A large reserve, in their eyes, meant the possibility of a socialistic state that controlled private initiatives. There was some support for lower taxes and larger benefits, but the foundation for this support was a concern that America was moving too far in the direction of socialism. In this sense, most business or industrial organizations did not seek out Social Security; rather, Social Security bureaucrats eventually needed to accommodate these interests in order to ensure the political viability of the system. More than business or industry seeking the state for relief, state bureaucrats sought out sympathetic members of these groups to exemplify business support for Social Security.

Time is an important organizational variable, and another example of this is evident in a cohort effect in the administration of Social Security. The early cohort of personnel was partly responsible for counteracting the early instability of the program. These individuals were carefully selected, visionary professionals, committed to Social Security. Wilson discusses this cohort of SSA employees:

When the Social Security system was founded in 1935, key leaders, especially Arthur J. Altmeyer and John G. Winant, pressed hard and successfully for winning an exemption from standard civil service rules so that they could hire especially talented persons, usually with a social-science background, who shared the liberal commitment to a universal retirement system in which benefits would be guaranteed to all contributors as a matter of right and without a means test. . . .

Altmeyer and Winant devoted many hours to handpicking the managers of local field offices to insure that they were fully imbued with the client-serving ethos. Recruitment and training programs emphasized not just the procedures but the "philosophy" of Social Security (by which was meant the commitment to serving beneficiaries). (1989: 100–101)

The early baptism-by-fire years no doubt tested the commitment and creativity of the original personnel. In many ways an entrenched bureaucracy may not attract entrepreneurial spirits or encourage major innovation to the same degree as do early organizational forms. This cohort cycle and its implications are often evident in organizations that experience waves of recruitment.

The relevance of the idea of timing is also evident here. To quote

Carolyn Weaver: "The outcome of what appears to be a democratic voting process may reflect little more than citizen demands among a narrow array of predetermined alternatives. . . . Existing and potential public suppliers including Roosevelt, the CES, and other social insurance advocates played disproportionate roles in the timing and form of the Social Security Act" (1982: 72). The timing of broader historical events is also central to the developments noted here. The onset of World War II was fortuitous in many ways for Social Security. This will be discussed in depth in the next chapter, but there were five developments during the war that benefited the Social Security program initially. (1) World War II deflected most of the attention away from Social Security. Though this may have had certain negative effects, the deflection of criticism gave SSB bureaucrats time to establish the program. (2) Many uncovered workers worked in covered employment during World War II, thereby creating a clientele to lobby for expanded coverage after the war. (3) The trust funds grew because of the high rate of employment in industries that could pay well. (4) The continuing payment of Social Security benefits built up a growing interest group that was concerned about the maintenance and expansion of the system; even the Townsendites could not compete with the provision of real cash benefits, and they and other alternative programs grew increasingly less threatening. (5) Wartime inflation eroded the purchasing power of Social Security benefits, thereby increasing the potential pressure for incremental expansion.

We also gain a sense of the importance of ideology in political organizations' lives. Immediately after the constitutionality of the program was established in the 1930s, the analogy to private insurance was heavily emphasized in documents published by the SSB. Legitimacy was a key concern of the early Social Security Board and Roosevelt. It was believed that this would help to increase the acceptability of the new payroll tax; in retrospect, the analogy appears to have worked, although in later years it was downplayed as less important than the social benefits of programmatic expansion. But it was significant that levels of autonomy varied among state actors in the early years. There was a continuum of autonomy. Roosevelt had some autonomy from powerful interests because of his general popularity. He attempted, often successfully, to stack the decks in favor of Social Security. The CES, the first Advisory Council, and his Supreme Court reorganization plan exemplified this autonomy.

On the other hand, state bureaucrats in the SSB had considerably less autonomy from powerful interests because they had to figure out ways of ensuring the viability of the program by making concessions to various organizations. Altmeyer and other administrators therefore could not institute a full-fledged social insurance program at once but had to wait until the program became more politically entrenched.

Further, it is evident that the role of Congress from 1935 to 1949 was far more cautious and far less autonomous with regard to Social Security than it was during the 1950s and 1960s. The very nature of elective positions, which generally span more years than does the presidency, require more frequent accountability to the general public, hence Congress often proceeds more slowly than presidents or state bureaucrats. During the early years, the Social Security system was new, untried, and controversial. Employers and employees complained of an added payroll tax; the Townsendites and their followers said that the program did not go far enough; and some conservatives and state's rights advocates complained of the federal domination inherent in the program. Social Security was obviously a controversial and risky issue for senators and representatives during these first years. The legislation that was drafted during this period reflected the influence of the insurance industry (no voluntary annuities to be sold by the government), manufacturers and retailers (low tax rates), and the Southern tenant farm economy (the exclusion of agricultural and domestic workers). Congress was held increasingly accountable for its actions by powerful interests as well as by the public. There was little if any autonomy for Congress.

In addition, ideological shifts, especially the validity of radical flank effects, are also evident during this time period. The popularity of the Townsend Plan and the other more radical alternatives stemmed from their promises of generous pensions, short work weeks, and other tantalizing utopian attractions. These groups or individuals were political outsiders, with radical agendas, and they clamored for relief. But the exact form the relief would take, and the administrative mechanisms for extending benefits, were not clearly articulated by the leaders or members of these more radical social movements. Both Paul Burstein (1985) and John Kingdon (1984) have noted that popular protest most often mandates change in a general direction, rather than specifying particular legislative details. The general public was indeed a factor in that high unemployment rates were an economic and political mandate for change, but this pressure was very indirect in terms of program development. The resulting legislation was therefore not a compromise among all the alternatives presented. A true political compromise would have been much more radical and much more favorable toward the working class than the program that emerged. For example, it might have extended coverage to all workers, including agricultural and domestic workers; unemployment compensation might have been federally administered, hence more uniform; disability and hospital insurance might have been included; and benefits might have been more substantial. The alternative, relatively radical proposals served mainly to underline the seriousness of the crisis. They forced the hand of Congress into doing something to alleviate the economic hardship, but the program that was eventually adopted did not overwhelmingly offend powerful interests, and it was not a radical departure from cherished American ideologies or institutions. Most importantly with regard to social movements or interest groups and their organizational persistence, influence in pressing for a nebulous form of legislation is not the same as influence in writing the legislation or influence in its implementation. It was in the latter stages that more powerful interests clearly had an edge, including those groups that had voiced their opposition in the earlier stages of the political process. In a funneling process, a large number of actors registered their discontent, while a smaller number were invited to participate on the Advisory Council. Finally, since Congress is the place where legislation is actually hammered out, powerful interests attempted, often successfully, to pressure Congress to satisfy their interests through the now inevitable reform. The NAM and the U.S. Chamber of Commerce opposed the legislation in its early form, but that did not mean that they passively accepted the specific provisions embodied in the final bill. It was in the later stages of the process that these more powerful groups were to have enormous, if subtle, influence. Southern congressional representatives made sure that agricultural and domestic workers were excluded, and employers made sure that the tax rate remained low. And as we shall see, organizations representing more powerful interests were eventually even more effective, proving that organizational persistence yields returns in the long run. Business, industry, and finance began to accept the fact that the program was there to stay. The Business Advisory Council, the NAM, and the U.S. Chamber of Commerce all developed proposals for amendments that were in line with their interests. These groups were an important factor in the passage of the 1939 amendments. Especially after Roosevelt's reelection in 1936, the big question for these groups changed from "Should we have a system such as Social Security?" to "Now that we have it, how can we influence the direction and shape of policymaking?"

An organizational framework also lends itself to the conclusion that during periods of crisis, organizations are much more likely to be affected by their environment than vice versa. Rather than being an independent, autonomous actor, the early SSB was required to make numerous political compromises. Over time, if the organization survives, we see a process highlighted by organizational theorists—of bureaucracies taking on a life of their own. The SSB sought to expand its reach and increase benefits, all in an effort to garner support for the program. During the 1950s and 1960s, the Social Security bureaucracy was able to affect its environment. Arthur Altmeyer commented: "Administration consists of more than organization, procedures, and personnel. . . . Administration also consists of interpreting social legislation in such a manner that it achieves its fundamental purpose most fully" (1966: 262–63). But it was not until the 1950s and 1960s that state bureaucratic administrators were able to carve out their own vision of the ideal social insurance system.

CHAPTER FOUR

Bureaucratic Expansion, 1950-1969

> Since this legislation was originally passed in 1935, we have increased the total burden of Federal expenditures from about $9.7 billion a year to a prospective $45 billion a year, included in which are about $23 billion for defense and European aid—most of which constitutes the cost of the cold war. Already our economy is up to the limit of endurance under this load. I believe we should go slow and hold further additions to this burden to the absolute minimum. When the cold war is over, we can afford many more domestic improvements.
>
> —Herbert Hoover, in a letter to the chairman of the House Ways and Means Committee (USNA, "SS—OASI Misc.")

> In the Cold War we are judged by the peoples of the world on our social performance on behalf of our mothers, our young, our infirm and our aged. As a representative of the million members of our union, I urge you not to pass ammunition to our totalitarian foes but instead to reconsider and reinstate these provisions which give meaning to the word democracy.
>
> —Walter P. Reuther, President International Union of United Automobile Workers of America, regarding 1950 Senate removing House provisions for disability insurance and other more liberal Social Security measures (USNA, "SS [Misc. May–June, 1950]")

IN THE ENTIRE HISTORY of Social Security, there was no period more crucial for the program's expansion than the 1950s and 1960s. First, the frequency and regularity of legislation to expand the program was notable; in the 1950s, every election year, legislation was enacted to expand the program. Second, in terms of new groups brought under the Social Security umbrella (e.g., agricultural and domestic workers), sheer numerical expansion of those covered was phenomenal. Third, there were significant increases in benefits, even controlling for inflation (see Table 4). And finally, philosophically, the program encompassed more insurance against the hardships of life. The addition of disability insurance in 1956, hospital insurance, or Medicare, in 1965, and the movement

TABLE 4
Social Security Benefit Increases, 1950–1977

Date effective	Pct. increase	Date effective	Pct. increase
Sept. 1950	77.0	Jan. 1971	10.0
Sept. 1952	12.5	Sept. 1972	20.0
Sept. 1954	13.0	June 1974	11.0
Jan. 1959	7.0	June 1975 [a]	8.0
Feb. 1968	13.0	June 1976 [a]	6.4
Jan. 1970	15.0	June 1977 [a]	5.9

SOURCE: *Congressional Record* 123 (1977): 39021.
[a] Automatic cost-of-living increases, as provided in the Social Security amendments of 1972.

away from a "floor" of protection toward "adequate" protection, all reflected this change in philosophy.

This chapter discusses events that occurred beginning with the post–World War II period through the late 1960s. Organizational theory and the organizational dynamics presented earlier are very useful in explaining and understanding the developments during this time period. Before the first payment of benefits in 1940, the Social Security system did not yet have a clientele interested in its expansion. As an organization, the Social Security bureaucracy at this point was vulnerable to competing political demands and much more reactive than active. This changed drastically with the legislation of the 1950s and 1960s. Now, the organization was capable of having a real effect on the larger political and economic environment.

By the 1950s, the Social Security bureaucracy had succeeded in creating several communities of interest for the cash benefits program—not only groups that were receiving benefits but also groups that were excluded and now began lobbying for coverage. This process lowered the likelihood of competition in the political arena, and in a non–zero-sum economic climate, the counterbalancing forces of negotiation and compromise were less common. This meant that the dramatic expansion of benefits, and the addition of disability and hospital insurance, occurred in a context of relatively little countervailing opinion. These situations made it possible for organizations to have an impact on their larger environment. It is much more likely that organizations will be able to have an effect on their environment during periods of stability than during periods of crisis.

It is also clear that in the political arena, prior events or outcomes are often used as precedent to justify changes at a later point: effects at time one become causes at time two. This dynamic occurred in the expansion of coverage to disability insurance. The first step was to offer means-tested assistance for the needy disabled. This program then served later on as the precedent for instituting a full-fledged, non–means-tested disability insurance program. Economic prosperity and stability eventually allowed the Social Security Administration (SSA) to institute certain social insurance programs that it had wanted from the start.

In addition, I argue that power resides in organizations that operate within a particular economic and political context. Power is not equally distributed or expended. State bureaucrats often have the inside track in promoting their agenda during periods of stability, and the provision of cash benefits often negates the voices of compromise or economic rationality. However, there are few all-powerful or omnipotent organizational actors evident here. State bureaucracies may have long-range plans, but most organizational actors operate with an eye toward the near future. I also argue that the SSA had more autonomy from powerful, but isolated, organizational interests during this period than they did during the Great Depression. This is not to imply that this autonomous political power is evident if several powerful organizations are opposed; indeed, the political success of Social Security was ensured by generally catering to most other powerful organizations.

The chapter begins with a discussion of how World War II and the cold war affected Social Security legislation of the early 1950s. Following this, I address the support and opposition to the changes that occurred between 1950 and 1969, and the nature of these changes. Finally, I discuss the organizational dynamics presented earlier, in view of the developments surrounding the legislation of the 1950s and 1960s.

The Economic and Political Context

Common-sense notions of the inverse relationship between "guns or butter" (military versus domestic expenditures) make the expansion of Social Security during the 1950s and 1960s seem anomalous. World War II, the cold war, and the Korean War could have deflected resources away from Social Security. Wars tend to encourage debates about the relative merits of foreign versus domestic spending, and the petitions that Congress receives tend to support one over the other. In the early 1950s, with the loss of China, and the Soviet Union's development of atomic power, many Americans believed that the communists were winning the cold war (D. Mitchell 1950).

Harold Wilensky, in a comparative analysis of sixteen countries, found that these troublesome times did indeed affect social programs: "The beginnings of the cold war locate the most obvious, powerful, depressing effect of warfare on welfare. In those years of 1950–52, the superpowers launched a nuclear arms race, developed rigid doctrines of international conspiracy and enemy encirclement, and demonstrated their willingness to be tough and take risks in such crises as Berlin and Korea. The resulting swift increase in military spending from 1950–1952 cast the die for a poor welfare performance for those countries most swept up in the crisis atmosphere" (1975: 75). If government resources are viewed as zero-sum, war-related expenses should have meant a retraction of Social Security, or at least stagnation. Further, the cold war and increasing concern with the threat of communism meant that Social Security could be denounced as a socialist program that was meant to undermine capitalism from within. Some opponents of the program in the 1950s claimed that the only "social security" was defensive, and they argued that domestic programs drained the lifeblood of our nation that should have been expended for military preparedness. As evidence, they cited Lenin's statement, made years earlier: "We shall force the United States to spend itself to destruction" (USNA, "Special SS Files—Private Pension Plans"). A letter from a Maryland doctor, sent to Walter F. George, chairman of the Senate Finance Committee, highlights this position well:

I am writing to urge that you help kill this bill in conference. Any money that we have lying around should be used for our national defense, instead of for Social Security hand-outs. The paramount desideratum we need in this country today is Physical Security, not Social Security. If we ever become physically secure (which is probably as far off as the next millennium), we can then begin to think about being soft and worrying about Social Security. The gross neglect of the Administration is the cause of the present war in Korea. The blood of those dead and wounded boys in Korea is on the hands of the Administration. One would have thought that Munich would have taught us a lesson in appeasement. We have spent billions to appease the Reds since 1945 and what have we to show for it— nothing but the grim reality of war. If we had spent those billions to stay armed, we would not have the war. Every realist knows that there is only one thing which will stop the Russians and that one thing is force and more force, applied in such a realistic manner that they dare not attack. In the name of God, let us stop spending our money for the soft things in life! The only thing that will save our country is the *vigor*, and the *force*, and the *character* that was exemplified in 1776. I cannot see how any patriot can vote for an extension of so-called Social Security in times like these. (USNA, "OASI Misc.—June–August, 1950")

Nor was the threat of communism only a matter of external foes. By the early 1950s, Senator Joseph R. McCarthy (R-Wisconsin) had accused the Roosevelt and Truman administrations of being rife with Communists, and he directly accused many liberal Democrats of being Communists. In 1949 and 1950, CIO-affiliated unions conducted a massive housecleaning to rid themselves of Communist members. A leading article in *U.S. News and World Report* in 1953 concluded: "In the 20 years since one little Communist cell was started in Washington, the U.S. has lost its ally, China; its big secret, the atom bomb; and its entry to Eastern Europe. All those losses were big gains for Russia, the country that the Washington spies worked for" (in Warren 1955: 208).

In light of these considerations, it becomes all the more interesting that the decades of the 1950s and 1960s were the time of greatest expansion for the Social Security program. By 1950, the momentum for expansion of the Social Security system was strong. And though some of the pressure for expansion came because of inflation resulting from the Korean War, the interesting question for this period is what fueled this expansion in the context of war and criticism.

Unlike the zero-sum context where large military expenditures mean that domestic programs are cut back, Table 5 shows that, contrary to Wilensky's contention, national defense expenditures

TABLE 5
Defense and Social Security Outlays of the Federal Government, 1940–1970, and Percent of GNP of Expenditures
(in millions of dollars, except percentages)

Year	National defense		Social Security	
	Absolute	Pct.	Absolute	Pct.
1940	1,504	1.5	1,508	1.5
1941	6,062	4.8	1,681	1.3
1942	23,970	15.1	1,515	0.9
1943	63,212	32.9	1,209	0.6
1944	76,874	36.5	1,232	0.6
1945	81,585	38.4	1,359	0.6
1946	44,731	21.3	2,682	1.3
1947	13,059	5.6	2,908	1.2
1948	13,015	5.0	2,932	1.1
1949	13,097	5.1	3,763	1.5
1950	13,119	4.6	4,959	1.7
1951	22,544	6.8	4,749	1.4
1952	44,015	12.6	5,536	1.6
1953	50,413	13.7	6,446	1.8
1954	46,645	12.7	8,048	2.2
1955	40,245	10.1	9,393	2.3
1956	40,305	9.6	10,131	2.4
1957	42,760	9.6	11,983	2.7
1958	44,371	9.9	15,556	3.5
1959	46,617	9.6	17,901	3.7
1960	45,908	9.1	18,959	3.7
1961	47,381	9.0	22,100	4.2
1962	51,097	9.0	23,660	4.2
1963	52,257	8.8	25,463	4.3
1964	53,591	8.4	26,826	4.2
1965	49,578	7.2	27,406	4.0
1966	56,785	7.5	31,525	4.2
1967	70,081	8.8	37,831	4.7
1968	80,517	9.2	43,716	5.0
1969	81,232	8.6	49,310	5.2
1970	80,295	8.1	56,697	5.7

NOTE: Source for outlays, *Historical Statistics of the United States: Colonial Times to 1970*, Bicentennial ed., Part 2, Washington, D.C.: U.S. Bureau of the Census, 1975: 1116; source for GNP percentages, The National Income and Product Accounts of the United States, 1929–76: 1–2.
Pearson's Correlation = .62.

were positively correlated with Social Security expenditures during this period. A study of Great Britain similarly found that major wars necessitated and enabled the government to expand its fiscal base; further, since much of this structure and capacity remained after the war, expanded social provision could be more easily instituted (Peacock and Wiseman 1961).

Guns and butter are not necessarily mutually exclusive, and war can stimulate certain types of social spending (Amenta and Skocpol 1988). Even though World War II, the cold war, and the Korean War demanded that a larger portion of the gross national product be used for national defense, this increased expenditure had little effect on absolute expenditures for Social Security old-age insurance. This is especially so when we exclude World War II, a period when Social Security expenditures were reduced because of the elderly's participation in production. With only three exceptions between 1940 and 1970, Social Security budget amounts increased steadily through World War II, the cold war, and the Korean War. Each new budget set a plateau below which expenditures have rarely fallen. Whereas national defense expenditures fluctuate depending on our involvement in wars, the absolute expenditures for Social Security have generally increased.

Support for Social Security

In addition to the favorable economic context, three developments brought on by World War II contributed greatly to the growing support for Social Security expansion. These were the opportunities in industrial plants in the North, inflation, and the growth of private pensions. Edwin Amenta and Theda Skocpol have noted, "In a number of ways, the war aided the bureaucratic fortunes of the Social Security Board and set the stage for OASI to become the keystone of postwar U.S. public social provision" (1988: 120–21). Since this historic crisis or "accident" was largely outside the control of program bureaucrats or organizational actors, its effects on the program, though beneficial in retrospect, were really unforeseen shifts that organizational actors had to adapt to.

OPPORTUNITIES IN INDUSTRIAL EMPLOYMENT
IN NORTHERN STATES

During World War II, the opportunities for workers in wartime industries in the industrial sector resulted in three significant developments for Social Security. First and most importantly, during this four-year period, many workers moved from uncovered employment such as housework, agricultural work, and domestic work to covered employment. But many of these people returned to their former jobs when the war ended. This meant that, although they had paid Social Security payroll taxes for several years, most of them would never qualify for even limited Social Security benefits because their time in covered employment was too short. Because the system was constructed on the principle that jobs were covered and not individuals (as in private insurance), the movement of labor during World War II brought inequities in taxing and benefits coverage. This was not a development that was obscured by technicalities; the inequity was well understood by those workers affected. Before the 1950 amendments, 80,000,000 Social Security accounts existed. Yet only 35,000,000 persons actually remained insured because of movement into and out of covered employment during World War II. Thus there were 45,000,000 persons who, though they had had wage credits posted to their records during World War II (USNA, "Social Security Revision"), were not due to receive any benefits. They constituted a huge new interest group that could be counted on to support more universal coverage.

Second, the labor market shift of the war years drew many Southern blacks to industrial jobs in the North; most of them, owing to deteriorating job opportunities in the South, were unlikely to return there. In effect, the South underwent a selection process whereby the youngest and most able-bodied workers were fleeing the South because of lack of opportunities in an increasingly mechanized agricultural economy. Those who were left in the Southern states were the elderly and the very young—obviously a tremendous burden to local or county relief rolls. Since agricultural and domestic workers were excluded from coverage under old-age insurance, the assistance burden in the South was much heavier than in nonagricultural states.

Jill Quadagno (1985) documents how Southern congressmen offered less resistance to federally mandated old-age insurance in the 1950s than they had in the 1930s and 1940s. As noted earlier, when the Social Security program began in the 1930s, Southern congressional members were instrumental in seeing that agricultural and domestic workers were excluded from coverage under the federal program. Although those employed in agricultural or domestic work could be eligible for old-age assistance in the 1930s and 1940s, this program was administered by local relief agencies. The dollar amounts for the assistance programs in the Southern states were extremely miserly. Southern whites viewed the federal control of old-age insurance as infringing on local authority, and as a threat to their tenant-farm economy; essentially they feared that blacks' incentive to work for low wages would be hindered under any program of federal relief.

The movement of labor out of the South during World War II, along with the mechanization of agricultural work and the increasingly burdensome dependency ratios and assistance loads in the Southern states, quieted the resistance by Southern congressional members to expansion of old-age insurance. It should also be noted that there is evidence that not only the Southern states but *all* states that had high relief costs pressured the federal government to liberalize old-age insurance by 1950 (USNA, "OASI Misc.—April, 1950").

The third development brought about by wartime job opportunities was the reentry of many elderly and previously retired persons into the workforce. Because of the earnings test whereby benefits were reduced when beneficiaries earned over $14.99 a month, most of these workers were now drawing fewer Social Security benefits but at the same time, in the payroll tax, contributing directly to a growing trust fund.

INFLATION

Inflation, another critical consequence of World War II, also affected old-age insurance benefits. First, the buying power of benefits, which remained at 1940 levels throughout the 1940s, was drastically eroded. From 1937 to 1949, the purchasing power of the dollar declined from 96.3 cents to 59.1 cents (USNA, "OASI

Misc.—June–August, 1950"). In 1940, the average benefit represented approximately 20 percent of the average monthly wage of all employees in industry; by 1950, it represented only 11 percent of the average wage (AFLA 1950: 166). The second, related effect was the growth of old-age assistance payments relative to old-age insurance payments. The old-age assistance program was amended in 1946, 1947, and 1948; the effect of each of these amendments was in the direction of liberalizing public assistance. The original intent of old-age assistance, however, was to provide a temporary safety net for those who were already aged, in need, and were not covered by the insurance system from the start. Social Security planners intended this needs-based safety net to disappear as the more universal old-age insurance system took hold. But the relative growth of the two programs actually developed in such a way that old-age assistance monthly payments averaged $48 in 1949 while old-age insurance benefit payments averaged only $24. A letter to Senator Walter F. George dated June 7, 1950, from the American Retail Federation stated:

In order that the public assistance programs be subordinated in importance to the federal contributory system of old-age and survivors insurance, the latter system should be expanded to provide for universal coverage, and there should be no increase in the extent of federal participation in assistance programs. In fact, serious consideration should be given to cutting back, gradually, the extent of federal participation so that it represents a smaller portion of the total outlay than at present. (USNA, "SS [Misc. May–June 1950])

Welfare programs are generally less palatable to Americans than the more incentive-based social insurance program. The more rapid growth of old-age assistance allowed those who supported higher old-age insurance benefits and universal coverage (under the insurance program) to point to the relative merits of the two approaches and argue for a reversal of the trend that occurred in the 1940s. Supporters also pointed out that with the aged population increasing, public assistance could be expected to continue to rise (USNA, "SS-OASI Misc. [May, 1949]").

THE GROWTH OF PRIVATE PENSIONS

A final development that occurred largely as the result of World War II was the growth of employer and union pensions. As a way to cap wage inflation during the war, the Stabilization Act of 1942 froze wages. At the same time, employer contributions to employee welfare and health programs "in a reasonable amount" were specifically exempted from the provisions of the Act (Perlick 1950: 683). Labor unions, unable to bargain for wage increases, took up the notion of bargaining for better retirement pensions. CIO-affiliated unions were especially effective in winning pensions of $100 per month. For example, under the plans of Bethlehem Steel and the Ford Motor Company, a worker was entitled to a monthly pension of $100 after a 25- or 30-year service record, and these plans were to be a combination of Social Security and employer pension plans. In October 1950, the evening before the Ford agreement was finally reached, Ernest Breech, Ford executive vice president, stated that the most satisfactory method of providing old-age security was through federal legislation. Further, he said that existing benefits were inadequate and needed to be increased. This was the first time that any major industrial executive had ever publicly advocated increased Social Security benefits (USNA, "SS-Misc. [October, 1950]"). In 1949, the death, accident, sickness benefits, annuities and saving plans cost the Standard Oil Company of New Jersey 15 percent of its total payrolls (USNA, "Special SS Files—Private Pension Plans"). By 1950, major corporations such as Bethlehem, U.S. Steel, Kaiser Steel, Ford, International Harvester, Westinghouse, Goodrich, General Electric, American Cyanamid, Frigidaire, and American Can had all adopted private pensions.

Such plans were beneficial to business and industry in three ways. First, during the war, many employers were faced with the problem of high labor turnover. They were willing to initiate fringe benefit plans in an attempt to keep their workforce intact and to attract additional employees. (Later on, this concession to workers also gave workers new bargaining leverage, and in 1949 the national economy was disrupted by coal miner and steelworker strikes. A key issue in these strikes was the demand for a substantial increase in old-age pensions.)

Corporations also used pensions as a way of avoiding income taxes. This was not illegal. A change in the income tax codes in 1942 stipulated that bona fide pension plan contributions were tax exempt. But an attorney representing several labor unions complained in a letter to Walter F. George, chairman of the Senate Finance Committee, of abuses by large corporations of the intent of Social Security:

> The practice of the Bell System and other corporations of deducting from their pension plans one-half of the Federal old-age retirement benefits takes advantage of the present state of the law whereby such private pension plans come within the tax exemption clauses of the Internal Revenue Code. At the same time, these pension plans secure to themselves one-half of the Federal old-age retirement benefits that were intended for aged individuals and not for huge corporations. The public welfare is thus perverted into private gain by private corporations. (USNA, "SS—OASI Misc.")

In addition, a high excess profits tax during World War II led business and industry to relax the control of costs, and renewed their interest in pensions in order to benefit from provisions for tax deductions. It was estimated that under wartime tax rates, each dollar contributed by an employer for pensions cost the employer only 14.5 cents because the balance would have gone to the government in taxes (in Perlik 1950: 686).

Finally, a conversation between Herschel Atkinson, a representative of the Chamber of Commerce, and Senator Eugene Millikin (R-Colorado) of the Senate Finance Committee nicely summarizes another reason for the Chamber's change of heart on Social Security. Atkinson was explaining that his organization favored broad coverage, higher benefits, and the use of private plans to supplement Social Security benefits but opposed an increase in the wage base to $3,600. Millikin replied:

> And of course, those companies that have the provision whereby their pension shall be reduced by the amount of the basic Federal pension — those companies, of course, are rooting and tooting for a better level of Government pensions?

ATKINSON: Yes.

MILLIKIN: Quite naturally and quite understandably.

ATKINSON: Yes; I think that those feelings are evident.

MILLIKIN: The system has gained some new and strange adherents in the last year or so. (USNA, "Social Security Revision")

For many business and industrial organizations, the growth of private pensions by 1950 meant that much of the earlier vehement opposition to old-age insurance increases had dissipated.

Both the AFL and the CIO were also instrumental in pressing for expansion of Social Security during this period, especially the AFL-affiliated unions. As noted earlier, AFL unions were less swift than CIO unions in adopting company pensions as a top priority, and they were consequently more vocal in their support of Social Security expansion during the debates over the 1950 amendments (AFLA 1948: 236). William Green AFL president, told the Senate Finance Committee in 1950: "The failure of Congress to act after the end of the war has created a vacuum in this field which there have been attempts to fill by other methods, some of them unsound and ill-advised. Today many unions in the American Federation of Labor are waiting to see what Congress does to revise the basic social-security structure. They cannot be restrained indefinitely" (USNA "Social Security Revision"). Overall, union-won pensions were criticized in the 1940s and 1950s as limiting worker mobility from employer to employer. Nonunionized workers argued that union pensions diluted political pressure for pensions for all workers, perhaps lowering the interest in expanding Social Security.

In some ways, too, union-won gains backfired. For those workers who had won large pensions during the automobile and steel strikes, for example, an increase in federal old-age security actually narrowed the gains of their unions. Although the settlements provided for noncontributory pensions—employers paid the entire amount—they also usually required employers to pay only the difference between the guaranteed amount (e.g., $100) and any Social Security benefits. The noncontributory pensions meant that workers had no pension deductions from their pay; yet to finance any increase in Social Security benefits, workers were required to pay higher payroll taxes. In other words, workers would be contributing to the government for exactly the same benefits that industry alone had provided for in the past (Perlik 1950: 713). The advantage of union-won employer pensions was that they were not limited in amount; therefore, depending on the strength of the union, they often provided the highest pension benefits. Private insurance pensions had the distinct advantage of not limiting worker mobility between employers, but the amount of the pensions was fixed and consequently they were susceptible to inflation erosion.

The entrenchment of the Social Security system was not surprising in light of this debate over employer pensions versus private insurance. In many ways, a universal social insurance program answered both problems: workers could move from job to job, and if universal coverage were in place, they would not lose their pension rights; further, since Social Security is primarily a political organization and not solely concerned with economic factors, fiscal restraint was less evident and benefits could rise as they were eroded by inflation. Many business and industrial organizations no longer opposed such expansion. What occurred, however, was that Social Security adopted the most expensive aspects of both union and private pension plans—universal coverage and protection against inflation. These were major factors propelling the system toward economic crisis in later years.

Similar to the dissension among organizations representing capital, and dissension among organizations representing labor, organizations representing the insurance industry were also divided over Social Security in the 1930s and 1940s. However, by the 1950s, even their voices rang in harmony. In 1950, a variety of organizations representing the industry testified before Congress that there had been an increase in their business as a result of the Social Security Act (*CR* 1949: A. 2411–15). They now favored broad coverage, with subsistence-level benefits and a low wage base for collecting taxes. In addition, they opposed the payment of lump-sum death benefits to survivors of a Social Security beneficiary. With broad coverage, adverse selection would be less likely for those covered by private plans. In other words, those worst off in our society (both physically and economically) and therefore at highest risk, would at least be covered by the government plan, and would be less of a burden on private insurers. With low benefit levels, not only was the public sensitized to the advantages of insurance coverage, but the inadequacy of these benefits was used as a selling feature for more adequate private plans.

An insurance industry representative testified before the House Ways and Means Committee that Social Security had given them an "approach to people" and drew an analogy to what had occurred after World War I:

> We had every veteran coming out of the service with Government life insurance for $10,000. We held meetings, looked down our noses and thought, "There she goes, the life insurance business is all out." As a matter of fact, that is the one thing that has ever happened that made life insurance big, because all of the people to whom we had been selling $1,000 of insurance, and having a lot of trouble at that, they found that the Government was telling them, "You have got to have $10,000." So, when they got back, they remembered that, and they told their father and their uncle and everybody else, and if the kid had $10,000 of insurance, Dad could not go along with only $1,000, could he? (*CR* 1946: 439)

In essence, private insurance salespeople used Social Security as a base from which to sell private insurance (*CR* 1946: 434). It is noteworthy that insurance industry organizations were especially protective of a low wage base (they favored $3,000 per year instead of $3,600) because the higher the income taxed by Social Security, the less excess cash higher-income persons would have to purchase private insurance. The industry also felt that lump-sum benefits to survivors infringed upon an insurance option that was rightly theirs to offer (USNA, "SS-OASI Misc. [May, 1949]").

Finally, there is evidence that the federal Treasury had a growing interest in seeing Social Security benefits increase. Several veterans' organizations predicated their opposition to a veterans' pension (which would be paid by the federal government, not by a payroll tax on employers and employees) upon enactment of a general extension of OASI coverage (USNA, "SS-OASI Misc. [May, 1949]"). In other words, the federal government, instead of having to find independent sources of revenue, could dip into the existing trust fund to pay veterans. Politicians concerned about the impact of large deficits on the public's perceptions of their relative success or failure in office readily saw that this was the best course to pursue. This particular example reveals how intrastate organizations such as the Treasury Department also developed an interest in Social Security expansion.

In brief, opportunities in industrial plants in Northern states, inflation, and the growth of private pension plans all set the stage for the early 1950s legislation. The key point here is that business and industry were not alone in their new-found interest in the expansion of Social Security. Excluded groups of workers who had worked in covered employment during World War II, Southern legislators and individual states with burdensome assistance payments, private employers who witnessed rising pension costs or pensions linked to Social Security, AFL and CIO labor unions, insurance industry representatives, and the Treasury Department now turned to the SSA and Congress for relief. It was not merely organizations representing business and industry that favored expansion. At any rate, the slowness with which business and industry embraced the Social Security program is not very solid evidence of corporate liberal planning.

What we begin to see with regard to Social Security legislation in the 1950s was a majority of organizations speaking in favor of expansion—organizations representing employers, AFL labor unions, the insurance industry, state governments, the SSA, and even other federal government departments like the Treasury Department. Certainly groups such as agricultural and domestic workers, if they were inclined to register their support or opposition at all, would benefit from inclusion under the program at this stage. However, many members of Congress noted that they received very little feedback from farmers and agricultural and domestic workers regarding their position on inclusion under Social Security; these were, of course, by and large unorganized groups. Organizations representing blacks, however, such as the NAACP, stated their support for this extension (USNA, "SS-OASI Misc. [May, 1949]").

Opposition to Social Security

Not all organizational actors supported Social Security during this time period. Martha Derthick notes that many business organizations continued to offer "conservative resistance" (1979: 132). For example, in 1950 General Motors and the United Auto Workers reached an agreement that contained a provision whereby if Social Security increased, pensions for General Motors employees would go up correspondingly. A letter from the Ohio Chamber of Commerce explained the reasoning: "Thus, General Motors certainly is out of the classification of corporations which it might otherwise be assumed would welcome an increase in the OASI benefit amount as a means of immediately relieving the corporation of some costs. . . . Like industrial executives generally throughout the United States, GMC officials are gravely concerned with the fiscal problems ahead for the Government, corporations and workers in meeting the eventual liabilities of the Social Security program now in the process of revision" (USNA, "OASI Misc. [June, 1950]").

Also there were still groups that wanted the entire program replaced with an alternative. The Townsendites were still promoting a version of their ideas, though their alternative was muffled by the increasing monopolization of debates by the SSA. A Townsendite critic of the program complained to the chairman of the Senate Finance Committee in 1950:

It must be remembered, however, that the Advisory Council [of 1947–48] had at its disposal only those facts concerning the social security program which Dr. Altmeyer chose to make available to it. Only Dr. Altmeyer was permitted to appear personally before the Advisory Council. Moreover, the technical staff of the Advisory Council consisted of persons who both shared Dr. Altmeyer's point of view and were more or less under his control; the head of the staff, for example, while not then employed by the Social Security Administration, was on leave from a research group in which Dr. Altmeyer had a controlling voice. Various employees and ex-employees of the Social Security Administration, who were in possession of the full facts of the matter and who, on the basis of these full facts, disagreed with Dr. Altmeyer were unable to present their views personally either to the Advisory Council or to the Congressional Committees. (USNA, "Senate Finance Committee—SS [April, 1950]")

Altmeyer, it should be noted, was given four days for testimony to the Advisory Council while opponents were given as little as twenty minutes. It was also reported that Altmeyer gave confidential wage data to John L. Lewis, president of the CIO, in order to enhance Lewis's congressional testimony (USNA, "SS—OASI Misc. [Dec., 1949]").

In addition, assorted groups of professional and public service employees—teachers, firefighters, federal, state, and local government employees—were quite opposed to coverage under Social Security. Whether they wanted it depended mostly on the relative generosity of their own pension plans when compared with the Social Security program. Some of those who opposed mandatory universal coverage were physicians, accountants, lawyers, and other professional people who claimed that they very often did not retire at age 65, and that the pension offered by Social Security "would offer them very little inducement to do so" (USNA, "Committee Attention").

Congress was careful not to alienate the groups that offered opposition to Social Security coverage. They shaped the 1950 amendments to exclude coverage of those groups opposing it. At this point the Social Security program could not compete with these more generous pension programs in terms of benefit levels. Congress responded to this difference of opinion by allowing coverage, but not requiring it, and left the decision regarding inclusion under Social Security up to local groups. The 1950 amendments tailored the program in such a fashion.

The amendments that were passed on August 28, 1950, with a vote of 81–2 in the Senate (the two nay votes were Republican), involved the most significant expansion of old-age insurance coverage in the entire history of the program. Benefits were increased 77 percent and were constructed in such a way as to lighten the load on old-age assistance. Benefit increases ranged from 50 percent for the highest benefit groups to 150 percent for the lowest. Compulsory coverage was extended to the non-farm self-employed (except for certain professional groups such as doctors, lawyers, and accountants), and to regularly employed domestic and farm workers. Optional coverage for employees of state and local governments and nonprofit organizations was authorized.

Before these amendments, approximately 35,000,000 workers were covered; the new legislation added about 10,000,000 more. Eligibility requirements for workers to receive benefits were greatly liberalized. Whereas under the old law, in most cases, ten years in covered employment were required, under the 1950 law, all workers over the age of 61 could acquire insured status with as little as eighteen months in covered employment. The tax rate was allowed to rise from 1 percent to 1.5 percent in 1950. Finally, earnings of beneficiaries had previously been limited to $14.99 per month; in 1950 this earnings test was increased to $50.00, with no limitation after age 75. The wage base was raised to $3,600 in 1951, a minor defeat for insurance companies.

In general, most groups were pleased with the 1950 legislation, and for Congress, the opportunity to increase benefits without simultaneously increasing taxes was as attractive as it was historically rare. There were groups on each side who argued that the program had either gone too far, or not far enough. For example, the amendments were a major defeat for alternative programs, such as the Townsend Plan; with the passage of the amendments, the Social Security bureaucracy clearly prevailed over the Townsendites. Others argued that more massive domestic expenditures would undermine military expenditures. Those groups on the other end of the continuum, like the radical CIO-affiliated unions that wholeheartedly supported expansion, argued that the wage base was too low, full disability benefits should be restored, and even more groups should be covered. Later amendments in the 1950s and 1960s would do much to appease the proponents of expansion.

The election of 1952 brought the first Republican President since Herbert Hoover was elected in 1928. Several reasons explain this political shift. Women were said to be repeatedly disappointed with the Democratic Party because of the intransigence of the Southern contingent. Large numbers of women voted for Eisenhower, and they were especially likely to welcome his implied promise to bring the boys back from Korea, and his promise to check high prices (Hammond 1953). McCarthy's attacks on communism in government, which had been primarily directed at liberal Democrats, led even more voters to support Eisenhower. Ironically the successes of the Democratic Party between 1932 and 1952 also helped Eisenhower and the Republicans. In the 1950s, in the context of unprecedented prosperity, many Americans had moved into the middle class, and to them "the danger of depression and economic insecurity seemed remote. Instead, income taxes and inflation that devoured a large portion of the economic gains of the postwar period loomed as the immediate threat to their economic welfare" (N. Graebner 1956: 71). Moreover, Social Security was no longer the favorite child of just the Democrats. "Through 20 years of defeat G.O.P. managers had become educated to the fact that the American people as a whole accepted economic legislation as a normal aspect of the functioning of the American economy. Candidate Dwight D. Eisenhower promised to maintain the gains of the New Deal, assuring the nation that it would enjoy tax reduction and the halting of inflation besides" (N. Graebner 1956: 71). Eisenhower would not wreck Social Security's progress, and throughout his term in office, he worked with Congress to extend coverage to an additional 10 million Americans. Indeed, the 1952 election in many ways clinched the bipartisan nature of the program; every Republican candidate since Landon had endorsed it (Albjerg 1952).

Eisenhower's message bore this out: "Banishing of destitution and cushioning the shock of personal disaster on the individual are proper concerns of all levels of government, including the federal government" (in N. Graebner 1960: 232). The gains made by Social Security during this Republican administration were significant. In Congress, normal party-line distinctions were blurred in creating Social Security legislation, making consensus and expansion more likely.

The 1952 amendments further increased benefits, and in 1954, coverage was made almost universal, with the exception of federal government employees. Provisions were made for a disability "freeze," which meant that old-age benefit rights were not impaired during periods of total disability. This was a second, seemingly minor step toward disability insurance.

After years of debate, disability insurance was finally included as an insurable risk under Social Security in 1956. Benefits were payable at age 50. After only six years, disability coverage had moved from welfare-tainted assistance to the more honorable ideology of insurance. Another important liberalization in Social Security that occurred in 1956 was the payment of reduced retirement benefits for women at the age of 62. The reasoning was that most women were younger than their husbands, and in order to be equitable, women should have the option of reduced benefits at an earlier age. Of course, this opened the door as a precedent for men to claim reduced benefits at age 62, as the 1961 amendments did.

The 1958 amendments increased old-age benefits, raised the wage base, increased the tax rate, and gave benefits to dependents of disability insurance recipients. The eligibility standard for disability insurance was also liberalized, so that less time in the active labor force was required for eligibility. (The original requirement was that six quarters of employment out of the preceding thirteen calendar quarters were required to attain eligibility; this was dropped in 1958.)

A 1959 *Current History* article proclaimed: "Not even the conservatives who fiercely opposed social security would now think of abolishing it." The Eisenhower administration indeed boasted of its achievements in this field. Increases in benefits and rates were made with a minimum of opposition (Starr 1959). Never before had a national political party been forced to operate so completely outside its philosophical boundaries.

By the early 1960s, inflation was no longer the threat it had been during the 1950s, but other problems arose. Sputnik, mounting racial tensions, and a sluggish economy were of great concern. The Social Security program expanded nevertheless. The 1960 amendments eliminated the age-50 limitation for monthly disability benefits. And the 1964 Johnson-Goldwater contest showed just how sacred Social Security had become. Lyndon Johnson promised a "War on Poverty" and a "Great Society," while conservative opponent Barry Goldwater suggested putting the Social Security system on a voluntary basis. The media, rival Republican candidates, and the Democrats all cited this as "a symbol of Goldwater's radical conservatism." As such, it figured conspicuously in the campaign. Theodore H. White, the chronicler of presidential campaigns, reported, "Out of the vast mass of his many statements and speeches, [the Democrats] chose to hook and hang him on one issue: Social Security" (in Derthick 1979: 187).

The next priorty on the list of the Social Security Administration was health insurance for the elderly. In 1935, "Unwilling to risk the entire Social Security Act by including health insurance, both Roosevelt and the Committee on Economic Security agreed to avoid the subject until Congress had enacted the bill"; opposition to a national health insurance program had grown out of the medical profession's concern that the greater the degree of government involvement, the less would remain of an individual physician's discretion, freedom, and status (Lubove 1963: 82, 77).

The momentum for hospital insurance had been building for years, as increasingly effective and highly technological health services resulted in increased cost and increased demand. The positive experience with disability insurance (benefit levels were reasonable, and the trust fund was sound) served as a precedent and lowered the American Medical Association's resistance to hospital insurance. President Johnson strongly supported health insurance for the elderly: "Health insurance for our senior citizens is the most important health proposal pending before the Congress. We urgently need this legislation—and we need it now" (in Cohen 1963: 119). By 1963, it was pointed out that the reserve fund had once again crept up to approximately $18 billion. In 1965, hospital insurance for the elderly became law. Old-age benefits were also increased, as were the tax rate and wage base.

Amendments in 1968 and 1969 increased benefits again. Primarily because of favorable employment conditions and low dependency ratios, the Social Security trust funds grew to be a larger and larger proportion of the federal budget. Before the fiscal year 1969 there were three budgets—the administrative, consolidated cash, and national income accounts. In 1967 Johnson appointed a President's Commission on Budget Concepts, which recommended that a unified budget be utilized that overlooked any surplus or deficit calculated for the administrative budget. Because of this change, the 1969 federal budget showed a "surplus" only because of the sizable excess in the Social Security trust funds. Some argued that Johnson made this accounting shift to cover the large Vietnam wartime deficit.

The late 1960s signaled the final stages of a comprehensive Social Security plan. There were few frontiers left to conquer, either in terms of clientele or in terms of philosophy. Except for benefit levels, the organization had expanded to its limits.

Organizational Dynamics

The developments of the 1950s and 1960s are instructive in relation to the organizational dynamics set forth earlier. Much of the political action occurred at the level of organizations, and by following this action over time, we gain a clearer picture of legislative change. Significantly, during the 1950s and 1960s, the Social Security Administration was able to act upon the larger political and economic environment. Once again, organizational persistence, interests, incentives, coalition formation, timing, time, and ideology are important conceptual categories for understanding the legislative turning points.

The entrenchment of the Social Security program during the 1950s and 1960s, and the resources available to the bureaucracy in the way of trust fund reserves and expert personnel were noteworthy in terms of organizational persistence. To a great extent the program gained acceptance and trust by the public because, as time elapsed, the impact of Social Security was deemed reasonable, and because payoffs in the early years were much higher than were taxes paid in. Indeed, the first person to retire under the system began drawing benefits January 1, 1940, after paying a mere $22.54 in payroll taxes. By the time of her death in 1975, she had drawn $21,000 in benefits (Brock 1982: 17). This public acceptance meant that Social Security was less of a political hot potato for Congress, which then felt encouraged to make changes suggested by the SSA that in effect, made the package a much more attractive one than the original. This is an excellent example of the role of slack, irrationality, or loose coupling in a system. The ability to add entire new categories of workers, and the fact that the program remained in the start-up phase (hence the numbers of persons drawing benefits was still relatively low), meant that benefits could be increased without corresponding changes in contribution amounts. This development was unique to this expansionary phase, and the system became more tightly coupled as time passed.

Further, the SSA had developed a clientele that had a stake in the program's endurance and expansion, even though the SSA and other groups voiced concerns regarding economic efficiency or rationality over the long run. Arthur Altmeyer and the SSA had firmly believed that benefit increases should always be accompanied by tax increases in order to make the public aware of the crucial link between the two. The SSA also believed that this would make it easier for Congress to initiate tax increases with every increase in benefits. But in 1950, with so much money in reserve, the idea of increasing this "temptation to government extravagance" (the reserve) by raising the tax rates was an unpopular option. At any rate, because of broadened coverage, nearly full employment, and a relatively young population, the trust fund continued to grow.

The strength of the trust funds throughout the 1950s and 1960s can only be viewed as yet another factor that increased confidence in the system and made possible the bold new additions of disability (1956) and hospital (1965) insurance. James Q. Wilson notes, "Obviously, a staff has the freedom to explore new objectives only when organizational maintenance problems have been solved; hence, the apparent paradox that it is in associations that have managed to win obvious respectability and assured member loyalty where one often finds elites willing, indeed, eager, to take on new political tasks" (1973: 209).

These programmatic developments and changes in the broader political and economic environment also influenced various political actors' perceptions of their interests. By 1950, Social Security had been in existence for fifteen years, taxes had been paid for thirteen years, and benefits had been paid for ten years. Many people who retired in the late 1940s and early 1950s were in their prime earning years during the Depression and had already used their savings, or were unable to save for retirement. Workers who had been employed in covered jobs were becoming increasingly committed to seeing the system maintained and expanded. Many people who requested larger benefits cited the millions of dollars spent to fend off communism, and to help foreign countries rebuild. In addition, by 1950, a variety of published sources had revealed that the costs of Social Security were passed on to the general public in the guise of higher prices, and to workers in the form of lower wages. This of course allowed persons and groups that were not yet included in Social Security coverage to complain that they were contributing indirectly to costs of the system without receiving their due benefits. Similarly, various business organizations developed agreements with unions whereby workers would benefit from increases in the federal old-age insurance program. The events of World War II and the wartime freezing of wages (but not benefits), and the linking of private pensions with the federal pension plan changed many of these groups' interests with regard to Social Security.

Before the 1950 Amendments there was also a great deal of discussion to the effect that a large reserve meant that the public was paying perhaps three times for their Social Security benefits. First, covered workers paid a payroll tax that went into the trust fund; but because this money was not set aside from general revenues, the federal government could borrow from the trust funds and sell bonds to the public to replace the funds. Marjorie Shearon, a vocal critic of Social Security, complained: "The OASI Trust Fund has been raided. . . . Trust Fund reserves have been siphoned off and IOU's substituted" (*CR* 1949: A. 2411–15). These bonds constituted the second instance in which the American public was financing government expenditures. Finally, if someone wanted to sell his or her bonds back to the government, the government would be forced to borrow yet a third time—from the American taxpayer.

Clearly, the changing context and shift in interests also influenced incentives to rally around the issue of Social Security. Beginning in the late 1950s there was an unprecedented burgeoning of groups representing the elderly (Pratt 1976). In 1956, Ethel Percy Andrus, a 72-year-old retired high school principal, conceived the idea of forming an organization to help older people obtain health, automobile, and home insurance. Two years later, Andrus and two of her friends met at the Woodner Hotel in Washington and voted to incorporate the American Association of Retired Persons (AARP). By this time, AARP was envisioned as more than a mere source of health insurance (Benac 1989a: J10).

This organization grew rapidly, and its political force is well known. Jack L. Walker describes its attraction:

The secret of this phenomenal growth, however, was not the attractiveness of the policies being advocated by the group; rather, it was the special medical insurance policies available to older people only through membership, the tours and vacation trips conducted by the group with the special needs of the elderly in mind, the commercial discounts and many useful personal services available for retired persons through membership. In Olson's terms . . . [this group grew] because of their ability to provide selective material benefits for their members, not because of the devotion of their members to the common interests of the elderly . . . its reliance on selective benefits is also quite *unusual*. (1983: 396)

Without selective incentives, voluntary organizations generally face the free-rider problem, whereby there is no specific benefit that accrues to any particular member by joining an organization that works toward group goals anyway. The AARP employs selective incentives in a highly successful manner by providing a wide range of services. Further, these services are offered while membership dues are kept at a minimum, and any person 50 years of age or older is included as a potential member. By these methods, AARP has overcome many of the impediments to successful organization that have been outlined by various scholars (Olson 1965; Salisbury 1969; Wilson 1973). Today, more than twenty organizations represent the elderly in Washington, D.C., including AARP, the National Council of Senior Citizens (NCSC), the National Council on Aging (NCOA), the National Association of Retired Federal Employees (NARFE), and the National Committee to Preserve Social Security and Medicare (NCPSSM) (Torres-Gil 1993).

The addition of disability insurance also illustrates how coalitions of actors can win out over very powerful but isolated interests. It is important to understand how disability insurance was linked to the regular program. Roosevelt, the Committee on Economic Security, and the early Social Security Board desired disability insurance from the very beginnings of the Social Security program in the 1930s. Arthur Altmeyer was the U.S. representative in the 1930s to the International Labor Organization (ILO), a socialistic organization that worked for the enactment of social insurance legislation. Its long-range objectives, set in the mid-1930s, were universal coverage, disability and hospital insurance and, eventually, general revenue financing (USNA, "SS—OASI Misc. [May, 1949]"). Many who were aware of the ILO program and Altmeyer's connection with it criticized the entire Social Security system as "un-American, having been imported via the ILO at Geneva in 1934" (USNA, "Non-profit Form Telegram"). However, because the program was new and still controversial in the 1930s, pursuit of disability and hospital insurance was put on hold until the basic program was instituted (Derthick 1979:296).

The SSB began recommending disability insurance to Congress in the early 1940s, but throughout that decade it appeared unlikely that it would ever get congressional approval. A House bill in 1949 that included other major changes to Social Security also included provision of benefits to workers who had been permanently or totally disabled before reaching retirement age, but the final bill that passed in the Senate removed these disability provisions. Senator Walter F. George, a Democrat from Georgia and Chairman of the Senate Finance Committee, and the two ranking GOP members, Robert A. Taft of Ohio and Eugene Millikin of Colorado, succeeded in eliminating the House proposal for disability insurance in the final 1950 amendments.

The main groups opposing disability insurance were the U.S. Chamber of Commerce, private insurance companies, and the AMA. The Chamber of Commerce was especially worried about the unforeseen costs of disability provisions, and private insurers had particularly bad experiences with disability insurance during the Depression when the rate of disability climbed sharply with widespread unemployment. The insurance industry's chief arguments were that costs were unpredictable, insurance discouraged rehabilitation, deceit was common, and administration required a great deal of discretion, which, of course, could be abused (USNA, "SS—OASI Misc. [May, 1949]"). The AMA argued that whereas age and dependency were objective conditions, disability was a subjective condition that encouraged malingering and that disability insurance would discourage rehabilitation. According to the AMA, disability insurance was one step toward socialized medicine (USNA, "Social Security Revision"). The AMA is a very powerful lobby, and archival evidence indicates that it overwhelmed Congress with letter-writing campaigns.

The SSA was joined in the fight for disability insurance by AFL-CIO unions. Union representatives argued that disability could quickly wipe out a life's savings, which would eventually mean an increased burden on welfare or public assistance. Not only was disability insurance administratively feasible according to them, but also the negative experience of private insurers was no indication of danger. Various labor union representatives explained that many of the private insurers tied their disability insurance to ordinary life policies in an effort to boost sales of the latter. This led to careless administration of the disability aspects. When private insurers tried to tighten up on disability insurance, they ran into adverse selection (USNA, "Social Security Revision").

In the 1940s and early 1950s, in comparison with discussions regarding the by-now comfortable old-age insurance, disability insurance polarized the debates. To overcome legislative opposition, the SSA pursued a policy linking disability to the regular insurance program. Supporters of disability coverage won a minor, and hardly noticeable victory in the 1950 amendments, which allowed benefits for the needy disabled by means of federal grants to individual states. The conservative opposition viewed this as a compromise, for they had wanted assistance to be a substitute for insurance, but certainly it was a very minor compromise. In the context of major legislative amendments, legislative watchdogs were somewhat lax in their review of what appeared to be minor bones of contention. Compared with the concern over expanding benefits and coverage, a minor concession to needy, disabled persons seemed insignificant. Once those opposing disability insurance had compromised on this particular point, they felt the issue was closed and turned their attentions elsewhere. Further, given the other broad changes brought about by this legislation, inclusion of this relatively obscure component did not attract much attention.

In some ways, however, these seemingly minor concessions were a giant leap, from no provisions to at least some. Certainly to the coalition of organizational actors that favored disability insurance, this victory acted as a spur, so that it was only a matter of time before they began working on an expanded program.

Given the pressures for expansion, the opposition from relatively powerful organizations was relatively muted, and disability insurance was enacted, while the tax rate and earnings base moved slowly upward. Once Social Security was entrenched, administrators and representatives of the Social Security bureaucracy were in a much better position to make autonomous gestures to relatively disenfranchised groups. A central reason for this was that the coalition of interests that had evolved made it easier for the SSA and Congress to enact legislation that was vehemently opposed by powerful political organizations.

Disability insurance also provides an excellent example of the dynamic in which outcomes at time one are causes at time two. In terms of broadening coverage and adding new programs like disability insurance, the strategy used was, first, to bring in those groups that desired coverage, and second, to move incrementally. During this period, coverage was not coercive, and by making benefits more attractive while simultaneously proposing broader coverage, the benefits of inclusion for many groups overshadowed the costs. These events set the stage for actors to group together, organize political and economic resources, collect information, garner support from outsiders, nurture constituents, and lobby for more. Executives of the SSA viewed the assistance provisions as complementary to insurance provisions, like old-age assistance and old-age insurance. Having achieved their top priority in 1950 of expanding coverage, the SSA set to work on moving disability from assistance to insurance. Disability insurance began as a needs-based program, was later extended to all disabled over the age of 50, and finally was extended to cover all disabled persons and their dependents.

It is through the mechanism of incrementalism that we can understand why the state bureaucracy had more autonomy from active, powerful interests during this period. In many ways, political energy and resources for any individual or group are zero-sum: there are opportunity costs involved in pursuing some policies; the cost is ignoring others. For example, legislators and interest groups have a broad agenda of items to consider, and limited staff and other resources with which to consider these issues; therefore they choose to pursue policies that have the greatest chances of success. But because the SSA pursues a narrower range of policies, it is more likely to be persistent and its interests are more likely to prevail over the long run. So while looking at one cross-sectional moment it may appear as though the SSA has suffered defeat (e.g., the disability amendments in 1950), in reality, a minor concession (e.g., welfare benefits for the disabled) is later turned into a full-blown program of benefits. Benefits expand the clientele, who in turn help the SSA to spread the word on how to collect benefits. The powerful but relatively isolated organizations that opposed expansion thus became captives of those concerned with the expansion of the program. Again, this is not to imply that powerful interests were overlooked; it was simply that, as time passed, they eventually molded the program to their needs.

The increasing complexity and technicality of the Social Security program also began to overwhelm most legislators during this time period, even key committee chairmen. At the time of the 1950 Amendments, Robert L. Doughton, chairman of the House Ways and Means Committee, stated, "I do not have the technical staff to analyze in detail the effect of the amendments to previous legislation" (USNA, "SS-OASI Misc. [April, 1949]"). The education, information, time, energy, advisers, and staff that were required to understand the legislation were scarce political resources. If groups do not fully understand the issues, they cannot play an effective part in political debates, and there is a corresponding lessening of the number of "competing" interests.

During this time period, organizations representing capital could still be classified as divided over the best policies to pursue. General Motors was more cautious than Ford, and the insurance industry's desired package (lower benefits) was different from the package sought by unionized sectors of industry. Considering monopoly capital as one unified group that socializes the costs of production ignores the variation within monopoly capital. Most importantly, an instrumentalist argument is misleading in terms of assessing cause and effect. In general, groups representing monopoly capital did not pursue Social Security so much as Social Security pursued them. Many representatives of business and industry offered conservative resistance to the program until the changes had been introduced, at which point they at last realized that they could live with, and even benefit from, Social Security. The tactic of incrementalism meant that this conservative resistance was eventually overcome. Martha Derthick summarizes this dynamic for the opposition surrounding disability insurance:

Perhaps a better explanation for the failure of business groups to sustain the intensity of their opposition is that crowding of the policy agenda compelled them to overlook much that they might have wished to attend to. Besides being incremental, the bits and pieces of disability legislation that passed after 1956 were not isolated. They were invariably part of a large and complicated legislative bundle for social security, which was itself just one part of a long agenda of domestic legislation. Pressure groups with limited resources have to choose their targets from a large universe. . . . The AMA feared that the disability program would be the federal government's first step in controlling medical practice. In fact it hardly disturbed the nation's doctors, the AMA calmed down, and the issue lost the intense symbolism that had been imparted by the AMA's earlier cry of "socialized medicine." (1979: 311–12)

So while the SSA had more autonomy from powerful interest groups during the period of expansion than at any other period, we again see that, over time, the program did not pose a threat to powerful groups because it accommodated their concerns and interests. This ensured the program's long-term political success.

Another key organizational development relates to timing and time, the former referring to the fortuitous nature of World War II for the Social Security program, and the latter referring to the origins or start-up phase of the system. The developments brought about by the war stimulated interest in Social Security. The problem of moving from covered to uncovered employment, the passing on of costs to the entire population, the investment of those who had paid in, an early actuarial imbalance, and the siphoning off of trust fund monies all led to pressures to expand the program. Not only was there pressure to expand, but the overall economic climate was also conducive to such growth.

During the fifteen-year start-up phase, the actuarial balance was such that taxes paid in were much greater than benefits paid out. A relatively large number of workers were paying in, compared with those who had worked enough years in covered employment to gain benefits. This, along with the fact that benefit payments did not increase for the first ten years of the program, added to the imbalance. Most importantly, the near full-employment of the wartime years meant that more workers were paying taxes and fewer persons were collecting retirement benefits. The effect of these unusual circumstances on the trust fund reserve was an enormous increase—from $368 million in 1940 to nearly $3 billion by 1950 (SSA 1989: 130). As discussed earlier, the reserve, under the control of the Secretary of the Treasury, had been a major point of contention in the 1930s; its growth in the 1940s meant that an increase in benefits became more acceptable. For business organizations like the U.S. Chamber of Commerce, the prospect of greater pension payments going to consumers was more acceptable than a piling up of massive reserves in the federal coffers. For the Congress, the existence of a large reserve was a politician's dream, for it made it possible to raise benefits without raising taxes. It was a rare and wonderful opportunity: the ability to increase benefits by 77 percent and yet increase taxes by only half a percent.

The importance of ideology is also evident during the 1950s and 1960s. First, the McCarthy era and charges of Communist infiltration of CIO unions forced a major housecleaning, and in 1955 the CIO merged with the AFL once again. This meant that labor spoke with a more unified voice after 1955 than it had when the two groups were split and had different political strategies. Similarly, over time, the relatively radical Townsendites were less successful than the more reformist AARP in having their agenda met.

Second, the ideology surrounding the Social Security program also shifted during these years of expansion. The Social Security bureaucracy gained in power and legitimacy during the 1950s and 1960s. An insurance industry executive summed up the change: "For 3 years after the Social Security Act was passed, if you went into a man's office and talked with him and said, 'What about your social security?' . . . at least half of them would have said, 'Forget it; I do not think I will ever get it.' . . . Now, that attitude has changed, . . . and the fellow who is not covered is beginning to say, 'Well, I think it is kind of an unjust thing that the Government is providing certain benefits for other people and I do not get them. After all, I am a citizen too.' That is a marked trend at the present time" (*CR* 1946: 436). Nelson Cruikshank, head of the AFL Social Security staff, said, "I think that is one of the most significant things that the people who are under the system longest and most fully under it are the people who like it best" (USNA, "Social Security Revision"). Social Security had achieved a great deal of legitimacy.

Support from a wide range of groups meant that the SSA could now pursue many of its most controversial programs, programs that incited the wrath of powerful interests—disability and hospital insurance. This autonomy stemmed from the clientele developed and the trust engendered after more than a decade in operation. The SSA took an active role in disseminating information about the vast array of benefits available. Arthur E. Hess, acting commissioner of the SSA, testified at a congressional hearing: "We do have a very extensive program of informing people through informational literature and through the new media. Just before an individual attains age 65 we have a computer exchange of information with Internal Revenue which gives us a lead on his current address" (*HWMCH* 1973: 690). State bureaucracies are active, not passive, in creating communities of interests that evolve over time, and the Social Security Administration has been especially successful in this respect.

Another ideological shift involved a change from concerns of "equity," prevalent during the origins period, to concern over the "adequacy" of benefits during the expansionary phase. The analogy to private insurance was now abandoned. The Social Security technical staff of the House Ways and Means Committee reported: "In these early steps [the 1930s] the influence of orthodox insurance practices, and a strong sense of equity which required a quid pro quo from the individual for old-age benefits, are quite apparent. But it was almost immediately obvious that strict attention to these ideas of equity limited most seriously what could be done in developing the social value of the plan and, after all, this was the purpose of its creation" (*HWMCH* 1946: 665). Social Security is a political program with social value concerns that sometimes prevail over economic rationality. No private insurer could pay benefits that were adjusted for inflation. Further, private companies have to insure that their premiums cover their commitments. The concern with a large and misused Social Security trust fund meant that we developed what amounted to a pay-as-you-go system. Congress could also give away benefits gratis. For example, World War II veterans, who paid no taxes and received no credit toward pensions, were credited as though they paid tax on $160 per month while in the service (USNA, "SS—OASI Misc. [Oct.,

1949]"). These benefits were paid from general revenues, not from Social Security trust funds.

This was a highly significant shift in the American public's perception of the role of Social Security. Gone were the days of Social Security supporters walking the legislative tightrope by stating that, in actuality, Social Security was designed to provide a minimum floor of protection. Supporters of Social Security abandoned the rhetoric of a "floor" and began to speak of the inadequacy of benefits in terms of meeting living costs (*HWMCH* 1950: 50). During this period of entrenchment in the 1950s and 1960s there was much indication, by letters to representatives and in testimony before Congress, that the public did not remember (or chose not to remember), that Social Security had never originally been intended to provide a comfortable living. There were few others who were willing to point out this fact.

Harold Wilensky has said: "Time will count if a welfare bureaucracy acquires a vested interest in expanding budget and personnel in its area vis-a-vis others, if it successfully cultivates a committed clientele and powerful political allies, and if it effectively spreads information about its benefits and programs" (1975: 10). Social Security in the United States was highly successful in political terms during the 1950s and 1960s. There were dramatic changes that would occur during the 1970s, and these are addressed in Chapter 5.

CHAPTER FIVE

The Tipping Point, 1970-1976

> If we enact the 20-percent increase . . . I can assure the
> membership of this House that we will over the forthcoming
> 75-year period take in each year more money than we will be
> paying out.
>
> —Wilbur Mills (D-Arkansas), chairman of the House Ways
> and Means Committee, regarding the 1972 amendments
> (*CQA* 1972: 402)

THE ONE TURNING POINT in Social Security's entire history that probably sheds the most light on its economic and political dimensions is the passage of the 1972 amendments. There are three ways in which the 1972 legislation can be said to represent the historic tipping point of the program. First, expansion occurred up to and including the 1972 amendments, whereas later changes involved retrenchment, in the form of slowed growth in the program. Second, when evaluating the ideal size of an organization and its political efficacy, the concept of a tipping point is an important one. As I shall discuss in this chapter, the 1972 amendments were pivotal in this respect also. Third, because Social Security was now a mature old-age insurance program, dependency ratios could no longer be altered solely by bringing in more workers. Further, the changing demographic profile of the American population would be cause for alarm in later years. Several of the key theoretical issues addressed earlier are illustrated by the developments that occurred from 1970 to 1976; but first, it is important to place this legislation in its larger economic and political context.

The Economic and Political Context

Between 1970 and 1976, shifts occurred in the economic, political, and demographic context. These shifts shaped the relative power and interests of many organizational actors involved in the debates surrounding Social Security.

Despite the strong economic performance of the 1960s (low un-

TABLE 6

Percent of Civilian Labor Force Unemployed and Percentage Increase
in Consumer Price Index, 1965–1985

Year	Pct. unemployed	Pct. increase in CPI	Year	Pct. unemployed	Pct. increase in CPI
1965	4.5	1.7	1976	7.7	5.8
1966	3.8	2.9	1977	7.1	6.5
1967	3.8	2.9	1978	6.1	7.7
1968	3.6	4.2	1979	5.8	11.3
1969	3.5	5.4	1980	7.1	13.5
1970	4.9	5.9	1981	7.6	10.4
1971	5.9	4.3	1982	9.7	6.1
1972	5.6	3.3	1983	9.6	3.2
1973	4.9	6.2	1984	7.5	4.3
1974	5.6	11.0	1985	7.3	3.6
1975	8.5	9.1			

SOURCE: *Statistical Abstract of the United States*, annual editions, 1965–85, U.S. Bureau of the Census, Washington, D.C.

employment and inflation, as seen in Table 6), certain groups did not benefit from this economic prosperity. Setting the stage for expanding Social Security benefits in the early 1970s was the fact that elderly and female-headed households were the only two groups to experience an increase in poverty (*HWMCH* 1970: 1339). In 1970, Walter P. Reuther, president of the United Auto Workers, testified before the House Ways and Means Committee that the poverty problem existed because Americans had not yet made a commitment to eradicate it. The reason Neil Armstrong could leave footprints on the moon, he said, was that the United States made a commitment to that end, and he urged the same type of commitment to deal with the domestic poverty problem (*HWMCH* 1970: 2212). Reuther argued, "Support of our men in Vietnam, of programs to ease the problems of our cities, and of the space program, should not require neglect of our elderly" (*HWMCH* 1970: 2228).

The specter of inflation also loomed large during the early 1970s, although it was not until the late 1970s that double-digit inflation took hold. To try to combat inflation, on August 15, 1971, President Richard M. Nixon imposed a 90-day wage-price freeze. Inflation hit especially hard on the elderly living on fixed incomes, and in 1971 the elderly still represented the nation's largest group living under the poverty line (AFLA 1971: 137).

Support and Opposition

The increasing poverty of the elderly was accompanied by significant growth in the organization and membership of elderly advocate groups. In 1972, the American Association of Retired Persons (AARP), founded in 1958, claimed nearly three and one-half million paid members aged 50 and over, and the National Council of Senior Citizens (NCSC), founded in 1961, had 4,800 clubs (Gruber 1987). Added to these two large and politically active organizations, the Gray Panthers, founded in 1970 by activist Maggie Kuhn, served as another energetic, vocal, and well-organized group of senior citizens. These groups represented strength in numbers, and because virtually all of them were eligible to vote, and usually did, they could nearly guarantee politicans a unified vote.

Changing demographics also contributed to the growth in membership, and latent or actual political influence, of these elderly advocate groups (see Table 7 for the growth of AARP). As Charles E. Lindblom writes: "Voting aside, in democratic and many authoritarian systems, ordinary citizens impose constraints on policy makers. . . . Citizens often need neither to speak nor act, if rulers fear that at any time they may do so. They need not deliberately try to achieve control or even realize that they exercise control" (1980: 44). The political muscle of elderly advocate groups, as evidenced both as potential political support or opposition and as actual lobbying before congressional committees, was an important factor in the continuing reluctance of Congress to alter benefit calculations.

Further, as time progressed, the elderly as a group reached retirement with higher and higher expectations. Part of the reason for these increasing expectations was that as the program matured, people had paid Social Security taxes over more and more of their working lifetimes. Another reason for increasing expectations was that in the 1950s and 1960s the program had in fact promised to do more than ever before. Expansion and optimism ruled the day.

TABLE 7
Membership of American Association of Retired Persons, 1959–1985

Year	No. of paid members	Year	No. of paid members	Year	No. of paid members
1959	50,000	1968	1,192,647	1977	9,975,982
1960	300,000	1969	1,606,390	1978	11,000,999
1961	381,000	1970	1,886,858	1979	11,840,082
1962	429,750	1971	2,487,783	1980	12,200,000
1963	496,100	1972	3,454,449	1981	12,574,747
1964	543,601	1973	4,852,625	1982	13,281,839
1965	731,110	1974	6,218,998	1983	14,309,991
1966	850,233	1975	7,451,272	1984	15,773,639
1967	914,140	1976	8,717,966	1985	18,237,790

SOURCE: *Encyclopedia of Associations*, Detroit: Gale Research Co., various editions.

What this meant for the program in the early 1970s was that the elderly were more invested in the system, more vocal about setting agendas, and more numerous and better organized as a group than they had ever been in the past.

Because of the relatively strong economy and the political influence of these elderly advocate groups, the primary focus in the early 1970s remained on benefits and on adequacy. Nelson Cruikshank, for many years the director of the AFL-CIO Social Security department, was president of the National Council of Senior Citizens at this time. In testifying before Congress, he reiterated the concept of adequacy: "Social security falls far short of doing what it was intended to do, namely, replace income lost due to retirement, disability, or death" (*HWMCH* 1970: 1339).

Cruikshank's statement reflected the ideology surrounding Social Security legislation in the 1950s and 1960s more than it did the intent of the original congressional framers, or the direction the program would take in the later 1970s. Indeed, the 1971 Advisory Council Report contained the reminder, "Social insurance cannot and should not be expected to do the whole job of income maintenance" (House Document no. 92-80: 2). Nonetheless, the majority of this Advisory Council recommended that old-age insurance benefits be linked to the Consumer Price Index (CPI) to maintain beneficiaries' purchasing power. This recommendation involved establishing a formula to index benefits automatically to the CPI, a procedure that had been done in the past by Congress on an ad hoc basis. A key concern of the SSA, AARP, and NCSC was that benefit increases lagged too far behind actual increases in the CPI; Social Security represented the major or sole source of income for the majority of beneficiaries, and any lag meant temporary economic hardship (House Document no. 92-80: 12). It was also believed by many, including the Nixon administration, that by automatically indexing benefits to the CPI, benefit increases would be less political and less pressure would be placed on Congress. James Q. Wilson writes:

> Tying one's hands also seemed to be good politics in the case of certain indexed or automatic expenditures. Republicans did not like the fact that the Democrats (who usually controlled Congress) were always getting the credit for increasing Social Security benefits. The only politically feasible way to end this advantage was to make such increases automatic. Indexing also had another advantage to fiscal conservatives: it would keep benefit increases in line with the cost of living and thus prevent bidding wars among members of Congress eager to portray themselves as the "senior citizen's best friend." And so the biggest part of the budget of the biggest (in dollars spent) agency in Washington was put on automatic pilot. Once on, it could not easily be taken off except by new, politically costly legislation. Congress had weakened its own powers. (1989: 239)

In spite of the fact that Nixon favored linking benefits to the CPI, it was because of inflation that Nixon was very opposed to a major increase in Social Security. He viewed any major increase in Social Security benefits as further fueling inflation. The original Social Security bill in the House in 1971 proposed a 5 percent increase in benefits. The 5 percent increase was supported originally by party leaders on both sides, including Wilbur Mills (D-Arkansas), Chairman of the House Ways and Means Committee.

Later that year, however, Mills became a candidate for the Democratic presidential nomination. Mills changed his mind about the adequacy of a 5 percent increase in benefits, and on February 23, 1972, he recommended a 20 percent increase. As noted in the *Congressional Record*, "13 days before the New Hampshire primary and 21 days before large numbers of elderly citizens were to vote in Florida's primary—Mills introduced his bill" (*CR* 1972: 17715). John D. Ehrlichman, assistant to the President for Domestic Affairs, said, "We think 20 percent is a political ploy and cannot be considered seriously" (*CR* 1972: 17716).

Dissenting members of the Advisory Council and representatives of the U.S. Chamber of Commerce and the National Association of Manufacturers, however, opposed the link to the CPI. They asked how we could fight inflation by automatically adjusting to it. They reiterated that Social Security was never intended to be the sole source of income, and pointed out that this would represent a "very substantial departure from relating benefits to past earnings records" that would make it impossible to estimate the costs for the program. Furthermore, they argued, it would not reduce the demands for liberalization but would simply result in additional benefits above and beyond the automatic increases (House Document no. 92-80: 83).

Early 1970s Expansion

The supporters of expansion of benefits prevailed. From 1969 to 1972, three across-the-board benefit increases were legislated: 15 percent effective for January 1970, then 10 percent effective for January 1971, and 20 percent effective for September 1972. The result was that real benefit levels increased by 23 percent in three years (USNA, "Correspondence with Commission Members, July 6–November 5, 1982").

These changes in the early 1970s reflected the unlimited expectations for the program in the past and the inherent optimism about the strength of the economy, based on the experiences of the preceding two and a half decades. The optimism embodied in the bill took the form of neglecting fertility trends toward zero-population growth and assuming that wage growth would outstrip inflation by 2–2.25 percent per year. The optimism was, however, consistent with the population growth and economic expansion of the 1950s and 1960s.

The 20 percent increase in benefits was accomplished primarily by altering the actuarial assumptions that had been used up until 1972. Before 1972, when Social Security Administration actuaries calculated trust fund income, they had used what was known as level-wage assumptions—that is, they assumed that wages would not increase. When in fact wages did rise, the additional amount received in the trust funds was generally used to increase benefits. This was a relatively safe, conservative way to estimate income, but when wages began to go up year after year, more liberal members of the SSA and Congress, and the 1971 Advisory Council, recommended using a rising-wage assumption.

Robert J. Myers, a fiscally conservative Republican and former Chief Actuary for the SSA, called the dynamic assumption "expansionist" and argued that it would be unwise to assume ever increasing U.S. productivity. He also pointed out a danger: "Very small errors in estimating the spread between price increases and wage gains . . . could cause 'terrific differences' in cost calculations" (*CR* 1972: 17714). The U.S. Chamber of Commerce echoed Myers's concerns. These concerns were to go unheeded, and a change in accounting principles was one actuarial key that allowed Congress to raise Social Security benefits 20 percent in 1972. Confident because of the strong economic record of the past two decades, and under pressure from increasingly activist elderly groups with only isolated resistance, Congress acted accordingly.

Overall, the 1972 amendments were extremely generous. Congress increased benefits by 20 percent, effective June 1972. Of course, the $6 billion surplus in the trust funds, as reported by the 1971 Advisory Council, did little to discourage massive expansion. Many organizations, as mentioned earlier, opposed the accumulation of large reserves. This large surplus, combined with the dynamic-wage assumptions, meant that the trust fund reserves were pronounced in great shape.

But another interesting question, whatever the actuarial assumptions, is why Nixon chose not to veto this huge increase in Social Security, which he had so vocally opposed as inflationary. Nixon supported a mere 5 percent increase in benefits but was faced with a Democrat-proposed 20 percent. A new tactic would become a common feature of Social Security turning points during the 1970s and 1980s. This was the tactic of linking Social Security changes to nongermane or omnibus legislation. The 1972 Social Security legislation was presented with a bill setting a debt ceiling that was designed to increase the allowable federal debt. Nixon was forced to choose between increasing the debt ceiling and accepting the 20 percent increase, or opposing an increase in Social Security and not obtaining the desired increase in the allowable debt ceiling. Rather than veto a large Social Security benefit increase in an election year, and in doing so also kill the debt ceiling proposal, Nixon chose to sign the bill into law. Not incidentally perhaps, it can be noted that Presidents who sign Social Security legislation that raises benefits, get much credit with voters. A notice is enclosed with the increased Social Security checks, informing beneficiaries that they received the extra amount because of a law signed by the President, even though the President may have opposed the legislation.

The 1972 amendments had other important provisions. They linked future Social Security increases to changes in the CPI (effective January 1, 1975); increased from $1,680 to $2,100 the amount that a Social Security beneficiary under age 72 could earn and still receive full benefits (there was no earning limit for those age 72 and over); provided a minimum monthly benefit of $170 for persons who worked in Social Security–covered employment for at least 30 years; and changed to age 62 for men the same computation that was used for early retirement for women (*CQA* 1972: 23). World War II Japanese internees who were eighteen or older at the time of internment were awarded wage credits in the 1972 amendments; Social Security trust funds would be reimbursed from general revenues for these last benefits.

The bill also federalized existing federal and state programs of assistance to the aged, disabled, and blind, effective January 1, 1974. This new program, known as Supplemental Security Income, gave persons with no outside income a minimum monthly federal payment of $130 ($195 for a couple). Individual states were permitted to supplement this federal payment if they wished to do so. Political pressure for federalizing these payments was exerted by individual states, elderly advocate groups, and the National Federation of Independent Business (*CQA* 1972: 900). In fact, many state representatives who testified (e.g., governors) argued that SSI did not go far enough in alleviating the assistance burden (*CQA* 1972: 901).

The states were, of course, concerned with an increasingly burdensome assistance load, but elderly advocate groups pointed out that many states reduced their old-age assistance payments after each increase in federal old-age insurance benefits was enacted by Congress. The elderly poor were thus no better off than they had been before the increase (*HWMCH* 1970: 1338). They lobbied for higher benefits in both programs and were successful with the 1972 legislation.

To finance these new benefits, there was a change to the dynamic-wage assumption, the tax rate was modestly increased from 5.2 percent to 5.5 percent, effective January 1, 1973, and the taxable wage base was increased from $9,000 to $10,800 in 1973, and to $12,000 in 1974. This increase in the wage base was strongly opposed by the American Life Convention, the Life Insurance Association of America, and the Life Insurers Conference, all of which maintained that any increase in the wage base distorted the "proper balance between the Social Security system and the private retirement media" (*CQA* 1972: 900). Again, organizations representing the life insurance industry generally opposed increases in the taxable wage base, primarily on the grounds that this represented increased taxation of higher income employees. Theoretically, this would mean less disposable income for this group, or a lowered propensity to purchase more insurance from private providers.

The use of price indexing (linking benefit increases to changes in the CPI) was expected to be less costly than using wage indexing, given that increases in wages had heretofore exceeded increases in prices. Although the indexing procedure adopted in the 1972 amendments was actually the same as what Congress had done on an ad hoc, or as-needed, basis during the 1950s and 1960s, the proponents of automatic indexing believed that the new method would eliminate any lag time between changes in the cost of living and increases in benefits.

In summarizing the importance of the 1972 legislation, we must consider both substantive and conceptual issues. Since these amendments represented the last major expansion of Social Security, it is instructive to note the political and economic context that preceded them. Unemployment was still low, and although inflation had risen slightly, it did not represent a major threat to the trust funds. Pressure for increased benefits was preceded by three factors: the strong economy and focus on the adequacy of benefits in the 1950s and 1960s, increasing rates of poverty among the elderly, and an increasingly activist aged population.

The added significance of the 1972 amendments is that they were the last in a long line of expansionary efforts. Complacency evident in the congressional debates reflected just how successful the program had been. Changes were instituted by SSA bureaucrats, primarily with a change in how the estimates were calculated, coupled with only minor changes in the wage base and tax rate. The fact that decision making with regard to Social Security had settled primarily in the bureaucracy is an indication of how many organizations had accommodated, or had been accommodated by, the Social Security program. With the exceptions of the AARP, the NCSC, and certain organizations representing conservative business resistance, most interest groups, having won the important battles, had turned their attentions elsewhere. The shortened debates regarding these amendments and the small numbers of outsider interest groups that testified regarding their positions indicated considerable trust and faith in the Social Security system. The system worked, guided largely by the bureaucracy and Congress, and therefore few organizations questioned their authority.

Again, we see that both the SSA and Congress had much more autonomy from powerful interests during the expansionary phase of Social Security than they had during the crisis periods of the Great Depression and the 1980s. Powerful insurance lobbies opposed the increase in the wage base that was mandated by the 1972 legislation, mainly because they perceived such increases as infringing on their potential business. The U.S. Chamber of Commerce and the NAM opposed linking benefits to the CPI, arguing that indexing made costs incalculable. These two organizations also opposed the shift to a dynamic-wage assumption, but this, too, was accomplished anyway. These organizations that opposed various changes in Social Security legislation, all of them powerful political actors, lost important battles in 1972.

The economic, political, and demographic context that led to the 1972 amendments would provide a stark contrast indeed to the events that would soon occur. In light of later developments, these politically expedient changes would appear to be economically catastrophic. In the following decade, the ill-considered, unfunded expansions would drain the reserves, and complacency would be replaced by concern with dwindling trust fund reserves, both short-term and long-term.

The Beginnings of Retrenchment

The events that occurred between 1972 and 1977 had devastating effects on the Social Security program. Though there has been retrenchment, it has had nothing to do with benefits. Benefits have not been cut, but programmatic growth and rising expectations have been curtailed by the developments of the late 1970s and early 1980s. Participation in the program became mandatory for federal workers, and others were not allowed to opt out. Social Security became much more coercive.

The 1975 Annual Report of the Social Security Administration touted that one out of every seven Americans got Social Security benefits each month (1975: 1); but it was also in 1975 that for the first time in the program's history the trust fund showed a deficit. Outgoing benefits exceeded incoming contributions. This was the first year benefits were indexed to the CPI.

In the mid-1970s, both inflation and unemployment soared (see Table 6). Since benefits were linked to inflation and contributions were affected by unemployment, the trust funds were depleted rapidly. Moreover, as high unemployment reduced the income for the trust funds, more people applied for all types of Social Security benefits. Persons in their early sixties who were out of work chose retirement, and that further swelled the massive number of persons depending on Social Security benefits. Legislators did not welcome the prospect of lowering benefits, but legislative change of some form was politically and economically warranted.

The most controversial issue in the mid-1970s was a proposal to mandatorily cover federal, state, local, and nonprofit employees and forbid withdrawal of groups that had elected coverage. The only workers not yet covered were various federal, state, local, and nonprofit employees. Employees who had not yet elected coverage argued that their own pension plans were superior to the Social Security system. A study conducted by the Office of Personnel Management found that the average monthly civil service benefit was $1,047, whereas Social Security benefits were only $406. Civil service benefits were indeed very generous. The Civil Service Retirement System (CSRS) cost 36 percent of total payroll, but employees paid only 7 percent of the total costs of their pensions; because the CSRS was also on a pay-as-you-go basis, the remaining 29 percent came from general revenues. (This factor would be used against CSRS-covered employees in 1983 when proponents of mandatory universal coverage under Social Security showed that it would not actually cost the general Treasury any more to bring these workers under Social Security.) In addition, federal workers could collect a full pension if they retired at age 55 with 30 years of service, age 60 with 20 years, and age 62 with 5 years. Social Security recipients could retire at age 62 with reduced benefits and at age 65 with full benefits (*CQA* 1983: 574).

A good many other groups had elected Social Security coverage voluntarily during the 1950s and 1960s when the program was very healthy, with the option of withdrawing from Social Security coverage after giving two years' notice. In the mid-1970s local and state governments began to complain about the high cost of Social Security. New York City and the state of Ohio filed notices of intent to withdraw from the program precisely because of the high costs; and various other state and municipal administrators protested that local revenues, already inadequate, would not be able to continue to carry the load of paying the required employer's share of one-half the Social Security payroll tax. New York City finance administrators estimated that they could save as much as $43 million in the final quarter of the 1977–78 fiscal year (*HWMCH* 1976a: 51). New York City had already made several other cuts, but to preclude massive layoffs and impairment of essential city services, it argued that the option to withdraw from Social Security was a necessary consideration.

These administrators were worried not simply about current costs; they feared future increases. Raymond D. Horton, staff director of the Temporary Commission on City Finance for New York City, testified at a House Ways and Means Committee hearing in 1976:

If the city could be certain that social security costs would not escalate further in the future, there obviously would be less reason to consider withdrawing from the system. However, given the huge revenue needs of the social security system and the history of increases both in the social security tax rate and base, it is predictable that the city's social security costs will continue to rise sharply if the city stays in the system. Since the city first entered the system, the maximum social security tax per employee has risen 965 percent, from $84 in 1956 to its present level of $895. (*HWMCH* 1976a: 55)

The high costs to state and local governments of Social Security coverage for their employees, and generally declining confidence in the solvency of the trust funds were important factors in their decisions to opt out. One additional reason for the opposition to mandatory coverage was that nonprofit organizations and state and local governments did not have the same tax breaks as corporations in writing off nearly half of the employer share of the Social Security tax (*CR* 1977: 36452). Of course, this could be remedied by providing these groups with the appropriate tax incentives. (This was done in the 1983 amendments.) Federal unions and some state and local governments lobbied long and hard against compulsory coverage (*CQA* 1983: 574). They organized a mailing campaign, and many members of Congress reported being flooded with mail from constituents opposing mandatory coverage (*CR* 1977: 35236).

A central problem connected with the absence of compulsory universal coverage was that many of these workers got windfall benefits. Both those who were excluded and did not want in and those who were included and wanted out posed problems. Even though coverage was terminated for these workers, Social Security benefits had already accrued for many of the temporarily covered workers. This meant that they could collect two pensions when they retired. This "double-dipping" was well publicized and it was estimated that it cost Social Security $1 billion per year. Only six quarters of employment in covered jobs were required to accumulate benefit rights. Therefore by choosing to withdraw from the program, although one's contributions to the trust funds ceased, even the minimum amount of contributions entitled one to benefits. Further, the benefit formula was weighted to favor low-paid personnel; since many government employees had only a few years of employment covered by Social Security, they were analogous, in effect, to low-paid workers and their benefits rose accordingly. For a working lifetime's contribution of as little as $111, these retirees could draw $114 in Social Security for their first month of retirement. If married, they could get 50 percent more. Medicare and disability insurance were also provided for life. This amounted to a windfall for these workers. Double-dipping was legally practiced by 43 percent of all Federal Civil Service retirees (*CR* 1977: 35266). Representative Sam Gibbons (D-Florida) declared: "Sure, they do not want to come into the system. They have the best of all worlds" (*CR* 1977: 35298). James Burke (D-Florida), a member of the House Ways and Means Committee, argued that double-dipping was "costly to the system and unfair to the majority of contributors to the system, who do not have the option of voluntary participation" (*HWMCH* 1976b: 33).

The groups mandatorily covered under Social Security were a ready-made constituency to oppose double-dipping. Many legitimately covered groups demanded universal coverage. The larger employer organizations like the U.S. Chamber of Commerce and the NAM advocated compulsory coverage for noncovered employees. The AFL-CIO favored less coercion and therefore opposed mandatory coverage of all employees; they advocated the use of collective bargaining to sort out the employees' best interests.

Clearly, the draining of the trust funds as a result of unemployment and inflation was creating paranoia; those groups not yet covered or those who could opt out attempted to reject coverage. This massive exodus was alarming to the SSA. In a statement before the House Ways and Means Committee, James B. Cardwell, commissioner of the SSA in 1976, summarized the scope of the problem:

Since social security coverage was first made available to State and local employees in the 1950s, their coverage under the program has increased dramatically, and during the 1960s there were very few terminations of coverage—in almost all cases the terminations resulted from dissolution of political subdivisions. However, in the past 4 years there has been a trend for more groups of covered State and local employees to request the States to terminate their coverage. Through March 1972, coverage has been terminated for 133 entities employing less than 10,000 workers. In the following 4 years, by March 1976, the number of entities terminated had increased by 2.5 times, and the number of employees involved by more than four times. In the next 2 years, based on current requests, coverage could be terminated for an additional 232 entities employing about 454,000 workers. (*HWMCH* 1976a: 35)

This movement out of coverage reflected declining confidence in the program. Representative Barber Conable (R-New York) summed up the dilemma well: "Our concern, of course, is that this action by as large a municipality as New York carries with it some interesting implications for the system. We are concerned that there not be a run on the system because of concurrent publicity relating to social security which has given a wide number of Americans the idea that it is not going to be as good a deal in the future as it has been in the past" (*HWMCH* 1976a: 60). Representative Steven Allen (R-Alabama) lamented, "Whereas the social security system was once looked on as a haven of security for the people, it is beginning to be looked on as a tremendous burden for the working people of our country" (*CR* 1977: 364329).

Organizational Dynamics

In view of the interaction between the larger economic and political environment and organizations, the early 1970s was the period in which the SSA and Congress were most capable of influencing the environment. With such a strong economy, they could aggressively attack the problem of poverty among the elderly. And the economy also made it easier to secure goals politically: considering the drastic changes embodied in the 1972 amendments, very little debate occurred. Inflation was relatively low, wages rose, and dependency ratios remained at an acceptable level. The increasing political influence of elderly advocate groups did little to temper the debates.

The SSA was successful in a number of ways. It had the respect of Presidents, the Office of Management and Budget (OMB), and the public. Along with this favorable opinion, a major factor behind its survival and ability to persist in promoting a long-range plan, it had kept its administrative costs low, and this, too, gained it respect. Nelson W. Polsby writes that in setting agency administrative budgets, both Congress and the President take into account

"(1) What agencies received last year. . . . (2) World developments. . . . (3) Agency reputations for accurate estimating, hard work, and 'integrity.' . . . (4) Prior programmatic commitments. (5) Interest group demands. . . . (6) Economic ideologies and general economic conditions" (1986: 185–86). A counterexample here is to note how NASA's appropriations were cut during the late 1980s and early 1990s because of various problems it experienced.

For Social Security, the developments from 1972 through 1977 vividly illustrate that "organizational decisions depend on information, estimates, and expectations that ordinarily differ appreciably from reality" (Cyert and March 1963: 83). As the trust funds were drained by high inflation and high unemployment, public confidence in Social Security began to falter. Regarding the later 1970s, Martha Derthick notes: "The picture that emerges . . . is of an agency badly buffeted by external forces. . . . It is not viewed as a valuable public resource to be husbanded, nor as a tool that needs care and maintenance and can be used effectively only by those who comprehend how it functions" (1990: 175).

The 1972 amendments are perhaps the most forceful example of how the coinciding interests of bureaucracies, elected officials, and beneficiaries can obviate compromise in any true sense of the word. Many political observers in the late 1970s and early 1980s would question where the counterbalancing forces were during the debates over the 1972 amendments. These developments clearly show that it is not simply organizations representing capital that have economic interests or political power. Wilbur Mills, a politically ambitious congressman, and elderly advocate groups were key forces behind the 1972 legislative turning point. Yet, as congressional documents reveal, no representatives of business, industry, or insurance were in favor of the massive increase in benefits brought about by these amendments, the CPI indexing provisions, or increasing the wage base.

In terms of incentives to organize, Robert H. Salisbury's analysis is pertinent:

[First] . . . institutions are *far* more likely to be part of relatively small, similarly situated groups . . . and thus be able to organize more readily and to anticipate being more effective politically than most individual citizens can expect. Second, although a given individual may hold a large number of distinct values or interests and even embrace a considerable set of political causes, available resources for participation are quickly exhausted, and multiple modes of individual participation are comparatively uncommon. Institutions possess more resources which, combined with a greater sense of efficacy in political action, lead to a considerable increased probability of participation at any given level of intensity of interest or concern. (1984: 69)

Aside from institutions, we might have expected taxpaying workers to organize in protest of the increasingly burdensome Social Security payroll tax. There are several reasons this did not occur. Jack L. Walker writes:

Citizen groups face an entirely different set of initial circumstances. Their potential membership is extremely large and, in most cases, unknown to one another. There is no ready-made community waiting to be organized, no readily available sources of money, and often not even a clearly articulated common interest in creating an organization. Citizen groups must begin with a fairly large staff, or they will have little chance of reaching enough of their far-flung potential membership to create a stable organizational base. (1983: 398)

Another reason for the lack of effective political organization of taxpayers was that tax increases were incremental. For most employees, take-home pay is the critical variable. Since a slight increase in Social Security taxes made only a small dent in a paycheck, there was less incentive to organize politically. Changes in Social Security were therefore viewed by workers as less important in the short run than cost-of-living or merit raises. In retrospect, however, and utilizing a long-range perspective, these tax increases were extremely significant.

Social Security created an anomalous coalition of interests. A wide variety of groups, aside from the elderly, either actively supported the program, or at the very least, offered no organized resistance to the 1972 amendments. There was no common incentive. Persons not receiving benefits but paying taxes expected to retire and collect benefits themselves. There were also many taxpaying persons who benefited indirectly from Social Security through the care provided to a family member who would otherwise have to be provided for privately. And the fact that other Social Security programs, besides old-age insurance, served younger persons further enhanced its acceptability and constituency. Employer organizations like the U.S. Chamber of Commerce and the NAM wanted other groups to be required to participate in the program (e.g., civil service workers). Finally, organizations like the AFL-CIO lobbied hard to increase Social Security benefits in the 1950s, 1960s, and early 1970s. All these factors served as disincentives for the organization of a protest movement to suggest that Social Security benefits should be scaled back. Barring more drastic measures, widening the coverage and increasing the wage base or payroll tax were the only solutions that remained.

It is only in recent years, as the Social Security dependency ratio has grown more onerous in the form of tax burdens on younger workers, that we have seen slightly more opposition from taxpaying workers. The National Taxpayers Union (founded in 1969) and its opposition to the heavy taxes levied by the 1977 amendments are indicative of this trend. In 1984, Senator David F. Durenberger (R-Minnesota) formed a group called Americans for Generational Equity (AGE), which later merged with the American Association of Boomers (AAB). These groups promote intergenerational equity over time and work to equalize the relative benefits that accrue to a range of age groups.

With regard to the idea of timing, the economic context and cohort-related demographic developments provide good examples. The unanticipated, historically rare stagflation of the mid 1970s, when both inflation and unemployment rose, had a tremendous impact on Social Security. The "pig in the python" demographic bulge of the baby boomers was another development that also greatly influenced the Social Security program.

As far as the concept of time being a central organizational variable, the Social Security program was gradually becoming a mature program. It was becoming more zero-sum and more tightly coupled. More and more workers were covered, and more people had paid into the program for more of their working lives. With an increasing percentage of the workforce in covered employment, the trust funds could not be bolstered significantly solely by including large numbers of previously uncovered workers.

As the program matured and expanded, it had a significant

TABLE 8
Percent of Persons Aged 65+ Living Under the Poverty Level

Year	Pct. elderly poor	Year	Pct. elderly poor	Year	Pct. elderly poor
1959	35.2	1974	15.7	1981	15.3
1962	34.0	1975	15.3	1982	14.6
1963	35.0	1977	14.1	1983	14.2
1970	24.6	1978	14.0	1984	12.4
1972	18.6	1979	15.2	1985	12.6
1973	16.3	1980	15.7	1990	11.4

SOURCE: *Statistical Abstract of the United States*, U.S. Bureau of the Census, various editions.

impact on the economic status of the elderly in the U.S. Largely because of Social Security, the elderly in the late 1970s and 1980s were about as well off financially as the non-aged. Poverty rates for those 65 and over decreased, largely as a result of Social Security benefits (see Table 8). But benefit expansion slowed down with the 1977 amendments. An organizational framework suggests that there may be a tipping point for the effectiveness of various organizations within any particular constituency. Gary Becker's notion that the relative size of an interest group is inversely related to political influence is relevant in regard to Social Security recipients and taxpayers. Becker writes: "Since an increase in the number of persons taxed reduces the tax required on each person to obtain a given revenue and thereby reduces the . . . cost of taxation, an increase in the number of taxpayers would reduce their production of pressure. . . . The optimal size of a subsidized group is smaller . . . because an increase in the number of members reduces the net income per member if efficiency does not significantly increase. . . . Politically successful groups tend to be small relative to the size of groups taxed to pay their subsidies" (1983: 384–85). Becker uses the example of farm subsidies for farmers in wealthy countries, where farmers constitute a relatively small group, and urban dwellers in poor countries, who likewise constitute a relatively small group. He notes that both these groups have been fairly successful politically.

The analogy extends to Social Security lobbying as well. Relatively speaking, old-age insurance benefited, and still benefits, a

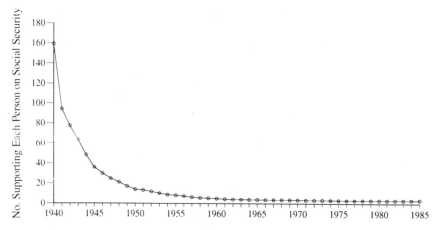

Fig. 3. Dependency ratios for old-age insurance, 1940–1985. (Source: Annual Statistical Supplement to Social Security Bulletin)

smaller group than those paying taxes, hence the beneficiaries' ability to prevail has been greater. The importance of dependency ratios cannot be overstated. In a system that took approximately 50 years to encompass the entire population, the number of taxpayers relative to the number of beneficiaries in the early years was quite high. Figure 3 shows that when benefits were first paid in 1940, there were 159 taxpaying workers supporting each person aged 65 and over receiving Social Security benefits. By 1941 this number had fallen to 100, and after a steady decline to 1960, it has now, for several decades, been approximately three workers paying for each elderly beneficiary.

During the early decades of old-age insurance, these ratios were kept low by adding entirely new categories of workers. And though it is true that an increasing number of elderly dependents will be somewhat offset by a decline in fertility rates (hence the number of young dependents), it is not a one-for-one correspondence from the standpoint of dependency because the relative costs of maintenance are less for a child than for an aged person. An often-proposed solution to the "pig in the python" baby boomers' retirement is in our conceptualization of "dependency." Alice Rossi points out that the traditional computation of dependency ratios uses age 15 and under, and 65 and over, to define "dependency." She notes that age 20 and under, and age 75 and over, might be more appropriate in defining "dependency." Using 65 as the cutoff in 1980 makes 11 percent of the population "elderly"; by 2030, there would be 21 percent "elderly." But if 75 were the cutoff age, by 2030 there would be only 10 percent elderly. She points out that there is plenty of time to study, formulate policy, and effect such a transition in legislation (1993: 210).

Becker's argument about the importance of relative size also means that, whereas in the past a relatively small increase in the payroll tax yielded large amounts, a similar situation will occur with regard to cuts in benefits. In other words, once past a certain tipping point, with large numbers of people receiving benefits, a relatively small cut or adjustment in these benefits will yield greater savings than if there are fewer beneficiaries or if taxes are raised for contributors. Because of past increases in benefits, there is also a consequent growth in the ability of upper-income elderly beneficiaries to absorb cutbacks.

In terms of the idea of organizations becoming more tightly coupled over time, Martha Derthick, discussing the SSA, notes the following:

None of this is to suggest that enactments a generation ago were any less likely than modern ones to have unanticipated consequences. Yet the older Congress had greater room for error. When government was smaller, simpler, and in its program-building phase, new laws had fewer consequences. As government programs grew in number, an action in any one was increasingly likely to have unanticipated effects on others. As more and more citizens became clients and beneficiaries of more and more programs, changes in programs had wider and deeper effects on their lives. . . . Lawmaking has become unstable largely because it has come to have such a wide range of impacts. (1990: 204)

Within the changing economic and political context, the ideology surrounding Social Security also shifted. The 1972 amendments were a major turning point in the history of Social Security, signaling a shift from a concern with adequacy (i.e., legislation from 1950 to 1972), to a concern with equity (i.e., legislation from 1977 on). Political debates during the 1950s and 1960s centered around the adequacy of benefits, while the debates surrounding the legislation of the mid-1970s and early 1980s would emphasize that the cutbacks were designed to affect everyone equitably. In addition, the increases of the 1950s and 1960s generally occurred in even-numbered election years. The 1972 amendments would underscore the importance of this dynamic even further: they occurred in an election year and benefits were increased 20 percent without any major increase in the tax rate or wage-base schedules. It was during the more prosperous, expansionary period of Social Security that the state bureaucracy was able to increase benefits, add new programs, and develop new policies to ensure adequacy of Social Security benefits. This move toward concern for the adequacy of benefits, which essentially redistributed income, was accomplished in this more prosperous, less crisis-driven environment.

Much like James Q. Wilson's ideas regarding the incompatibility of responsiveness and efficiency in political organizations, adequacy and equity often work against each other. Former Social Security Commissioner James B. Cardwell made this comment: "I would say at the risk of being thought too philosophical, that we are all members of a government that has a long concern with accountability, and being very concerned with equity. As someone once said before I got here, those two things are often mortal enemies" (in Derthick 1990: 155). The situation would become even more grave from 1977 to 1985, and it is to this period that we now turn.

CHAPTER SIX

Retrenchment of Social Security, 1977-1990

> There is no such thing as an easy way out of the social security dilemma. There are not going to be any more easy votes on social security. . . . Those who would tell us that there is some easy way to solve the social security problem are not telling us the way it is.
>
> —Al Ullman (D-Oregon), chairman of the House Ways and Means Committee (*CR* 1977: 39007)

> The SSA doesn't move today the way it used to. People aren't as inspired. Some sort of lethargy has set in. . . . Staying here in the SSA is not where the action will be this year.
>
> —Robert J. Myers, Chief Actuary for SSA, 1947–70, commenting on the SSA (USNA, "NAM," 1981)

> Social Security has become about as sound as a chain-letter.
>
> —Horace W. Brock, in the *New York Times* (1982: 17)

THE SOCIAL SECURITY dilemmas of the late 1970s and early 1980s were historically unique. It was a period of retrenchment, but not in the sense of cutbacks in benefits. As Martha Derthick writes:

The anticipated reactions of the public prevent social security policy-makers from seriously considering, let alone adopting, alterations of the social security program of a kind that would entail reduction of benefits for any portion of the constituent public. The withdrawal of a benefit or privilege once granted, which is difficult for the government to do in any of its programs, is uniquely difficult in the social insurance program because of the implied contractual content of the government's promise. Here the public psychology associated with insurance becomes very important. The public presumably believes, for it has been encouraged by policymakers to believe, that the benefits authorized in the law belong to it by right, as a just return for contributions. For the government to withhold or revise any of these benefits violates an implied moral contract, even if not a legal one. The usual political risks that accompany withdrawal of benefits are much compounded by the introduction of moral and psychological stakes peculiar to the program. The very integrity of the government, not just the election chances of incumbent officeholders, is put at risk. (1979: 204)

Following this, I use the word retrenchment to mean a backing off from previous programmatic plans. The retrenchments of the late 1970s and 1980s included delayed cost-of-living adjustments, cutting peripheral programs such as student benefits, and gradual increases in the retirement age.

This chapter reinforces several key points that are gained by an organizational analysis of Social Security legislation. The first section will sketch the economic and political context of the 1977–90 period. Section two discusses the 1977 and 1983 legislative turning points, with the supporters and opposition delineated. The last section will once again consider the insights of organizational theory.

The Economic and Political Context

The economic and political climate of the late 1970s and early 1980s was altogether different from that of the 1950s and 1960s, and in some ways, though to a lesser degree, analogous to the devasting conditions of the Great Depression. The economic crisis of this period was not as extreme as the collapse during the Great Depression, but the high rates of inflation and unemployment wreaked havoc with the Social Security trust funds. The 1972 amendments tied benefits to the Consumer Price Index (CPI), and the rampant inflation during the 1970s meant that benefits increased rapidly. At the same time, high levels of unemployment translated into fewer workers paying payroll taxes, and slowed growth in wages for those who were working reduced contributions to the trust funds even more. In 1966, the trust funds held 5.4 percent of the total estimated obligations; by 1974, the comparable estimate was 1.3 percent (*HWMCH* 1973: 680). There was further erosion of the trust funds as a result of the growth of non-taxable fringe benefits. In 1951, a huge 95 percent of all compensation was subject to Social Security taxes; in 1982, only 84 percent was taxable (USNA, "Correspondence with Commission Members, July 6–November 5, 1982"). Together, these developments created an actuarial nightmare. In addition to this short-term imbalance in the trust funds, declining fertility rates in the 1970s and 1980s, coupled with increasing life expectancies, did not bode well for the secure retirement of the massive cohort of baby boomers.

Like the legislation of 1935 and 1939, Social Security in the late 1970s and 1980s was highly controversial. The controversy was reflected in legislative retrenchments occurring in the odd-numbered, nonelection years of 1977 and 1983. Other reflections of the controversial nature of the legislation of this period were the use of the "all-or-nothing" piggybacking of changes in Social Security onto omnibus or nongermane legislation, and the use of bipartisan commissions (Light 1985). Similarly, whereas benefit increases legislated in the 1950s and 1960s took effect as quickly as possible, the legislation of the 1970s and 1980s would make these retrenchments effective in the years or decades to come. This was very similar to the early legislation, which reflected much more political restraint and caution. It was during the more plentiful middle years that the state bureaucracy had the most power and autonomy from economic interests. This was when the program assumed drastic new dimensions, with the addition of disability insurance, Medicare, student benefits, military benefits, special age-72 benefits, and so on, to name only a few.

However, it is also clear that this period was unique in a variety of ways. First, precisely because of the historical success of the program and the expansion that had occurred, a large clientele of beneficiaries existed who were actually dependent upon the continuance of the system. This made the 1970s and 1980s unlike any other period in several respects. Although the program had won legitimacy by its successes (unlike the situation during the early period), it was no longer the political gravy train that it had been in the 1950s and 1960s, when political agendas were well served by advocating massive expansion and benefit improvement, more or less regardless of either short- or long-term costs. And as the program evolved further and further from the original notions of an insurance program, adding gratuitous benefits that were not linked to contributions, the economic dimensions that concerned private insurers became increasingly clear. Thus during the late 1970s and 1980s there had to be political compromises to sort out the impending financial crisis.

Second, the program became much more coercive during this period (e.g., mandatory universal coverage), and a relatively less attractive option for those not yet covered by Social Security. It had not been difficult to convince various groups in the 1950s and 1960s that Social Security was a good thing, but during the 1970s and 1980s the force of law was required. The mandatory coverage of federal, state, local, and nonprofit workers is a prime example of Congress taking politically unpopular steps to shore up short-term revenues.

A third interesting and uncommon feature of this period was that Social Security had become a noteworthy example of the tail wagging the dog: the program was now dramatically influencing its larger environment. Old-age insurance consumed a larger and larger percentage of the federal budget, and as a result of its close tie-in with inflation and unemployment, many problems involving the economy and Social Security began to prove cyclical and self-reinforcing: increasing Social Security benefits with partial funding from general revenues increased the federal deficit, which in turn was reflected by a rise in inflation, which in turn pushed up Social Security benefits that were linked to the CPI, and so the cycle continued.

The sheer size of Social Security outlays made them a source of problems. Between 1962 and 1980, for example, the annual cost of Social Security increased from 2.6 to 4.5 percent of the total GNP (*WQ* 1986: 43). In addition, with lower retirement ages allowable (i.e., age 62), longer life expectancies, and higher benefits, Social Security encouraged early retirement (USNA, "Correspondence with Commission Members, July 6–November 5, 1982"). This simultaneously deprived the trust funds of the much-needed payroll tax contributions and increased the outlay. Representative Bill Gradison (R-Ohio), speaking about the 1983 amendments, stated the problem this way: "Social security and the political consideration of it, then, have reached a point of maturity which acknowledges the system's central role in our society . . . the willingness to make changes in benefits is a statement that social security is now so large that it not only is influenced by what happens to the economy, but it influences the economy, requiring adjustments . . . with the best interests of the overall economy in mind" (*CR* 1983:

H973). In other words, although the origin years (1930s), and retrenchment period (1970s and 1980s) both involved crises, the crisis in the 1930s was exogenous and played a key role in the emergence of Social Security, whereas the crisis in the 1970s and 1980s was much more an endogenous crisis. Many argued that Social Security was a root cause of the economic problems of the 1970s and 1980s (Murray 1984; Weaver 1982). And uncertainty regarding the future of Social Security was as evident during the 1970s and 1980s as was uncertainty regarding the future of capitalism during the Depression.

This uncertainty heightened awareness regarding the "crisis in Social Security." It was clear to many interest groups that there were now higher stakes in terms of potential losses. Political debates were now being carried on by more diverse groups, over more diverse alternatives. The power, influence, and autonomy experienced by the Social Security Administration during the golden years of expansion were gone. The Social Security bureaucracy had lost much of its political control of the program. The small cadre of SSA bureaucrats and Advisory Council appointees could no longer claim a monopoly on information relevant to the debates. The blank check so evident in the 1972 amendments was replaced by in-depth review of the program and how it had got into such a predicament. The advisory councils, SSA, and Congress were chastised for careless oversight of the program as evidenced by the state of the trust funds.

Seeds of doubt about the power and authority accorded the advisory councils, SSA, and certain congressional committees were actually sown in the early 1970s. Republican members of the Senate Special Committee on Aging had proposed an independent, bipartisan Social Security Commission. Their proposal stated:

With all due respect to the distinguished members of the 1971 Advisory Council on Social Security, and they are truly so, we do not believe such a function should be performed on a part-time or intermittent basis. Nor do we believe that the Social Security Administration, which has responsibility for conduct of the system's operation, should be the only source of information or the primary source of policy recommendations. . . . [This Commission should] provide opportunity for hearing all shades of expert opinion. . . . Social Security is too important to Americans of all ages to permit its future to depend on decisions by the Federal operating agency, a part-time advisory council, and intermittent review by Congress. It needs continuous supervision and review by a full-time agency independent of the program's administrators. The Senate Finance Committee and House Ways and Means Committee have in the past done a remarkable job on Social Security. It has been doubly remarkable in view of their limited staffs and their other important legislative responsibilities. (*CR* 1972: 17244)

Similarly, the advisory councils were admonished for their careless oversight of Social Security. Representative Elliott Levitas (D-Georgia) commented: "One of the problems with the present advisory councils is that, not only are they appointed by the Secretary of HEW and not by the President, making them in-house councils, but all they have done during their entire period of existence is to rearrange furniture on the deck of the Titanic, and they have not done anything at all about the fundamental long-term problems of social security" (*CR* 1977: 35269). Walter Klint, chairman of the Task Force on Social Security for the National Association of Manufacturers, argued that problems evident in the mid-1970s were due to the fact that "the Social Security Administration, when they made these short-range assumptions, did those through a pair of very rose-colored glasses" (*HWMCH* 1976b: 112).

While some people blamed the unforeseen factors of high inflation and high unemployment for the problems of the late 1970s, others faulted Congress for caving in too easily to politically popular expansions of benefits without legislating for a corresponding increase in contribution rates (*CR* 1977: 35250). Senator Strom Thurmond (R-South Carolina), speaking about the 1977 amendments, said: "In the past a vote for social security legislation has come much easier for many Members of this body. This is the first social security bill which has not been centered on increasing benefits for retirees" (*CR* 1977: 39147). Senator Carl T. Curtis (R-Nebraska), speaking on the day the 1977 amendments were passed, declared, "What is happening here today is that, indeed, we are having to pay the piper for the excessive and often somewhat mindless generosities of past Congresses" (*CR* 1977: 39136).

In all this economic and political turbulence, the voices of the advisory councils, SSA, and members of Congress were muffled. There was debate among a wider variety of groups, with various political actors receding in influence; some, out of choice, like Congress, and others, including the SSA itself, uncertain and overwhelmed in the effort to consider any alternatives. Social Security reform was precarious, and Congress tried to insulate itself from criticism while dealing at least with the short-run problems. There were two ways of doing this.

One method was the use of the closed rule. The closed rule of the House Ways and Means Committee was designed to curtail excessive debate and tinkering with the "intertwining complexity of tax legislation" (*CR* 1977: 35237); it was used to protect, intact, the Social Security amendments of 1977. This meant that other members of the House could not amend the bill on the floor. Debate concerning the 1977 amendments was limited to only four hours by the Rules Committee.

The second method for deflecting criticism was the use of bipartisan commissions. Control over the program, which was granted to the SSA and Congress during the expansion years, was now given over to bipartisan commissions, which were charged with saving the system and developing the tough compromises that were in order. Many in Congress, particularly those who were less sympathetic to the SSA, welcomed bipartisan commissions, arguing that the self-interested bureaucracy could not be trusted to develop new alternatives. The National Commission on Social Security (NCSS) and the National Commission on Social Security Reform (NCSSR) were made up of persons who were more politically insulated and could therefore make the decisions that some representatives knew were in order, but were in no position to recommend (Light 1985). Nevertheless, when possible, changes occurred in areas of least resistance or least visibility. Crediting the trust fund with Social Security checks that had gone uncashed for long periods, ceasing benefit payments to felons, maximizing trust fund investment income, and other such reforms were utilized when they were identified as an option.

It is also important to understand the dynamics of a fully mature social insurance program. Most groups of workers were now covered under the program, and many business, industrial, and labor organizations had molded their policies to the existing program; this all meant, of course, that a great portion of the population now had a vested interest in seeing the program maintained in its current form. For legislators, this popular stake placed an increasing constraint on their options in the matter of changing the system. Further, the slack in the system (e.g., the ability to extend coverage) was no longer such that changes could be made independently of each other. In the mid-1970s, the difficulties were all too apparent. High inflation, massive unemployment, an increasingly aging-activist society, and pressures for more of the same from interest groups, presented mutually exclusive demands. This relatively zero-sum economic context pitted powerful interest groups against each other. The American Association of Retired Persons (AARP) and the National Council of Senior Citizens (NCSC), for example, proposed general revenue financing to resolve the crisis in the trust funds, against the vehement opposition of the NAM and the U.S. Chamber of Commerce.

Support for the 1977 Amendments

Unlike earlier years, any support for the amendments of the later years meant supporting the retrenchment of old-age insurance. It was difficult for many members of Congress to support the large payroll tax increases that were being discussed as necessary to bolster the old-age insurance trust fund. The political difficulty of these decisions was reflected in the fact that retrenchment took place in nonelection years. Representative James Burke (D-Florida) noted: "We are unable to write a bill this year because 1976 is an election year, and I can understand it, being a practical man. . . . [This problem will be postponed until] 1977, which I say is going to be the year of atonement when everybody will have to face the music" (*HWMCH* 1976: 113–14). Congress was far from insulated from criticism that it had caused, or at least had not foreseen, the predicament the program was now in. In 1977, when the House Ways and Means Committee was criticized in floor debates for the crisis in Social Security, Barber Conable (R-New York), a member of the committee, retorted that it was not just the committee's problem, but rather could be attributed to Congress as a whole:

I want to recall to the Members that in 1972, in a bill that did not come from the Ways and Means Committee at all but was a Senate amendment to a debt ceiling bill, we provided for a 20-percent benefit increase with no financing whatsoever except a revision of the actuarial assumptions, and everybody who was in Congress at that time participated in that wonderful opportunity to provide benefits to people without the unpleasant other side of the obligation: the financing. (*CR* 1977: 35238)

It was politically difficult to support the large payroll taxes embodied in the 1977 amendments, but some members of Congress felt there were no acceptable alternatives.

With regard to the proposals for mandatory coverage of federal employees, Representative Levitas (D-Georgia) noted ironically: "You know, the American people are asking themselves this question: If the Commissioner of Social Security himself is not covered by social security, then something must be wrong with the system. If the Members of Congress are not covered by the system, it is no wonder Congress has let it become such a mess. Would you want to eat dinner at a restaurant where the chef would not eat his own cooking?" (*CR* 1977: 35269).

Opposition to the 1977 Amendments

One of the main critics of the 1977 amendments was Senator Barry Goldwater (R-Arizona), long a foe of the Social Security system. He said quite bluntly:

My personal opinion is that social security has failed, and we would be better off in this country if we pledged to every person who has ever paid a dime into the social security fund that that money would be returned, and then forget about the whole thing. There does not seem to me to be any way to have what we call social security and avoid the politics, every 2 years, of having the House feel that it must make additions to the social security payments regardless of whether the money is there. (*CR* 1977: 39140)

Other critics of the proposed payroll tax increases argued that these hikes would be inflationary since "it is an established economic fact that most employers pass on payroll tax increases to the consumer via higher prices" (*CR* 1977: 39025).

Some representatives of business and industry believed that Social Security had grown too quickly. Though these groups could write off some of the tax as a business expense, nontaxable fringe benefits had also grown, partly as a result of union bargaining (which also made it possible for business and industry to avoid paying the expanding Social Security taxes). Larger corporations also found a way of avoiding increasingly burdensome Social Security taxes simply by moving their more labor-intensive industries to other countries. Some congressional representatives argued that the relatively high Social Security tax rate imposed on employees and employers was a major reason for the flight of capital from the United States to foreign countries. In many foreign nations, labor costs were lower and Social Security programs were often financed by a tax split into thirds—one-third each for employers, employees, and the government. Others argued that high Social Security contribution rates encouraged capital to substitute machines for people whenever feasible (*CR* 1977: 39150). Therefore, although monopoly capital may have been able to socialize costs through Social Security, it may have backfired on them, providing an inducement for them to move their operations to foreign countries; Social Security programs are not the only method of socializing costs. At any rate, it is going too far to suggest that these groups were all-knowing, calculating, and aggressive in sponsoring the expansion of Social Security.

In December 1977, just before the holiday recess, Congress enacted the largest peacetime tax increase in history. In addition, the wage base was increased above and beyond the scheduled automatic adjustments, from $17,770 in 1978 to $22,900 for 1979, to $25,900 for 1980, and to $29,700 for 1981. In effect, this change meant that more workers had more of their earnings taxed for purposes of old-age insurance (see Table 9).

This emphasis on tax rate and wage base increases also represented a shift in strategy that is noted by Carolyn L. Weaver (1982). Weaver argues that SSA bureaucrats and congressional representatives showed the good judgment over the years of expansion, to use the method of financing that embodied the "least resistance." She points out how choices were made among the three possible ways of funding: tax rate increases, wage base increases, and expansion of coverage. Expansion of coverage was the method chosen in the early years because the high rates of return meant large numbers of groups clamored for coverage. By the late 1950s, when nine out of ten workers were covered, Congress turned to tax rate in-

TABLE 9

Percent of All Workers with Total Annual Earnings Below Annual Maximum Taxable, 1937–1984

Year	Annual maximum taxable	Pct.	Year	Annual maximum taxable	Pct.
1937	3,000	96.9	1966	6,600	75.8
1940	3,000	96.6	1967	6,600	73.6
1945	3,000	86.3	1968	7,800	78.6
1950	3,000	71.1	1969	7,800	75.5
1951	3,600	75.5	1970	7,800	74.0
1952	3,600	72.1	1971	7,800	71.7
1953	3,600	68.8	1972	9,000	75.0
1954	3,600	68.4	1973	10,800	79.7
1955	4,200	74.4	1974	13,200	84.9
1956	4,200	71.6	1975	14,100	84.9
1957	4,200	70.1	1976	15,300	85.1
1958	4,200	69.4	1977	16,500	85.2
1959	4,800	73.3	1978	17,770	84.6
1960	4,800	72.0	1979	22,900	90.0
1961	4,800	70.8	1980	25,900	91.2
1962	4,800	68.8	1981	29,700	92.4
1963	4,800	67.5	1982	32,400	92.9
1964	4,800	65.5	1983	35,700	93.8
1965	4,800	63.9	1984	37,800	94.1

SOURCE: *Social Security Bulletin, Annual Statistical Supplement*, 1986, p. 90.

creases. Why tax rate increases rather than wage base increases? (As Table 9 shows, wage base changes before this time were slight.) Workers who were not yet covered during this period tended to be highly paid professionals who would be less easily convinced of the advantages of universal coverage if wage base amounts were especially high. In 1965, coverage was extended to most of these highly paid, self-employed professionals, and once this occurred, ceiling increases provided a new option for Congress (Weaver 1982: 159–60). Table 10 illustrates the relatively substantial changes in the wage base as enacted by the 1977 amendments. However, these options became increasingly constrained, or tightly coupled over time, meaning that the SSA and Congress had utilized all options within the existing programmatic framework.

Although the 1977 amendments raised the payroll tax and wage

TABLE 10

Wage Base Under Prior Law and Amendments in 1977

Calendar year	Prior law	1977 amendments
1977	$16,500	$16,500
1978	17,700	17,700
1979	18,900	22,900
1980	20,400	25,900
1981	21,900	29,700
1982	23,400	32,100
1983	24,900	34,500
1984	26,400	36,900
1985	27,900	39,600
1986	29,400	42,000
1987	31,200	44,400

SOURCE: House Ways and Means Committee Hearings, "Summary of PL 95-216, Social Security Amendments of 1977," 1978, H782-32.

base and slowed benefit increases, these changes were not to take effect for two years (i.e., 1979). The reluctance to impose either of these in 1978, an election year, was evident in the debates, and it did not go unnoticed in the popular media. *New York Times* columnist Tom Wicker wrote: "Long-term tax increases totalling $227 billion would be imposed. . . . Note that the Congress that voted this body-blow to the American wallet prudently put off the first of the increases until *after* its members try to get themselves re-elected next year" (in *CR* 1977: 39019). Increasing taxes and the wage base and slowing benefit increases were not politically popular, and congressional representatives were understandably concerned. The closeness of the vote, in contrast to the lopsidedness of the votes on expansionary measures, also indicates the difficult decisions Congress now faced. The House vote on the 1977 amendments was 189 in favor, 163 opposed; the Senate vote was 56 in favor, 21 opposed.

In fact, the controversy and lobbying effort surrounding mandatory coverage of federal, state, local, and nonprofit employees had so divided Congress that the 1977 amendments merely provided for further study. They authorized the study of Social Security coverage for government workers and employees of nonprofit organizations. The study group was charged with reporting back to

Congress within two years on a sound procedure to cover public and nonprofit employees without doing them harm. Members of Congress who had opposed hasty action on mandatory universal coverage wanted to know what the transition plan would be before they voted on such a controversial measure. The lobbying efforts of federal, state, local, and nonprofit organizations were temporarily successful. Once again, we see how state actors embody a variety of interests, some opposed to each other.

The least controversial issue in 1977 involved "decoupling" the faulty indexing formula set into place in 1972. In effect, the 1972 amendments had double-indexed benefits. Benefits were linked to the Consumer Price Index, so that if wages did not rise at all, the initial benefits of current workers would be much higher than those of persons who would retire before 1975, when the indexing was to take effect. If wages climbed as an indirect result of inflation, this would place current workers in an even higher benefit category. By adopting indexing, Congress was trying to avoid constant review of Social Security; but in any indexing scheme there is considerable room for error, because it has built-in assumptions and during a highly volatile period can be very unpredictable. In 1977, it was decided that benefits would be decoupled, and benefits were indexed to wages rather than to prices. This had the effect of improving the trust fund balance, at least in the short term.

Finally, the 1977 amendments provided for the establishment of a bipartisan National Commission on Social Security (NCSS), to be independent of the executive branch and the SSA, composed of nine members who would be responsible for on-going review of all Social Security programs. This commission would consider all issues related to Social Security. Members would be appointed by the President, the House, and the Senate, and they were to consider any and all alternatives to the Social Security program. Some of the possible solutions suggested for review were substitution of the payroll tax by general revenues, mandatory participation in private insurance, and a choice of public or private insurance (*CR* 1977: 39027). Representatives of the private insurance industry and future beneficiaries were also to be included on the commission. It was "to be independent of the bureaucracy downtown and not fully dependent on the social security system itself" (*CR* 1977: 35396). The Secretary of Health, Education, and Welfare, and the SSA were vehemently opposed to this commission.

The institution of this commission was a drastic change from the authority and autonomy granted to the SSA in the 1950s and 1960s. Control was now removed from their sole purview, and options were considered that emanated from many potential adversaries. The SSA was less able to control the agenda. Representative Levitas (D-Georgia) stated: "In many ways the adoption of the National Commission on Social Security is revolutionary. It is not just another study. It marks a turning point, a milestone. The social security system will never be the same again" (*CR* 1977: 39027).

After passing the 1977 legislation, J. J. Pickle (D-Texas) declared, "In passing this bill, we can say to the American people that we are putting social security on a sound financial basis for the next 25 to 50 years"; and President Jimmy Carter, in signing the bill into law, stated, "Now this legislation will guarantee that from 1980 to the year 2030, that social security will be sound" (*CR* 1983: H964).

In 1980 the NCSS, appointed during President Carter's term in office, made a number of recommendations designed to address both the short-term and long-term problems of the system. To solve short-run financing problems, the commission recommended that there be interfund borrowing (i.e., between the relatively depleted Old-Age and Survivors Trust Fund and the more solvent Disability and Hospital Trust Funds), and an acceleration of the scheduled payroll tax increases. For the long term, they recommended phasing in a later retirement age and a later *early* retirement age (from 62 to 65). In addition, they recommended phasing out the earnings test for older workers and encouraging older workers to stay in the labor market and receive temporary unemployment rather than choose early retirement. The commission favored strengthening individual efforts to save for retirement, for example, through Individual Retirement Accounts (IRAs). Finally, they recommended that Social Security should not replace existing pension plans but that mandatory universal coverage should be extended to all workers. For this reason, they noted that the option allowing covered government and nonprofit groups to withdraw from the program should be terminated and that "those groups be encouraged to elect coverage prior to the effective date of mandatory coverage" (USNA, "Correspondence with Commission Members, February 10–June 21, 1982").

By the early 1980s it was clear to most careful observers that Social Security would have to retrench yet a second time, but President Ronald Reagan and Congress were unwilling to dive headlong into the reforms suggested by the NCSS. Reagan was able to improve the trust funds somewhat in the early 1980s through massive cuts in the means-tested entitlements. For example, although expenditures for these assistance programs represented approximately 18 percent of the total benefit payments, cuts in these programs enacted in 1981 accounted for 40 percent of the total reduction in benefit payments. Relatively speaking, changes in old-age insurance benefits went unscathed (USNA, "Correspondence with Committee Members, July 6–November 5, 1982").

In 1981, President Reagan proposed what turned out to be very controversial changes in the Social Security old-age and disability insurance programs. He proposed elimination of the $122 minimum monthly OASI benefit; a larger penalty for retirement at age 62; elimination of student benefits at ages 18–21; the introduction of a maximum on all disability benefits from government sources and more stringent requirements to qualify for these benefits; reduction of the maximum age for a child to qualify its mother or father for benefits; limitation of payment of lump-sum benefits to certain spouses and children; elimination of benefit payments for the month of entitlement unless it is a full month; and a change in the "bend points," which would essentially have lowered the overall benefit level over the long term (i.e., the average replacement rate would change from 41 percent to 38 percent; AFLA 1983: 408). These changes would have slashed benefits $8 billion in the first year alone.

Reagan was committed to changes in the Social Security program, but he faced massive opposition. He therefore appointed a bipartisan National Commission on Social Security Reform (NCSSR). Newly formed in January of 1982, it was criticized by many as a stalling tactic employed by the President in an election year. The commission consisted of fifteen members, eight of

TABLE 11

Members and Affiliations of the National Commission on Social Security Reform

Name	Affiliation
Alan Greenspan, Chair	President, Townsend-Greenspan Co.
Bill Archer	U.S. House of Representatives
William Armstrong	U.S. Senator
Robert M. Ball	Former Commissioner of Social Security
Robert A. Beck	Chairman of the Board, Prudential Insurance Co. of America
Barber Conable	U.S. House of Representatives
Robert Dole	U.S. Senator
Mary Falvey Fuller	Vice President, Finance, Shaklee Corp.
John Heinz	U.S. Senator
Martha E. Keys	Former Congresswoman, U.S. House of Representatives
Lane Kirkland	President, AFL-CIO
Daniel P. Moynihan	U.S. Senator
Claude Pepper	U.S. House of Representatives
Alexander B. Trowbridge	President, National Association of Manufacturers
Joe Waggonner	U.S. House of Representatives

SOURCE: List dated February 3, 1982, Records of Temporary Committees, Commissions, and Boards, National Commission on Social Security Reform, Record Group 220, National Archives, Washington, D.C.

whom were members of Congress; the chairman was Alan Greenspan, a Republican economist. (See Table 11 for a list of members and their affiliations.) Reagan specified that they had to develop a plan that would save $40 billion in the unified budget attributed to either benefit cuts or additional income to the Social Security trust funds; they were scheduled to make their recommendations by December 1982.

Reagan left it up to the commission to work out the details of the plan, but many were dissatisfied that Reagan's stipulations precluded some solutions to short-term aspects of the Social Security crisis. The concern centered around the fact that borrowing from general revenues or direct general revenue contributions to the trust funds would not affect the unified budget totals, even though they would resolve the Social Security trust fund shortfall.

This commission, along with its predecessor (the NCSS appointed by President Carter), was substantively different from past advisory councils. Expectations were that these commissions would study all options to Social Security, not just changes within the existing framework, and that they would foster widespread public debate. Representative Matthew J. Rinaldo (R-New Jersey), a member of the House Select Committee on Aging, wrote Greenspan:

> It is my strong hope and recommendation that the Commission will decide to open itself to public comments, either through hearings or other appropriate forums, in order to engage public attention and measure sentiment for its mission. . . . I believe that in order for recommendations emanating from the Commission to gain support in Congress, the public must have confidence in the Commission and an understanding that it is to find a solution that will shore up the system over the long term. (USNA, "Correspondence of Dr. Greenspan")

The political popularity of the Social Security system, so obviously present in the 1950s and 1960s, had been shaken, with the result that the SSA itself could not reassure Congress that its recommendations were politically and economically most acceptable to the voters. The only way to convince Congress that the reforms to emanate from the NCSSR were acceptable was to show that the public had knowledge of the dilemma and alternatives, and that among these difficult choices, voters preferred certain changes over others. The SSA could no longer set the agenda and help to influence the outcome.

Again, the NCSSR was explicitly charged with considering all options regarding reform, including phasing out the Social Security program as it was known. Unlike the Social Security advisory councils, this commission was staffed by and heard testimony from a much broader array of personnel in terms of backgrounds, philosophies, and recommendations. For example, one summary of the alternative Social Security reform proposals presented to the NCSSR included the following:

1. Complete privatization, with participation being compulsory to avoid adverse selection. The mechanism for accomplishing this implied that current taxpayers would have had to finance two retirement systems—one for those who were already retired and another for a genuine trust fund for their own retirement.

2. Retain pay-as-you-go as it would suffice until baby-boomers retire, so recommended postponing any tax increases. When these individuals begin to retire, the U.S. would allow massive immigration, or develop policies to encourage fertility, to prop up taxes.

3. Use general revenues to shore up the system. The major problem with this proposal as noted, is that it would not lessen the federal deficit or the overall tax burden.

4. Increase the retirement age in a phased-in manner, and increase rewards for choosing to postpone retirement.

5. Mandatory universal coverage to do away with the multiplicity of retirement systems, which allowed "double-dipping." (USNA, "Correspondence with Commission Members, July 6–November 5, 1982")

It is interesting to note that even though four of these five options involved the Social Security program as it existed, a proposal for privatization was now on the agenda as an alternative. And the historically volatile issue of general revenue financing received a 5–4 majority vote from the NCSSR. The closeness of the vote reflected the wariness to move overtly in this direction; but the fact that there was majority support for using general revenues when faced with all other options represented a shift in thinking.

Another example of this altered economic and political context is revealed in a letter from Robert J. Myers, former SSA Chief Actuary, to Alan Greenspan, chairman of the NCSSR, dated February 12, 1982. Myers was registering his opposition to taxing Social Security benefits as income, but he felt that Greenspan had to place this on the agenda of the NCSSR so that it could "be recognized as having been consciously eliminated" (USNA, "Correspondence of Dr. Greenspan"). In the past, legislators or advisory council members had the leeway to utilize such tactics. However, facing new constraints on action, it is noteworthy that this was placed on the congressional agenda, and eventually was approved in the 1983 amendments. Advocates of Social Security and insiders such as Myers could no longer count on the "conscious elimination" of any reforms.

Although the NCSSR was scheduled to make its recommendations by December 31, 1982, a fifteen-day extension was required because members had not yet reached agreement. Chairman Greenspan was quoted as saying, "All of us swallowed very hard and accepted individual notions that we personally could not actually support" (*CQA* 1983: 221). The NCSSR made its recommendations after a 12–3 vote in mid-January of 1983. The commission "agreed to disagree" on how to solve the projected Social Security shortfall in the early twenty-first century when the baby boom generation would begin to retire and dependency ratios become even more problematic (*CQA* 1983: 221).

Support for the 1983 Amendments

One idea for shoring up the old-age insurance trust fund was to gradually increase the retirement age. Proponents of this idea argued that such a policy would be quite consistent with the intent of the original legislation of 1935. The SSA published an article entitled "Equivalent Retirement Ages: 1940–2050," which explained historical and future (estimated) data as to equivalent retirement ages for different life-expectancy measures. Greenspan had asked Myers to make this calculation and Myers responded that for 1980, age 71 would be analogous to age 65 in 1940 in terms of life expectancy and number of years expected to collect benefits (USNA, "Correspondence of Dr. Greenspan").

Another controversial proposal concerned mandatory universal coverage. Since the 1977 amendments only recommended studying the issue of mandatory universal coverage, various federal, state, local, and nonprofit workers were not yet covered by Social Security in 1982. Myers and the SSA tried to convince federal employees that there were advantages to joining the Social Security system. Myers, in a memo to the NCSSR, listed the following advantages to these employees:

1. Family benefits, e.g., benefits to spouses and children;

2. 80% of those who leave federal retirement sometime before age 65 choose immediate refund of their Civil Service Retirement benefits; thus, they have no pension;

3. Because federal service is not covered by Social Security, even though many of these workers have some credits toward benefits, these benefits are smaller than they would be if they were covered;

4. Social Security benefits income is tax-free; Civil Service Retirement System (CSRS) benefits are taxed after they exceed the amount of the workers' contributions;

5. Spouses retain eligibility after divorce under Social Security if the marriage lasted 10 years; not so under CSRS;

6. Disability and survivors' benefits are better under Social Security;

7. Two-thirds of all federal workers leave federal service without CSRS

benefits, while their Social Security benefits are diminished because of their working in uncovered employment. (USNA, "Correspondence with Commission Members, July 6–November 5, 1982")

Mandatory universal coverage had the support of the National Conference of State Legislatures because it would decrease state expenditures for their own separate pension plans (USNA, "Correspondence of Dr. Greenspan"). State and local pension plans were hurt by the inflation of the 1970s and by the budget cuts of the 1980s. These developments made Social Security relatively more attractive to state and local officials than it had been in the late 1970s.

Not only had some state and local employers changed their minds about the cost-effectiveness of Social Security coverage, but also, in a context of ailing trust fund reserves, all those included under the program (hence, all those paying into the system) were potential supporters of mandatory universal coverage. The National Association of Manufacturers, the Business Roundtable, and the U.S. Chamber of Commerce actively supported mandatory universal coverage (USNA, "Correspondence of Dr. Greenspan").

Detailed review was also given to general revenue financing. There was a central difference between the overt form of general revenue financing (appropriating money from the general Treasury to the Social Security trust funds) and the more indirect forms of general revenue financing that were uncovered by review of the program in the late 1970s. (See Table 12 for the extent of general revenue financing.) It is worthwhile in understanding this issue to trace its historical background. A quote from Representative James A. Burke (D-Florida) summarizes the origin of the idea of general revenue financing in the 1935 Committee on Economic Security:

The original recommendation included a plan for general fund participation by the late 1960s. This recommendation was based on several grounds: the system was taking on an accrued liability in the form of early year retirees who had not contributed for any lengthy period; the recognition of broad national welfare interests served by a cash benefits program of a national scope; the limits to the utility of the payroll tax; and, the fact that Government participation was the prevailing public policy in other established foreign social insurance programs . . . in the final hours before the

TABLE 12

Reimbursements from General Revenues for OASI

(in millions)

Calendar year	Military wage credits	Special age-72 benefits	Total
1937–45	0	0	0
1946	<.5	0	<.5
1947	1	0	1
1948	3	0	3
1949	4	0	4
1950	4	0	4
1951	4	0	4
1952–65 [a]			
1966	78	0	78
1967	78	0	78
1968	156	226	382
1969	78	364	442
1970	78	371	449
1971	137	351	488
1972	138	337	475
1973	139	303	442
1974	140	307	447
1975	157	268	425
1976	378	236	614
1977	385 [b]	228	613
1978	384	230	614
1979	393	164	557
1980	390	150	540
1981	534	140	674

SOURCE: Memo to Staff at SSA from Robert J. Myers, dated April 1, 1982, File Folder "Staff Info. File," Records of Temporary Committees, Commissions, and Boards, NCSSR, Record Group 220, National Archives, Washington, D.C.

[a]Between 1952 and 1965, the additional costs arising from military service wage credits were financed by the OASI trust fund. The 1965 amendments provided that these costs would be reimbursed by the general fund over the 50-year period ending with 2015.

[b]Includes a $2.7 million one-time payment for the estimated costs of granting noncontributory wage credits to U.S. citizens of Japanese ancestry who were interned during World War II.

submittal to the Congress . . . in early 1935, the President had deleted from the report references to the deficits that were anticipated in the late 1960s. The Committee on Economic Security, however, had recommended that those deficits be met by general revenue contributions, eventually amounting to one-third of program costs. The 1938 and 1948 advisory councils both had the very same recommendation. (*CR* 1977: 36687)

Although overt general revenue financing was also advocated by CIO labor unions from the inception of the program, the arguments for general revenue financing became increasingly salient during this later period of dwindling reserves. This debate was a key issue during the late 1970s and early 1980s, and it continued to be regarded by some as a viable way to prop up the system. With universal coverage, high tax rates, and high wage bases already in place, general revenues were one of the last remaining options for Congress. It must be remembered, however, that Roosevelt, the early SSB, and the later SSA argued that general revenue financing would leave the program politically vulnerable, and generally avoided making such moves themselves.

During the early 1980s, AFL-CIO affiliated labor unions, the NCSC, and the AARP supported general revenue financing, while conservatives and business leaders were generally opposed to general revenue financing. Conservatives claimed that the existing system linked benefits to wages and that general revenue financing would destroy this relationship and turn old-age insurance into a welfare system. In theory this is true, but the close relationship between contributions and benefits began to be dismantled as far back as 1939, with the introduction of survivors' benefits. There was actually a great deal of general revenue financing occurring, though in a roundabout way.

The discovery and discussion of this indirect general revenue financing in the meticulous review of the program conducted during the late 1970s and early 1980s reflected the growing concern about Social Security. The fact that increasing amounts of general revenues were being used to prop up the program revealed just how unwilling Congress was to offend the many interests that had coalesced around this cash-benefits program.

This more indirect general revenue financing took the form of the Treasury's reimbursing the Social Security trust funds for various special benefits—such as the special age-72 benefit for persons who did not otherwise qualify for Social Security, wage credits posted for World War II military personnel who were not included under coverage, and credits to World War II Japanese internees. It also took the form of granting income tax deductions for employers' Social Security payroll tax costs. The line between general revenues and Social Security trust funds was increasingly blurred.

During the careful review of Social Security throughout this period, it emerged that other programs, initiated during the expansionary phase, were now deemed less important than the more central program of old-age insurance benefits. Many of these more peripheral programs were separated from the old-age benefits program. Student benefits provide a case in point. A proposal considered during this time was the phasing out of Social Security's student benefits. These benefits, added in 1965, were available to persons aged 18–21 who were unmarried, full-time student dependents of dead, disabled, or retired workers. The cost of these benefits in 1977 was in excess of $1.6 billion (*HWMCH* 1977: ix). It was suggested by the U.S. Chamber of Commerce that a more appropriate vehicle for student aid would be student loans (e.g., the needs-tested Basic Educational Opportunity Grant), and that Social Security should not be in the business of subsidizing student costs. Critics of student benefits argued that insurance involved the sharing of risks and was not a concept applicable to conduct such as attending school. The SSA countered that student benefits were not aid to students, but rather income to families. It *was* clear that Congress, in 1965, had underestimated how many students would apply and how much these benefits would cost (*HWMCH* 1976b). This is only one example of how far the reach of the SSA extended during the expansion phase. In the careful review of the program during the years of retrenchment, peripheral programs of this sort were now seen as redundant, unnecessary, and politically indefensible.

A number of influential persons who served on the NCSSR, including AFL-CIO President Lane Kirkland, NAM President Alexander Trowbridge, and Senators Claude Pepper and Robert Dole, in addition to key party leaders including President Ronald Reagan and House Speaker Thomas P. O'Neill, publicly stated their support of the NCSSR package and rallied their supporters around the delicate political compromise. Frank S. Swain, chief counsel for Advocacy of the U.S. Small Business Administration, wrote Alan Greenspan in March 1982, "For much of small business, Social Security represents the only retirement benefit to which a company can afford to contribute" (USNA, "General–No Response Correspondence to Robert J. Myers"). Certainly this organization represents competitive capital, and they too benefited from Social Security legislation. According to the *Congressional Quarterly Almanac*, "The widespread endorsement of the commission's package gave members of Congress—queasy about making any unpopular changes in Social Security—a relatively painless way to take the necessary, but politically difficult steps to keep the system from going broke" (1983: 222).

Another method for garnering consensus in the House of Representatives was the Rules Committee's decision, once again, to invoke a modified closed rule. Members of the House were allowed to vote on only two amendments to the 1983 legislation, and general floor debate was limited to four hours. The two amendments allowed for consideration were the Pepper amendment, which recommended higher tax rate increases, and the Pickle amendment, which raised the normal retirement age. Those opposed to the provision disallowing further amendments called this a "gag rule" (*CR* 1983: 947–48). It was, quite simply, one more reflection of the delicate nature of Social Security legislation in a crisis environment.

Opposition to the 1983 Amendments

The Democratic Party, AFL-CIO labor unions, AARP, NCSC, and the Gray Panthers lashed out at Reagan's proposals and many of the proposed changes recommended by the NCSSR. Democrats accused the administration of attempting to balance the budget on the backs of the elderly. The International Ladies' Garment Workers' Union resolved to fight Reagan. They wrote:

Workers have every justification to feel that Social Security is a sacred contract between them and government and that promises of protection when they are forced to cease work because of old age, disability or death must be kept. This splendid program now faces its greatest danger since it came into existence. This arises not from internal weaknesses of the Social Security system but from the massive assault by the Reagan Administration against it by ruthless elimination and wholesale slashing of benefits. The Reagan people justify this by alleging that Social Security faces imminent bankruptcy unless these drastic cuts are made. This allegation is false. . . . A simple re-allocation of the total Social Security tax among the three funds that make it up would solve the immediate problem without having to cut benefits at all. It is not Social Security that is bankrupt but the policies of the Reagan Administration by not doing anything about unemployment which causes the problem in the first place. (AFLA 1983: 412)

The AARP, the NCSC, and the Gray Panthers urged higher payroll taxes to finance the program (*CQA* 1983: 219), and these organizations as well as the AFL-CIO unions and current beneficiaries were opposed to the NCSSR's proposed six-month delay in the cost-of-living adjustment. They all argued that such benefit cuts constituted a breach of social contract, and many voiced support for general revenues to bolster the trust funds. They accused Reagan and the Republican Party of exaggerating the extent of the "crisis" to win support for cuts in other welfare and assistance programs. Further, these organizations along with the National Center on Black Aged and the National Taxpayers Union objected to the taxation of benefits (*CQA* 1983: 222). Nonetheless, in spite of this opposition and the strong opposition also of the SSA, this radical departure from traditional policies eventually occurred. Finally, the National Taxpayers Union and the National Federation of Independent Business objected to the proposed payroll tax increase.

Perhaps two of the most controversial issues in the early 1980s were the proposals to increase the retirement age and to institute mandatory universal coverage. One of the chief lobbying groups against an increase in the retirement age was the AARP, which allows persons to become members at the age of 50. Mandatory coverage was opposed by workers under the Civil Service Retirement System, and they had the support of the AFL-CIO.

All these groups cited concrete demographic reasons for optimism regarding the short-term health of the trust funds. It was projected that there would be a fairly large accumulation in the trust funds between 1985 and 2015, owing to two key factors. One was that the 1977 amendments involved a sharp increase in the scheduled tax rates. More importantly, the annual birthrate during the 1920s and 1930s was relatively small compared with earlier and later periods. With fewer persons drawing retirement benefits from 1985 to 2015, and more baby boom workers paying taxes in their prime earning years, the trust funds would burgeon (Weaver 1990).

But the short-term crisis in the trust funds and the impact of Social Security on the overall federal deficit could not be ignored any longer. This was especially so, given that Reagan had promised to get government off people's backs and out of their wallets. Alice M. Rivlin, director of the Congressional Budget Office (a nonpartisan congressional office that advised Congress on budgetary matters), testified, "If substantial reductions in spending are to be achieved, changes in areas of the budget that have thus far been excluded from major spending cuts—defense and pensions—will have to be considered" (USNA, "Correspondence with Commission Members, July 6–November 5, 1982").

The trust fund was indeed in poor shape in the late 1970s and early 1980s. In 1940, the Old-Age and Survivor's insurance trust fund had 3,276 percent of one year's benefits; in 1950 it had 1,343 percent. By 1972, it had less than 100 percent of one year's benefits, and in September 1982, the Old-Age and Survivors insurance trust fund had reached its lowest balance since its inception. The fund accumulated enough in September of 1982 to pay checks in early October, but it had to borrow from the disability and hospital insurance trust funds to pay benefits in November. By 1983, the trust fund was empty (*CR* 1983: H979).

In 1983, some 36 million Americans were receiving Social Security benefits. There were 116 million contributing workers and 140 million insured dependents and survivors (*CR* 1983: 947). Social Security represented 28 percent of the federal budget (*CR* 1983: H978–79); Representative Phil Gramm (R-Texas) called it "the dominant issue in the 1982 elections" (*CR* 1983: H972). Representative Carl Perkins (D-Kentucky), speaking about the 1983 amendments, said: "[With the 1977 amendments] we said 'We have saved social security. We will not have to have any more social security bailout legislation. Hooray for us.' We believed the propaganda that was put out then, so we all voted for the bill and went home for Christmas. Well, as it turns out we did not do anything of the kind. Here we are, 63 months later, puckering up to 'save social security again'" (*CR* 1983: H951).

Like the 1977 amendments, the 1983 amendments were retrenchments, and the difficulty that Congress had in passing these amendments during nonelection years bears testimony to the changing context within which Social Security was considered. The chairman of the House Ways and Means Committee, Dan Rostenkowski (D-Illinois), said, "The political fences were too high last Congress to make any headway against the crisis. Finally, the leaders of both parties turned to a bipartisan commission to lift the issue above the campaign fray" (*CR* 1983: H955).

Based partly on the recommendations of the bipartisan NCSSR, the 1983 amendments made a number of important changes. Scheduled tax rate increases were speeded up, and cost-of-living adjustments were delayed six months. To offset the 1984 payroll tax increase, employees were allowed a 0.3 percentage point tax credit. In effect, workers were required to pay 6.7 percent, with general revenues reimbursing the trust funds for the remaining 0.3 percent (*CQA* 1983: 219–20). The tax rate paid by the self-employed also increased, so that they now paid the combined employer-employee rate of tax; they were, however, given a tax credit to offset this increase—again, an indirect form of general revenue financing. And for the first time in the program's history, benefits were taxed for certain groups. Upper-income beneficiaries would have up to one-half of their benefits considered taxable income. This was a major defeat for SSA bureaucrats.

After years of debate and study, all federal civilian employees hired after December 31, 1983, current and future members of Congress, the President, Vice President, federal judges, all new employees of the judicial branch, and all employees of nonprofit organizations would be mandatorily covered by Social Security. Any deficit in the Civil Service Retirement System trust funds as a result of lost contributions of federal workers would be made up through general revenues. A provision was also included to eliminate the problem of double-dipping. State and local governments were prohibited from withdrawing from the system, and those who had previously withdrawn from the system were allowed to return voluntarily. State and local governments were also required to transfer *all* withheld payroll taxes over to the Treasury more quickly than they had in the past.

There was a one-time credit made to the Social Security trust funds in the amount of $1.3 billion, for the value of Social Security checks issued by the Treasury but (for various reasons) never cashed; previously, these amounts were credited to the Treasury's general revenue fund. Social Security was removed from the unified federal budget beginning in 1992, and until then, Social Security income and expenditure were to be shown as a separate portion of the budget.

Interfund borrowing was allowed through 1987. The Secretary of HEW was now allowed to contract with the states to receive death certificate information to avoid death fraud losses, and a notice was printed on all Social Security checks that cashing the checks issued to deceased persons was a felony. Benefits were restricted for convicted felons, and for survivors and dependents of nonresident aliens.

To improve the long-term outlook of the system, Congress approved a gradual increase in the age of retirement with full benefits from age 65 to 67 by the year 2027. Although workers would still be entitled to retire early under these amendments (at age 62), their benefits would be reduced even more than under prior law. These changes were justified by citing increase in life expectancy since 1935 (*SSB* 1986: 9).

The 1983 amendments also encouraged later retirement by increasing the bonus for delaying retirement past age 65. The earnings test, used to determine benefits of workers aged 65 or over who continued to work, was liberalized. Under the previous law, those aged 65–70 had their benefits reduced $1 for each $2 they earned over $6,600. The 1983 amendments changed this to $1 for each $3 earned, effective beginning in 1990. The reasoning behind the 1990 date was that current trust funds could not bear the short-term costs of the liberalization. It was estimated that repeal of the earnings test would cost $7.5 billion over a five-year period (*SSB* 1986: 9). Overall, this liberalization of the earnings test had the effect not of lowering costs but of increasing trust fund revenues, because working individuals contributed a payroll tax.

Cost-of-living adjustments were to be based on the lower of CPI or wage increases. And finally, investment policies were changed to maximize interest received from the trust funds, again a form of general revenue financing since interest income from government bonds was paid from the Treasury to the Social Security trust funds. The 1983 reforms raised a total of $168 billion for the calendar years 1983–89 (*CQA* 1983: 221). It was much more than what Reagan had requested (*CQA* 1983: 425). According to estimates, approximately one-third of this $168 billion would come from general revenues in the form of tax credits and deductions or direct transfers from general revenues. The tax deduction given to employers, employees, and the self-employed for a portion of their Social Security contribution was, in essence, a form of indirect general revenue financing. In addition, the special age-72 benefit, World War II military wage credits, World War II Japanese-American "prisoners of war" credits, and the 1983 coverage of federal workers meant that general Treasury funds were being used to pay Social Security benefits.

The Reagan budget for 1983 called for Social Security tax increases of $11.7 billion in fiscal 1984, of $12.5 billion in fiscal 1985, and of $63 billion in fiscal 1986. Included in these were increases in Social Security payroll taxes, new taxes on Social Security benefits, higher contributions to CSRS, and a proposal to tax employees on health insurance premiums (*CQA* 1983: 432).

Organizational Dynamics

The inviolability and persistence of the Social Security program were noteworthy throughout the crises of this period of retrenchment. The fact that the NCSSR considered privatization, although it did not seem to be a politically viable option, also reinforced the notion that Social Security remained a relatively untouchable institution. President Reagan learned quickly just how inviolate Social Security was. Given that the changes required were win-lose (rather than the win-win nature of changes during the expansion phase), most elected officials steered clear of setting policies or priorities. Actors within the state, both elected officials and appointed bureaucrats, were paralyzed, and bipartisan commissions provided political scapegoats.

Organizational persistence also refers to the ability of a group of people to mobilize their efforts on a sustained basis. As Charles E. Lindblom writes:

For political influence in the play of power, they need time, knowledge of public affairs, skill in partisan analysis, a persuasive tongue or pen, status in the community, influential associates, and success in interpersonal relations. Millions of citizens lack these skills, and only a few possess all of them. One can contrast New York City's Puerto Ricans with a graduating class at Harvard or Stanford. . . . Despite their great numbers, the poor can afford only poor political organizations, and the well-off finance a variety of better ones. It is not simply an inequality between the very affluent and the poor, inequality in organizations runs through the whole society. Union members, among the better paid American workers, mobilize far less money for political organizations than do business people. . . . Because wealthy people can reward other people, many habitually defer to them and confer authority on them. (1980: 100–101)

Organizational theory provides some valuable insights here. For example, even though taxpaying workers represent an obvious interest group when discussing Social Security, mobilization factors *do* matter. First, strong leadership in this area is not evident. Second, these groups offer few selective incentives to encourage taxpaying workers to unite. Third, no age group has as high a propensity to vote as do the elderly. A quote from Al Ullman (D-Oregon), chairman of the House Ways and Means Committee, illustrates the extent to which Congress heeds elderly voters. Ullman, concerned that Congress might not pass the Social Security bill before the Christmas recess of 1977, reminded his fellow representatives: "We simply cannot vote down a social security package when the fund is depleted and go home and say that we have responsibly faced up to our responsibilities in social security legislation. Just keep in mind that a bigger and bigger block of our constituencies are senior citizens who have to depend upon social security as a major part of their retirement program" (*CR* 1977: 39007). Unlike the AARP, groups representing taxpaying workers cannot guarantee legislators a unified vote. A fourth reason for the lack of effective organization by taxpaying workers is that tax increases are incremental, making the tax burden change ever so slightly from year to year. Fifth, social class and racial divisions make it hard to organize such a diverse group. Sixth, the relative size of interest groups is a factor: increases in taxes yield quite large returns to beneficiaries because of the number of workers involved;

yet for any individual taxpayer the burden certainly *began* as a relatively light one. Finally, given that we all anticipate growing older, urging cutbacks in Social Security is tantamount to arguing for reduced returns for elderly family members, or for our own old-age insurance benefits. All these factors help to explain why taxpaying workers were unable or unlikely to register their political opinions effectively. There are social, economic, cultural, and demographic prerequisites to political participation and organization.

Because certain social groups did not register their protests loudly or on a sustained basis, these groups ended up as the economic buffers for the retrenchment that occurred. The increasing poverty rate of children during this time period is a notable case in point, and it seems clear that children's interests will probably have to be represented by organizational actors with more long-term perspectives. Victories won in the political arena are victories over other *involved* parties, with the uninvolved acting as a buffer in system (Polsby 1986). But with the decreasing effectiveness of the buffer over time, tight coupling and narrowed options occur. In other words, options due to slack in the system lessen over time.

With regard to interests, during this period of crisis interest groups were more likely to register their opinions, partly because of increasing information circulating about the program and possible alternatives; however, this did not have much effect on their success or failure. Outraged and overloaded taxpayers organized into the National Taxpayers Union and Americans for Generational Equity; neither group was successful in opposing the massive increases in both Social Security payroll taxes and income taxes (which would eventually go into the Social Security trust funds), but it is significant that during this period of crisis various groups did organize and begin efforts to influence legislative outcomes. Bipartisan commissions had better representation than did many previous advisory councils in terms of being independent of the SSA. Many interests were represented on these commissions, and they were indeed more "revolutionary" in the ideas considered, if not in the ideas implemented.

With regard to the importance of selective incentives, AARP

provides an excellent example. This group claimed approximately 33 million members in the mid-1980s, and in the United States was surpassed in size only by the Catholic Church. Nancy Benac writes: "Its activities include a mail-order pharmacy service, educational publications and classes, a senior volunteer network, local chapter activities, circulation-leading *Modern Maturity* magazine, driver education courses, legal assistance, a discount purchase program, group health, home and auto insurance, a motor club, travel service, investment programs, and even help filling out tax forms" (1989a: J10). Certainly few organizations can compare with AARP's success in employing selective incentives in a politically productive way.

As the success of these selective incentives partially attests, AARP represents a broad coalition of social classes. A compelling argument made by AARP, in the face of a variety of proposals for programmatic retrenchment, is that the incomes of the elderly tend to erode, unlike those of younger Americans who have historically seen their incomes grow. Timothy Smeeding, an economist at Syracuse University, notes: "A retired couple is often forced to cash in some of its assets to pay medical bills, thereby reducing the amount of interest and dividends it will earn. In addition, most private pensions are not indexed to inflation, so their value typically erodes. And husbands on average die sooner than their wives, leaving widows with reduced Social Security benefits" (in DeParle 1993: A17). The AARP emphasizes just such cases.

With regard to coalition formation, interest groups often coalesce around perceived infringement of their rights and the status quo. For example, the 1970s and 1980s stirred interests with threats of benefit cuts or higher taxes. There was a coalescing of diverse groups around the existing program. In many ways, crises change the political calculus on which political alignments are structured. The point here is that even during the retrenchment period of the 1970s and 1980s, the game was not entirely zero-sum. More politically powerful interest groups like the elderly (the AARP and NCSC) won out over taxpayers, as evidenced by the expanding use of indirect general revenue financing. Accounting shifts and cutting back in peripheral or more obscure parts of the program were also common.

Numbers of supporters remained a key variable in legislative outcomes. Without the influence of elderly advocate groups, the review provoked here might have produced real cuts in benefits rather than just taxation of benefits for certain beneficiaries. It is clearly not in the best interests of younger workers to continue financing the Social Security system through the use of indirect general revenues; this merely obscures the real costs of old-age insurance. Many observers predict disaster when the baby boomers begin to retire. And though some may be comforted by the idea of more liberal immigration policies and government policies that encourage fertility (as bolstering the taxpaying workforce), the overall picture remains dire. Forty percent of American workers pay more in Social Security taxes than they do in federal income taxes, and yet the National Taxpayers Union, an organization that is concerned with this issue, has only 150,000 members (*CR* 1977: 39142; Gruber 1987). Variations in the ability to form effective broad-based political coalitions need to be addressed.

With regard to the timing of various external events, the continuing high unemployment and inflation of the late 1970s prevented the 1977 amendments from going as far as they should have gone. Reagan launched a trial balloon in his proposals to reform the Social Security program, but that only pointed the way to more politically viable options without achieving anything substantial. The touchy political nature of Social Security reform was reflected in the use of the bipartisan commissions and closed rule.

There is also a sense in which timing, and "being first," matters. In the first chapter I discussed the process of lock-in, whereby a program or method becomes standard, even though it might not be the most efficient when compared with other alternatives developed later. The passage of social insurance legislation in 1935 meant that privatization of old-age insurance would never be a truly viable option. The polity, in the form of Social Security, played an increasingly important role in the U.S. economy, and over time, interests had coalesced around the existing program; this made privatization untenable. House Representative Ronald Paul (R-Texas), addressing House members before the vote on the 1983 amendments, castigated the reforms Congress was about to enact by saying, "Anyone espousing the idea of making social security voluntary — not to mention phasing the program out altogether — is labeled an enemy of social security and our elderly. The real enemies of our present and future elderly, however, are those who continue to call this pay-as-you-go scheme security" (*CR* 1983: H980).

Time perspective also played a major role in these turning points. The push to include the few remaining groups not yet covered by Social Security reflected the short-term orientation of congressional representatives, as well as the use of mere accounting shifts instead of instituting real, more controversial changes. Bringing in more workers would indeed increase tax receipts in the short run, but it would also increase future benefit obligations. Moreover, this was another method of indirect general revenue financing, simply because federal agencies were the major employers of these workers and therefore general revenues would be required to pay the employer's half of the payroll tax. Unlike private business and industry, these added costs could not be passed on to consumers since in effect these consumers, as citizens of the United States, were the employer of the federal agencies. Finally, the overall budget would be adversely affected by lack of funds contributed to the CSRS from federal employees, even though Social Security trust funds would appear to be enhanced in the short run as a result of universal coverage under the program.

In addition, time was also a factor in our "middle-aged" Social Security program. Although the choices to shore up the system were much more controversial than were previous decisions on expansion or benefit increases, there were several smaller, less controversial methods proposed to increase the efficiency of the system. Though these changes were minor, as Robert J. Myers often pointed out, millions could be saved through small accounting changes (USNA, "NAM"). The SSA proposed and won the following changes in the program: separation of the trust funds from the general budget; avoiding death-fraud payments; maximizing trust fund investment income; crediting the trust funds with uncashed checks; disallowing payments to felons; interfund borrowing; and agreements with foreign countries to integrate pensions. These relatively noncontroversial changes served to enhance the appearance of the trust funds in the short term, and tightened up on the few remaining loopholes.

Ideology was reflected once again in the adequacy v. equity debate. This debate was directly related to the macroeconomic context, in that increasingly zero-sum contexts led to concerns with equity, while prosperity was conducive to concerns over adequacy. A distinct move away from the notions of adequacy, so prevalent during the years of expansion, was apparent during this period of programmatic retrenchment. The new emphasis was on the notion of equity. This was reflected in discussions of the crisis in the expectations of the public concerning Social Security. Elliot L. Richardson, Secretary of Health, Education, and Welfare, said in testimony before the Senate Finance Committee: "There is no denying that . . . more and more citizens are becoming more and more distrustful of our government. A major reason for this . . . is . . . an 'expectations gap,' as rising and totally unrealistic expectations outstrip the realistic possibilities of fulfillment by our programs" (*CQA* 1972: 904). In the context of a crisis regarding the trust funds of the late 1970s and early 1980s, the new ideology cast reminders that Social Security was not intended to provide total replacement for lost income. Representative Levitas (D-Georgia) noted: "The supplementary nature of social security benefits has never been adequately publicized and is realized by only a few Americans. All too many people work the bulk of their lives confidently expecting social security alone or in tandem with a pension to maintain them during retirement at their same level of living, and by the time they realize otherwise, it is too late" (*CR* 1977: 39027).

The dangerously low level of the trust funds also led groups not yet included in the program to question the equity or fairness of being mandatorily included in the system. As reported in the 1975 SSA *Annual Report,* challenges to the constitutionality of the program were increasing (SSA 1975: 11). These charges were leveled by groups that did not want to be included but were threatened with compulsory coverage, as well as by groups that had voluntarily elected coverage and now wanted to get out. The issue of equity was also relevant for workers who were mandatorily covered for most of their working lives. For them, equity meant the justice inherent in a larger group of covered workers being forced to remain under an increasingly leaky umbrella, while small groups of government workers were opting out yet still receiving benefits.

Equity also became relevant during this period owing to increasing concern with intergenerational fairness. Senator David F. Durenberger's organization, Americans for Generational Equity (AGE), attempted to rally taxpayers around real Social Security reform. This group complained that in a program that only slowly encompassed everyone but began paying benefits immediately, early beneficiaries got a much higher return on their contributions than did workers who came into the system later, either because they were not covered originally or because they were born later. This made Social Security, as some writers have dubbed it, an intergenerational chain letter. Workers who came into the program later had a growing sense of entitlement to their benefits, and this made cutbacks in benefits much more difficult to legislate. For their part, the elderly argued that social insurance represented a pact between generations, and that because they had paid into the system, they were *entitled* to benefits. They neglected to mention that, generally speaking, they received far more in benefits than they paid in taxes. Their agenda also emphasized "the elderly" as if they were a monolithic group. To enhance their claims of entitlement and need they downplayed the socioeconomic variation that existed in their midst.

Thus, whereas adequacy was the key issue in the 1950s and 1960s, equity was the key issue in the early and later years. It is important to note, however, that the equity discussed in the early period (especially the 1940s) centered around the equity of being excluded from what was proving to be a good program for beneficiaries. The equity discussed during the 1970s and 1980s was the equity of being compulsorily included in an ailing program, or intergenerational equity.

The emerging trend toward encouraging the elderly to work also reflected the importance of equity in a period of crisis or retrenchment. Encouraging the elderly to work was justified as consistent with the original intent of the 1935 legislation, as well as being good for the system and good for the elderly. Raising the retirement age and increasing the amount allowable under the earnings test were important developments in the history of the program when it is recalled that during the 1930s, a key factor in the initiation of the program was high Depression-era unemployment rates; Social Security was viewed as a relatively acceptable method of moving large numbers of people out of the labor force. Labor unions were instrumental in making sure the original legislation included an earnings test. Indeed, the two key factors behind the earnings test were the AFL-CIO affiliated unions, which favored some restrictions on earnings, and the prohibitive costs to the trust funds of repealing the test.

Historically, the earnings test had been one of the most unpopular features of the program, with AARP, NCSC, and the Gray Panthers drastically opposed to it. Further, many independent professionals who continue to work after age 65 and various conservative representatives have recommended repeal of the test. Senator Goldwater, recommending repeal in 1972, stated:

Social Security payments are not gratuities from a benevolent central government. They are essentially a repayment of our own earnings. . . . As the program was first reported by the Committee on Ways and Means in 1935, there was no earnings test at all. Thus, a repeal of the test today would restore the program to its original form. . . . The earnings test is wrong morally because Social Security should not be a contract to quit work. It is wrong logically because the person who is penalized is often the one with the greatest need for more income than his Social Security benefits can provide. (*CQA* 1972: 902)

In light of the equity issue, this quote is interesting for several reasons. It was viewed as unfair that Social Security beneficiaries were required to quit work in order to collect benefits. Note the reiteration of *entitlement* to benefits. But Social Security benefits, for most persons, were much more than a "repayment" of their earnings. In the context of the Great Depression, some disincentive to continue work was eventually written into the 1935 Social Security Act in the form of an earnings test. It was viewed as fair or equitable. But in the context of retrenchment and a shrinking minimum-wage labor market, with a great deal of stratification among the elderly, the earnings test was viewed as fair game for revision.

The labor market during the late 1970s and early 1980s had changed drastically. During the 1970s, the civilian labor force grew 2.5 percent annually as the baby boom reached maturity, the Vietnam War ended, and women entered the labor force en masse. But as the influx of baby boomers into the labor force ended, and increases in women's labor force slowed and defense mobilization declined, the civilian labor force grew at only 1.2 percent annually through 1990, and only 0.8 percent from 1990 to 1995 (USNA, "General–No Response Correspondence to Robert J. Myers"). A further consideration was mentioned in the mid-1980s by Social Security Commissioner Dorcas R. Hardy. She complained to President Reagan that some Social Security beneficiaries tried to circumvent the earnings test by not reporting income to the government, and that in this way the test "has driven a large underground economy" (in Pear 1987: 6). Dr. Otis R. Bowen, Secretary of Health and Human Services, claimed that repealing the test would be "both good policy and good politics," because it would be "popular among elderly voters," would eliminate a work disincentive, and would bolster the economy by retaining skilled workers (in Pear 1987: 6). These changes, along with lower fertility levels (which reduce the number of younger minimum-wage workers), and a fiscal crisis in the Social Security trust funds, have led policymakers to view increasing the retirement age and liberalizing the earnings test (both of which encourage employment of the elderly) as justifiable and equitable.

In an increasingly zero-sum economic context, equity was an important issue. The crises of the origins phase of Social Security and this period of retrenchment created win-lose dilemmas, while prosperity created win-win successes. The 1977 and 1983 amendments also illustrated that during periods of crisis the state bureaucracy had to rely more heavily on its established constituency of beneficiaries to carry the flag. The SSA and Congress were clearly in no position to take strong stands on the issues, and politically insulated bipartisan commissions framed legislation. President Reagan was unable to implement his proposed Social Security reforms and was essentially forced to return to a bipartisan commission. Congress, for its part, welcomed the bipartisan option.

In the final chapter, I shall summarize some of the key theoretical and substantive points made so far, and I will briefly discuss some issues that are likely to dominate the Social Security agenda of the future.

CHAPTER SEVEN

Conclusions

> I have a sense of deja vu as we debate this bill today. . . . The words of Santayana come to mind: "Those who disregard the past are bound to repeat it."
>
> —Representative Elliott Levitas (D-Georgia) regarding the 1983 amendments (*CR* 1983: H974)

> Senator Carl T. Curtis (R-Nebraska): "What assurance do the future beneficiaries have that they will ever get their benefits?"
>
> Secretary of Health, Education, and Welfare Wilbur J. Cohen: "The assurance is that a particular generation of taxpayers will tax themselves to pay for it."
>
> —(*CR* 1977: 36470–71)

I BEGAN THIS PROJECT with both substantive and theoretical questions about legislative changes in Social Security. In this final chapter, I summarize the key points presented thus far and also suggest some possible outcomes for the future of old-age insurance in the United States. The theoretical and methodological questions are primarily of academic interest, but the substantive questions are relevant for all Americans.

What have we learned from this book that we could not have learned from earlier works? With regard to theory and methods, this work promotes a fresh approach to the study of social policy in the United States. First, it is clear that our historical focus influences the conclusions we reach about which actors hold political power. The long-term framework used in this analysis captures the unique effects of different economic and political contexts. It is impossible to sort out what is idiosyncratic or what constitutes a pattern without longer historical perspectives. For example, in many ways both the origins and expansion phases were atypical. The Great Depression with its massive unemployment and unrest was historically unique, and certainly the post–World War II era of economic growth and expansion was also unusual. The period after World War II was atypical in that there was an economic climate conducive to expansion *and* pressure to expand.

An analysis that employs a broader time frame does not simply allow us to determine what is unique and what reappears as a pattern. It also allows us to assess causality. What instrumentalists call corporate liberal planning is actually adaptation and implementation of certain business, industrial, and financial interests *after* these groups were forced to deal with the new legislation. Indeed, the realization that many representatives of capital were opposed to Social Security legislation in the 1930s is precisely what makes the idea of the relative autonomy of the state so compelling. The recognition of state autonomy is often applied to state policymaking developments in the 1930s. However, the emphasis on certain cross-sectional moments overlooks the fact that powerful interests eventually prevailed. A focus on more isolated time periods also overlooks the centrality of the economic, political, social, and demographic context.

The second point that emerges from this research relates to the importance of treating the state, capital, labor, and other interest groups as central explanatory variables while focusing on specifiable organizational actors. The advantages of highlighting organizational actors stem in part from the ease with which later scholars can replicate one's findings. And certainly, the more abstract theoretical concepts of "the state," "capital," "labor," and "elderly advocate groups" obscure interesting dissension, or shifts in political power, that occur *within* these groups. For example, the relative autonomy of the state during the Great Depression was primarily the autonomy of President Roosevelt; even then, it is difficult to separate Roosevelt's autonomy from the very real fears of domestic anarchy that prevailed in the early 1930s. The Great Depression created a crisis that undercut the long-standing leverage of powerful organizations, yet the state autonomy that existed ranged from only some to little. Roosevelt had some autonomy, the Social Security Board had less than Roosevelt but more than Congress, and Congress had the least.

The important point is that there are different pressures and different opportunities evident in the roles of President, congressional representative, and state bureaucrat. Though the President and congressional representatives are elected by the people, their terms in office, degree of authority vested, and visibility of roles are very different. And state bureaucrats are quite another category, which, depending on the economic and political climate, can assume either a lesser or a greater role in the political debates.

Autonomy among state actors varies not only at one point in time but also *across* time (Polsby 1986: 152, 204). In the early years, partly because of resistance from organizations representing capital and Southern congressional Democrats, Congress was fairly constrained, but in the later years, when old-age insurance was more widely accepted, it managed to pass many of the more liberal programs that program bureaucrats wanted from the beginning. Similarly, the more controversial Social Security legislation of 1977 and 1983 occurred in odd-numbered, nonelection years, whereas the extensions or expansions of the 1950s and 1960s occurred during even-numbered years.

And though the early SSB had more autonomy than Congress, it was not an entirely autonomous force during the origins period; Social Security bureaucrats actually had more autonomy during the prosperity of the 1950s and 1960s. The success of the program contributed to its legitimacy, and in a context of low unemployment, rising wages, and low dependency ratios, radical new programs were adopted. It was during this time that disability and hospital insurance benefits were enacted. These long-desired programs had heretofore been opposed by the powerful lobbies of the American Medical Association and the insurance industry, which later discovered ways to turn the programs to their advantage.

The model presented here uses organizational actors as the unit of analysis. In this way, we add precision to our methodology by specifying which political organizations or state bureaucracies are being addressed. Beginning with organizations as the unit of analysis, generalizations can then be made, using organizational actors as evidence. When more abstract terms are employed at the outset (e.g., labor, capital, and the state), it is not always clear which organizational actors are being considered as representative of these more macrolevel categories.

Through organizational specification, we can analyze these organizations to determine in what ways they resemble or differ from other organizations of a similar type. For example, the early Business Advisory Council was not an independently formed group of business representatives. It was an arm of the Department of

Commerce under the Roosevelt administration. This sort of group cannot be compared with the National Association of Manufacturers or the U.S. Chamber of Commerce in terms of their support of Social Security. Representatives of capital were divided in their attitudes toward Social Security in 1935. More specifically, once the NAM and the U.S. Chamber of Commerce had lost some of the initial battles over Social Security, they attempted to mold existing legislation to their best interests. The bulk of historical evidence from various studies indicates that welfare reform legislation is enacted in steps, and that "although some employers supported the laws, they did so because they had lost the battle at an earlier stage" (Steinberg 1982: 214).

There was also interest in the cash benefits of Social Security from many other groups besides those representing capital. Some labor unions in the 1930s had emptied their unemployment, strike, and pension funds, and embraced the notion of social insurance. Groups of workers who were excluded from the original legislation began lobbying Congress for inclusion soon after the first benefits were paid in 1940. Business and industrial associations also began to accept and push for increases in Social Security, but to single them out as the only important set of key lobbyists is a dubious conclusion given the overall context. This is not to say that Social Security has offended or alienated business, industry, the medical profession, or the insurance industry. On the contrary, these groups have used Social Security to their advantage.

In addition, this analysis treats as variables the concepts of organizational persistence, interests and incentives, coalition formation, time and timing, and ideology. In this way, it highlights both *variations within organizations over time* and *variations between organizations at a given point in time.* The emphasis on organization-environment interrelationships over time illustrates the variation within organizations such as the Social Security Administration, the NAM, the U.S. Chamber of Commerce, the AFL-CIO, and the AARP regarding their ability to promote their agenda. During periods of crisis, organizations tend to be affected by their environment, whereas during periods of calm they are in a better position to act upon that environment.

Major crises or changes require hypothetical thinking. Organizational persistence is not as big a factor during crises periods because interests are harder to define, especially for groups. For these reasons, social movements and radical ideas are most likely to have an audience—windows of opportunity—during these critical junctures. All institutions and organizations have the *potential* to act autonomously at all times, but issues related to timing and time greatly affect their visibility and long-term success.

Organizational persistence renders some groups more effective than others in having their agenda met. Organizations that persist over time are less distracted by issues related to timing, and because of this continuity they are more likely to be the key players when the time is ripe for a new idea. A fundamental reason that the early SSB was unable to institute a full-fledged Social Security program was that it was a new organization, struggling to attain acceptance and legitimacy, but its organizational persistence eventually secured the program that embodied the dreams of the early founders. Organizational persistence is one important factor that sets apart organizations such as the SSA, NAM, and the U.S. Chamber of Commerce from the more sporadic or relatively short-lived and resource-poor social movements such as those led by Dr. Townsend, Huey Long, and Father Coughlin.

Three noteworthy features of old-age insurance demonstrate its organizational persistence. First, the SSA has generally faced less uncertainty than many organizations. It is a monopoly provider that, historically, has had access to coercion. In the early years, supporters of Social Security used many "state" resources (e.g., the Supreme Court, the President, and the Congress) to ensure passage of the original legislation and compliance with the law.

Second, Social Security is currently a seemingly inviolable institution in American culture. When President Reagan proposed changes to the program in the 1980s, the public outcry was deafening. Indeed, if we view institutionalization as a variable, the Social Security program has a thriving history. The personnel of the SSA have generally been careerist executives with long-term vision, and there is a strong emphasis on service in the organizational culture. For example, "When a new SSA administrator announced that she wanted more field offices to open during the evening and on weekends and to allow beneficiaries to make appointments (rather than show up and wait in line), the field offices . . . welcomed what many other government agencies would have viewed as an objectionable burden" (Wilson 1989: 35–36). Because of this administrative success, the SSA has never had to face a serious challenge to its jurisdiction (Kaufman 1981: 161–64). The American public is generally accepting of the payroll tax, Social Security identification numbers, and the prospects of benefits during retirement. During the early years, political discourse reflected no such complacency about these issues.

Finally, the sheer number of people affected by old-age insurance also contributes to its organizational persistence. These numbers influence the relative and absolute dollar amounts of Social Security income and expenditures compared with other federal programs. Much like the concept "too big to fail" in private organizations, such as banks and auto manufacturers, the Social Security program generally commands much political attention. The main point here is that each of these atypical features contributes to the bureaucracy's ability to shape its environment. Other political organizations are more often subjected to being *acted upon*.

The interactions between organizations and the larger economic, political, social, and demographic environment are essential pieces of any political puzzle. Clearly, the context within which organizational actors attempt to exercise power or influence greatly shapes both their perceptions of their interests and their success in promoting policies that address those interests. Issues related to timing and windows of opportunity are influenced by the larger environmental context. Even though these circumstances are beyond organizational control, organizations that persist are better positioned to articulate their interests when the time is right. It follows that such organizations have more control over the environment in which they operate. Once entrenched, the SSA was a powerful force in advocating and justifying program expansion.

Coalition formation is also important in pushing forward new political initiatives. State actors involved with old-age insurance legislation were not generally neutral arbiters. The degree to which Roosevelt and his hand-picked lieutenants shaped the direction of Social Security does not accord with a pluralist image of outcomes negotiated between a myriad of relatively equal political actors. Interested actors within the state, from Roosevelt and the early SSB, to the SSA, Congress, and the Treasury Department, were able, at various times, to shape Social Security legislation. The pluralist view that state actors simply absorb and respond to what outsiders demand ignores the fact that state actors often bring to the political debates unique perspectives and interests of their own. And as political insiders, with ready access to each other, important information, and other political resources, they often have an advantage over political outsiders. It was true that political outsiders, such as the unemployed and the Townsendites in the 1930s, were important voices in the call for change. But in the case of Social Security, it was a very diffuse, indirect pressure that called for something to be done. It was not an equal sharing of power wherein all interests had a role in writing the actual legislation. In addition, the cross-class coalitions created by old-age insurance have been central to its endurance and political acceptability.

Time perspective and timing are also important variables for organizational actors in the political arena. This is overlooked by instrumentalist arguments, which assume too much foresight and rationality on the part of representatives of business and industry. James O'Connor maintains that powerful economic interests sought Social Security legislation as a way of socializing the costs of an inefficient mode of production; but in the 1930s, the NAM and the U.S. Chamber of Commerce did not anticipate the benefits of Social Security. Although these groups did eventually learn to socialize the costs of the payroll tax by lowering wages and increasing prices, it was an unplanned adaptation that occurred several years after the original legislation.

What we witnessed in the period of expansion during the 1950s and 1960s was the coincidence of interests of the SSA, the AFL-CIO, the NAM, the U.S. Chamber of Commerce, and elderly advocate groups like the American Association of Retired Persons and the National Council of Senior Citizens. This concurrence of interests was what fueled the massive expansion. It was not simply one elite group of powerful people pushing for expansion. In the long-term evolution of legislation, powerful interests did, quite clearly, have an impact, but it was far more the result of limited rationality and an unplanned adaptation than the outcome of a conscious, rational, forward-looking strategy.

The time perspective of state actors varies as well. Certainly for Presidents, success is measured using a relatively short-term perspective. Members of Congress, too, do not generally focus on long-term actuarial estimates but instead concentrate on what influential constituents want at a particular point. At the opposite end of the continuum, the SSA was generally staffed with personnel who had a long-term agenda that they pursued in an incremental fashion.

Ideological shifts in the broader society and those promoted by old-age insurance supporters are also vital to this analysis. Before the massive poverty brought on by the Great Depression, most Americans were philosophically opposed to a mandatory tax for old-age insurance. With the onset of the Great Depression and Dr. Townsend's proposal for $200 monthly pensions, Americans considered social security in a new light. The radical flank effect of the Townsend Plan made Social Security look reasonable by comparison, and in that way it provided some of the impetus for this dramatic social experiment.

Similarly, over time, the American public's expectations about the program have changed. Social Security altered people's way of thinking about aging and retirement. The gradual shift from discussions of equity to discussions of adequacy reflects the power of the SSA to promote its ideology regarding old-age insurance. Entrenched bureaucracies can be a powerful force that can affect the broader environment by mobilizing constituents and thus ensuring their own longevity. Both versions of conflict theory discussed here (i.e., instrumentalist and structuralist) downplay the importance of ideas and the relative autonomy of noneconomic aspects of society.

To come to any conclusions for theory construction, we need theoretical frameworks that squarely situate political events in their appropriate macroeconomic context. We must also address organizational-level and ideological dynamics. Our understanding of the interactions between organizations and environments is enhanced by considering the variables of organizational persistence, interests and incentives, coalition formation, time and timing, and ideology. To do this, we need more middle-level specification of notions such as the state, capital, labor, and elderly advocate groups. Different organizational actors under these more abstract categories behave in very different ways.

Good theoretical frameworks should also have predictive capabilities. Generally, it is tenuous to extrapolate to the future, and certainly it is difficult to predict the exact contextual dynamics of the future. Nevertheless, there are some possibilities that are more likely than others, given the organizational framework suggested here. The following possibilities are based on discussions of the future of Social Security, as recorded in government documents.

The Future of Social Security

A review of the events of the past 55 years of Social Security legislation strongly indicates that the economic, political, and demographic context will continue to shape Social Security legislation as well as the power exercised by different interest groups. In suggesting issues of the future, we can also look to other advanced industrial countries, many of which developed old-age insurance programs well before the United States. They are not thriving:

Since the 1970s all such democracies have endured a fiscal crisis. . . . International economic recession has brought the cold grip of "stagflation" to many nations at a time when Keynesian strategies of macroeconomic management no longer seem certain to ensure steady economic growth without rising unemployment. Large population cohorts covered by mature pensions systems are aging and retiring, while increasing numbers of individuals cannot depend upon traditional family ties for help during periods of difficulty. Economic pressures and social trends have thus combined to spur widespread consternation about the future of public social programs in the Western nations. (Weir, Orloff, and Skocpol 1988: 3)

There is no question that high rates of unemployment and inflation will be detrimental to the trust funds in the future. At least until 2010, however, the overall effects of poor economic performance will not create the sort of crisis experienced in the late 1970s. The reason stems from a favorable demographic situation. A large number of baby boomers will be in their peak earning years, and because of the tax rate and earnings base increases instituted in the 1977 and 1983 amendments, they will contribute relatively large amounts to the trust funds (Weaver 1990). But it is this group of people who will pose enormous problems for Social Security when they reach retirement age.

The demographic profile of the American population reveals that baby boomers put pressure on existing hospitals when they were born, on school systems when they were educated, on the labor market when they looked for work, and on the housing market when they tried to buy homes. Landon Y. Jones writes, "Demographers use the vaguely discomfiting metaphor of a 'pig in a python' to describe the resulting motion of the baby-boom bulge through the decades as it ages" (1980: 2). It will be no different for Social Security. The low dependency ratios of the first few decades of the program are gone forever. Estimates are that by 2029, there will be 78 million baby boomers retired, making non-wage earners the largest group in the population; today's dependency ratio of 3.3 to 1 will fall to less than 2 to 1 (Dain Bosworth, Inc. 1990: 1).

Undeniably, unless there are major changes in coverage, there will be more burdensome dependency ratios in the future. In 1982, the *Annual Report* of the Social Security Board of Trustees estimated that by the year 2030, the tax rate for all three Social Security programs will have to be 33 percent of gross income simply to sustain existing benefit levels (see *CR* 1983: H981). Economists also point out that retirees in 1989 got back $3.50 for each dollar paid into the system, but persons in their twenties and thirties will get back less than $1 for each dollar they put into the pot (*San Antonio Light* 1989c: E4).

But it is not just the sheer number of persons retiring that is significant. It is also the expectations these individuals have for their retirement years. Unlike those who received Social Security benefits during the 1940s, baby boomers have contributed a great deal to the system, and they have higher expectations for their postretirement lifestyle. With life expectancy increasing over time, they will also place a further burden on the system by living longer and longer. Not surprisingly, long-term health care is now a major issue of concern to the elderly as well as to their children, who must make decisions about caring for them. Programs developed

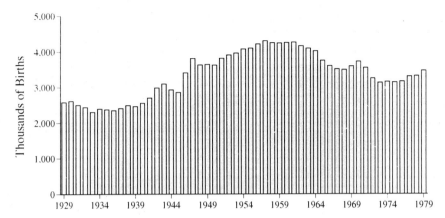

Fig. 4. The baby boom generation, annual births, 1929–1979. (Source: U.S. Bureau of the Census)

under Medicare to deal with this problem will only place a heavier burden on the trust funds.

Several conditions suggest that baby boomers will have a disproportionate degree of political power with regard to Social Security. First, the sheer number of persons involved means that elected officials will pay close attention to their concerns (see Fig. 4 for the imminent wave of retiring boomers). A Dallas-based American Association of Boomers claimed 21,000 members in the early 1990s (Hendricks 1992), and as boomers age, they are likely to follow the high-turnout voting patterns of contemporary elderly. In addition, because these workers will be the first major group of retirees to have paid into Social Security throughout their entire working lives, they are likely to reach retirement with a greater sense of entitlement than any other cohort of retirees. Finally, the Congressional Research Service estimates that by 2030, it will take average retirees eighteen years to get back the equivalent of what they and their employers paid into the system, with interest; in 1980, that figure was 2.8 years (DeParle 1993). For all these reasons, the SSA and Congress will probably have to respond to this group for a certain amount of policy direction, or face the electoral consequences.

It is also unlikely that any state actor will have the kind of autonomy given Roosevelt during the Depression or the SSA during the 1950s and 1960s. In the first place, the political and economic visibility of the Social Security program has increased over time, and as increasing numbers of citizens are covered by the program, it has come under closer scrutiny on account of its fiscal weight. Second, the maturing of Social Security means that legislative options are increasingly constrained, tightly coupled, and zero-sum.

The constraints facing Social Security bureaucrats and the incredible political power of elderly advocate groups indicate the nature of the policies that will probably be advocated. For example, in addition to an increasing number of elderly who live longer, more recent fertility trends have created a shortage of lower-paid young workers. Taken together, these demographic developments lead to an obvious solution. We now encourage the elderly to work longer in various jobs. McDonald's restaurants actively recruit older workers to fill the void left by teenagers; they report that these workers are more reliable, mature, and responsible (Ritzer 1993). Newspaper executives have also experienced the shortage of younger workers to deliver newspapers and have turned to the elderly as replacements (Bacha, personal communication).

I expect this trend to continue, both in these low-paid positions and also for more highly paid individuals. For the latter group, it will not be the case that employers urge them to continue working so much as that they will fight for their rights to continue working if they so desire. There are also proposals to encourage the elderly to work longer in areas of great social need. For example, two members of a subcommittee of the House Select Committee on Aging, Representatives Tom Tauke (R-Iowa) and William Hughes (D-New Jersey), the acting chairman, introduced legislation to exempt the earnings of child-care workers aged 65 or older from the Social Security earning limits. They noted that the proposal would encourage older Americans to work longer and help meet the nation's daycare needs. Hughes asked, "Why shouldn't we attempt to match needs such as child care to the desire to get older Americans who have so much to offer back into the workforce?" (in Benac 1989b).

Hughes said that the earnings exemption could be extended to other areas in which there are shortages, such as skilled nursing, with the nation eventually repealing the earnings limit altogether. The SSA officially opposed the child-care connected plan for two reasons. First, cost estimates from the Congressional Budget Office were $85 million over five years. Deputy Social Security Commissioner Louis Enoff reiterated to the House subcommittee the concerns with the massive elimination of the earnings test. Second, he pointed out the difficulty of administering a method of picking and choosing which earnings would be exempt. However, Carolyn Golding, Deputy Assistant Labor Secretary, took no position on the legislation, but told the subcommittee that premature retirement "becomes a real cost to the individual workers, the employer and the nation. There is much to be gained by using older workers to meet the needs for day care" (in Benac 1989b).

Congressional documents reveal two other methods that have been suggested to ease the burden of these oppressive dependency ratios. One is for the government to develop policies to encourage increased fertility. This policy has the obvious disadvantage of taking a number of years before labor force effects are felt in terms of creating a new group of workers who pay Social Security payroll taxes. The other method is for the government to encourage immigration from foreign countries. Both suggestions reflect the increasingly tight coupling of the Social Security system with other aspects of the economy and public policy, and the historic reliance on adding more taxpaying workers to the program to bolster the trust funds. Just as a chain letter requires new friends to add to the list, Social Security requires new groups to "pay as we go." This, plus the generally short-term orientation in the political arena means that immigration increases are likely to be the option chosen. Indeed, we have recently seen the raising of quotas in this area.

The use of indirect general revenue financing will probably continue. These strategies hide the overall economic costs of the programs, and they are a politically acceptable solution to shortfalls in the trust funds. In other words, this less visible method of taxation will continue to prop up the system for as long as the level of awareness remains low. Until some politically powerful group chooses to mobilize against this trend, it will be the method of choice for legislators.

These forms of indirect general revenue financing not only hide the overall costs of the Social Security program but also shift the emphasis from the health of the Social Security trust funds as a *separate* budget concern to the health of the overall federal budget. Whether this distinction is any longer truly meaningful is questionable: as Carolyn Weaver notes, "It is not immediately obvious whether the social security surpluses are being saved and invested for future years or spent on current consumption" (1990: 1). Members of Congress are, however, aware of the dynamics between general revenues, means testing, and political defensibility. Senator Carl T. Curtis (R-Nebraska), discussing old-age insurance, noted in the *Congressional Record*: "The minute you change it and dip into the general fund, you have ruined it; because after the appropriating process goes along here, somebody is going to get up and say, 'We can't pay it to certain groups. The tax is too high'" (*CR* 1977: 36450). What occurs is that general revenue financing places Social Security in more direct competition with other programs; indeed, the political debates of the 1990s often note that "even entitlements" will be placed on the agenda of potential budget cuts. These dynamics were the reason that Roosevelt wanted a payroll tax earmarked specifically for Social Security in 1935.

Means testing, in a variety of forms, is likely to be an issue in the future. During the 1992 presidential campaign, Ross Perot suggested that wealthy Americans who did not need their old-age insurance benefits could elect to return them to the trust fund. In the more zero-sum context envisioned in the future, with greater awareness that early participants in the program have received benefits vastly in excess of contributions, these sorts of appeals are likely to be heard more often. Perot's suggestion represents a "voluntary means testing," but it is means testing nevertheless.

In letters mailed to the National Commission on Social Security Reform during the early 1980s, many individuals favored a means test for the cost-of-living adjustments (USNA "Correspondence with Commission Members, July 6–November 5, 1982"). Gary Becker, a professor of economics and sociology at the University of Chicago, and former commerce secretary Peter Peterson were quoted on this issue in an interview published in *Business Week*. Becker noted:

"It makes little sense to give Social Security benefits to the many elderly households with sizable earnings and assets. The budget deficit and the tax burden on workers would greatly ease, and poorer households could be treated better, if only poorer households . . . were eligible for Social Security income." Becker is not the only person making this radical suggestion. Investment banker and former commerce secretary Peter Peterson told *Time* magazine: "The idea of spending hundreds of billions of dollars on entitlements . . . to people who really don't need it, when we could take a much smaller amount and really help the poor and the children, is really an unforgivable way of allocating resources at a time like this." (in *Hunger Action Forum* 1990: 1)

Katy Butler, in a June 1989 article in *Mother Jones* laments that she and other baby boomers have become "the first downwardly mobile generation since World War II." She suggests that younger people learn from the elderly, who organized into the powerful AARP, and lobby for more benefits for *their* generation—like the Earned Income Tax Credit, an income-support program for poor working families that Congress expanded in 1986. Butler notes that today, "the over-50 age group has a higher after-tax income per capita than the under-50 age group." And she adds: "On the last night of a [recent] visit with my parents, we all went to the movies. My mother and father got a senior-citizens' discount" (in *San Antonio Light* 1989a: 16). Large benefits to wealthy beneficiaries will be less politically defensible if other groups register their discontent; thus equity values might fade. This development is already occurring, as Lubove (1986: 180) observes: "Although the system has always been weighted in favor of lower-paid workers, the 'reforms' of 1977 and 1983 drastically increased the redistributionist and welfare component."

If the shift to means testing continues, however, there are important implications for old-age insurance. First, this will leave a vacuum in the provision of pensions for those whose incomes are higher. Given that private pension funds provide a pool of capital for private business and industry to invest, these private plans may fill the void left by Social Security. In the context of troublesome reserves, the SSA and Congress would welcome such relief. This development could grant private providers much political leverage.

Congress could also alter regulations pertaining to individual retirement accounts to encourage those who are able to provide for their own retirement. There is support for such a move. A recent study reported:

The U.S. savings rate fell sharply after Congress slashed tax deductions for individual retirement accounts. . . . [Senator Lloyd Bentsen (D-Texas)] called for restoring partial tax deductions on contributions to IRAs instead of cutting the capital gains tax. . . . "Now, if we're going to be less dependent on foreign investment and foreign loaning of money to us, then we have to increase the savings rate in this country. . . . [After the tax deductions regarding IRAs were changed in 1986] savings rates dropped substantially in this country—and they were already low. . . . IRAs generate savings which otherwise would not occur." (*San Antonio Light* 1989b: B7)

The second implication of means testing of old-age insurance, and an adverse effect of such a policy shift, would be that if the better off among us are taken care of by private initiatives, important political support for the program will be eroded. Members of the upper and middle classes, and interest groups representing them, must be attended to with regard to their positions on old-age insurance.

Many contemporary scholars of the Social Security program note the massive power of elderly advocate groups such as the AARP and the NCSC. The AARP is the largest citizens' lobby group in the United States. A large part of its success is that it acts as one homogeneous group. In truth, however, the elderly constitute an incredibly diverse group—with differences not only in physiological health but also in life experiences determined by social class, race, sex, religion, and ethnicity. Elderly advocate groups do not generally emphasize this heterogeneity when discussing Social Security.

One generalization that we can make, however, is that, as a group, the elderly are better off economically than they ever have been. Social Security is *the* most successful antipoverty program in the United States (Skocpol 1992)—though it must be acknowl-

TABLE 13

Poverty Rates Among Children, the Elderly, and the General Population, 1990

Category	Pct.
Total population poor	12.8
Age 65 and over poor	11.4
Children under 18 poor	19.6
Anglo children under 18 poor	15.1
Black children under 18 poor	44.2
Hispanic children under 18 poor	39.7
Whites	10.7
Blacks	31.9
Hispanics	28.1
White female householder, no husband present	28.1
White female householder with related children < 18	37.8
Whites, living alone, 65+	18.8
Black female householder, no husband present	49.4
Black female householder with related children < 18	56.1
Blacks, living alone, 65+	57.3
Hispanic female householder, no husband present	50.6
Hispanic female householder with related children < 18	58.4
Hispanics, living alone, 65+	39.4

SOURCES: U.S. Bureau of the Census, Current Population Reports, Series P-60, 175 and earlier reports. Numbers using household as a variable taken from CPS Reports, Series 169-RD, Measuring the Effect of Benefits and Taxes on Income and Poverty: 1989, U.S. Government Printing Office, Washington, D.C., 1990: 38–45.

edged that elderly women and members of minority groups are at a high risk of slipping below the poverty line. The poverty rate for children, and especially black and Hispanic children, and female-headed households with children under eighteen years of age is sobering (see Table 13). Approximately one out of every five children in the United States lives a life of poverty, and close to half of all black children do. The issue here is one of allocation of scarce resources and notions of equity across generations, social classes, and racial boundaries.

The Social Security program grew out of the desperate conditions of the Great Depression, and was designed to alleviate the poverty and destitution brought by massive unemployment. With the expansion of old-age insurance during the 1950s and 1960s and the establishment of powerful lobbies on behalf of the elderly, we have been relatively successful in meeting the social welfare needs of this age group. Nevertheless, as the program now exists, there will be little equity between generations. The current needs-based welfare programs show this:

> More than 60 percent of welfare recipients are children, aged people, or disabled; most of the rest are mothers with young children, and less than 5 percent are able-bodied men, most of them unskilled workers in areas of high unemployment. . . . Myths abound: that welfare recipients are mostly black (nearly two-thirds are white); that they have many children (most have two or fewer); that they are on welfare indefinitely (most receive it for less than two years); and that welfare is a terrible burden on the taxpayer (welfare represents 2 percent of the federal budget). (Robertson 1987: 278)

The middle-aged cohort of taxpayers in the U.S. is in a precarious position, however. They have paid all their working lives into a program that may require taxes of 33 percent by 2030 to sustain their retirement. More importantly, there is almost no consciousness of this fact among baby boomers. And given that most of taxpaying workers have parents or other relatives who benefit directly from Social Security, the implications for families, of any sort of cutbacks in the program are obvious. Someone must meet the needs of the elderly. If Social Security does not exist, the void will need to be met by others, and these "others" are likely to be family members.

The term "sandwich generation" is sometimes used to capture the demands on the middle-aged to care simultaneously for both their young children and aging parents; but to suggest that there is an intergenerational battle is not appropriate. Everyone ages, and since most of us have other family members, it seems unlikely, at least within families, that there would be huge disagreements about Social Security. As Schneider, a political analyst with the American Enterprise Institute, notes, another reason AARP, and the senior lobby as a whole, is so powerful is that most Americans do not look upon older people as just another special interest group: "The elderly are not seen as a special interest because everyone expects to get old. . . . It's impossible to get people of working age to oppose benefits for people of retirement age" (cited in Benac 1989a: J10). Clearly, one's perceptions of self-interest have some part here.

In *When the Bough Breaks: The Cost of Neglecting Our Children,* author Sylvia Ann Hewlett asks:

Why do we find it easy to ration measles vaccine for eight-month-olds but impossible to ration triple bypass surgery for eighty-year-olds? The core reasons center on self-interest. While we cannot recapture our own child-hoods, all of us anticipate being old someday. At some level we all perceive programs and benefits for the elderly as *mechanisms through which we trans-fer resources to ourselves in the future.* The logic is as follows: If we create these programs and give them our uncluttered political support, the odds are they will be there to feather our own retirement nests. There are, in fact, three types of self-interest behind our generosity to the elderly: the swelling ranks of the elderly themselves; working-age people who "vote" to subsidize older people rather than assume direct responsibility for their own elderly parents; and working-age people who "vote" on behalf of themselves in the future. (1991: 148–49)

Hewlett powerfully and persuasively points out the myriad socio-economic costs of our current course in not attending to chil-dren's welfare. Calculated self-interest is not behind every change in social welfare legislation, but we should attend to such dynamics nonetheless.

Thus we see that incentives to organize for future generations— our children—are lessened in several ways. First, as a particularly individualistic society historically, many Americans believe that the family should be a separate institution, protected from outsider or governmental meddling. At worst, this means that middle- or upper-class Americans are less concerned with the plight of all chil-dren, since their own families are "taken care of," both now and in the future. What we see historically is that often these debates are about social class and racial politics and the redistribution of income *across* different family units.

Second, there are very real time constraints faced by middle-aged cohorts in terms of political organizations, and children's welfare has not generally been defined as a vital national concern. Third, given the lack of long-term planning in the political arena, there are no incentives for politicians to tackle these tough issues. And finally, discussing welfare programs that *do* benefit children, Robert D. Reischauer argues that a key difference between the social welfare policy environment of the past and the contemporary situation lies in society's expectations concerning mothers' participation in the labor force. In the past, a benefit program that allowed mothers to remain at home with their children (AFDC) was "relatively uncontroversial because it conformed to the behavior pattern of the majority. By the 1980s this was no longer the case. Public opinion polls indicate that most Americans feel that it is both appropriate and desirable for mothers to work outside the home—a sentiment that reflects reality with a vengeance. . . . Hence the premise underlying the basic AFDC program has begun to diverge increasingly from the social norm. This has undoubtedly undermined public support for this program" (Reischauer 1989: 17).

If our society continues to neglect children's welfare issues such as hunger, lack of medical care, inadequate day care, and the accessibility and quality of education, then we must be willing to ask what are the long-term implications of a 20 percent poverty rate for children. Certainly, the issue of childhood poverty is linked to other social ills such as poor health, illiteracy, teen-age pregnancy, drug abuse, and juvenile delinquency.

Children cannot exercise a political voice as a generational group (Dahl 1989). Other age groups must lobby for their welfare; however, I reiterate that this is not an intergenerational issue but a battle over social priorities and resource expenditures. The important question for the future of children's welfare then becomes, what strategies or policies will work? I suggest that several factors will be central to success: organizations and coalitions, education on these issues, an informed national debate, and voting and funding. These are all essential components in the process of finding politically viable solutions to these problems.

ORGANIZATIONS AND COALITIONS

First, it is clear that in contemporary society, organizations and coalitions of organizations are often the vehicles of social change. Advocates for taxpayers in Washington, D.C., argue that we need an organization of "Future Senior Citizens." Even groups such as the AARP that typically advocate for the elderly are concerned about their grandchildren's futures and the world they will inhabit. A 1992 *New York Times* article reported:

Critics of Social Security and Medicare have long charged that as older adults get more, children get less. The accusation has promoted the belief that seniors are "greedy geezers" while the nation's children are ever more deprived. But now the seniors are fighting to restore their image by helping the kids. . . . The new president of the 33-million-member American Association of Retired Persons listed "intergenerational action" as her top priority when she got the job a few months ago. Just recently the AARP said it was teaming up with the nationwide Coalition for America's Children to promote issues like health care and education for youngsters. (*NYT* 1992)

Women's involvement will also be crucial to promoting changes in the area of social welfare. The social policies instituted in the New Deal and intervening years have generated new constituencies and bureaucracies, many of them explicitly oriented toward the needs and values of women and children (Piven and Cloward 1982). Women's increasing employment in the paid labor force is positively correlated with their role in instrumental organizations such as business and labor unions (Klobus-Edwards, Edwards, and Watts 1984). More women are being elected to local, state, and federal government positions. Nevertheless, the question remains—does the movement of women into these various arenas suggest that, as a group, women will alter social structures or social policies?

In an analysis of state-level data regarding the number of domestic relations legislative components, Patricia Murphy (1991) found that the number of women legislators in the states was positively related to policies favoring women's interests. These women's party affiliations did not matter; women legislators apparently relate to certain social policies in a manner different from men. Children's welfare might be just such an issue.

With regard to coalitions and social welfare policies specifically, Peter Baldwin (1990) notes that political solidarity emerges when there are cross-class coalitions of "risk communities" (that is, groups share similar relations to the means of security, and the redistributive implications of social welfare policies are held to a minimum). Indeed, the term welfare is highly stigmatized today, and welfare policies create serious value conflicts. On the other hand, however, "Broader strategies may be far more likely to garner long-term public support. Programs like Social Security have been very successful in reducing poverty among the elderly precisely because some redistribution was embedded in a broader program which aided the middle class" (Ellwood 1989: 279). Theda Skocpol's most recent work (1992) makes similar points: policies must meet the needs of both the middle class and the poor, and social welfare policies must be linked to socially valued contributions to the broader social community.

Both cross-generation and cross-class coalitions of organizations will be needed to facilitate sociopolitical changes in Social Security. A variety of studies of collective decision making at the local and national levels find extensive coalition-formation efforts, suggesting that networks of organizational actors and exchange are significant factors shaping the processes and outcomes of contemporary politics (Galaskiewicz 1979; Heclo 1978; Knoke 1983, 1986: 17; Knoke and Laumann 1983). It will require the massive, persistent organization of interested groups to retain or alter policies related to children's welfare. This will be best accomplished by pooling the resources, energy, and commitment of various groups.

EDUCATION

The musician Paul Simon has committed a great deal of money to financing medical clinics that specialize in children's medical needs in high-demand areas. Simon explains that potentially, there are a number of worthy causes for him to support, but he chose children's welfare because he knew it would be easy to get others excited about it too. Certainly we cannot blame poverty-stricken children for their predicament.

The government and popular media could do a better job of informing the American public about the future of Social Security and children's welfare needs. True democratic politics is founded on an educated public. There must be broader education on the dynamics of old-age insurance and social welfare policies more generally. In an increasingly zero-sum context, difficult choices will have to be made. Representative Bill Archer (R-Texas), discussing the 1983 amendments, drew a historical parallel: "In 1784 Samuel Adams, speaking on a major national issue said, and I quote, 'The necessity of the times demands our utmost circumspection, deliberation, and fortitude, for we must seriously consider that millions yet unborn may be miserable sharers in this event today.' I believe the impact of social security is our Nation's Number 1 economic problem in the long term" (*CR* 1983: H978).

AN INFORMED NATIONAL DEBATE

Means testing of old-age insurance and intergenerational equity will be key concerns in the decades ahead. Using the past as our guide, there are two possible strategies that we could use to make the tough decisions surrounding Social Security reform or "dedistribution" (Light 1985: 4). On the one hand, we could use Roosevelt's early model of setting up the Committee on Economic Security, or, as Carter and Reagan did, we could establish bipartisan commissions to facilitate action. Proponents of this strategy argue that Social Security policymaking is highly complicated and politically volatile, so much so, that truly broad-based democratic politics must be put aside.

Though congressional sunshine has many advantages—more accountability, less hidden influence, fewer abuses of power, more access for the unrepresented—it also brings problems, particularly on dedistributive issues. Leadership is clearly more difficult in an open congressional system . . . negotiating gangs may well become the standard device for resolving party differences outside the public spotlight. This may be the era of gangs in government. With the public and interest groups firmly opposed to most of the major options on the dedistributive agenda, Congress and the President are well advised to build pre-negotiated packages outside the constitutional system, returning to the normal process only at the last moment. (Light 1985: 234)

This orientation stems in part from concern regarding the proliferation of narrowly focused interest groups, which often thwart our liberal democracy (Olson 1982; Thurow 1980).

I believe that the strategy of removing Social Security reform from the public "sunshine" is too cynical a view of the capacities of the American public. It is true that there is a great deal of misunderstanding about old-age insurance; how else can one explain the popularity of the ideas about equity and entitlement, for a program that will pay out relatively more to those who joined early as opposed to those who joined later? Social Security is complicated, but the American public is capable of becoming educated about the broad outlines of important issues for the future. In addition, far more than in the past, the technological potential exists for widespread, accessible media coverage of these issues. An informed national debate means that we must have the basic facts straight about where we have been and where we might be going.

An *informed* national debate on these issues would allow people to exercise their vote wisely and plan for their futures. Politicians would have the protection of knowing what broad-based public opinion was, in order to develop policies supported by the public that are attuned to the longer term. Politics *could* be injected with more long-term planning, but as Nelson Polsby notes, controversy is necessary for an issue to become important enough to be the focus of our energies or research (1984: 155). Certainly, there will be no shortage of controversy on these issues. To assume that the American public is incapable of understanding some essential facts about the future of old-age insurance, and to assume that small gangs of Washington insiders know what is best for the future, is pessimistic at best, and arrogant at worst.

VOTING AND FUNDING

There are organizational and political dynamics suggested in this volume that might compromise the inclusiveness or outcomes of such a national debate, and children are noteworthy examples of political disenfranchisement. However, in a persuasively written account of "why Americans don't vote," Frances Fox Piven and Richard A. Cloward (1988) make three relevant points: (1) most people who register to vote, *do* vote; (2) registered voters are unrepresentative of the general population, and the resulting low voting rates are largely the result of historic exclusionary voter registration systems established at the end of the nineteenth century; (3) voting does make a difference in political outcomes. Piven and Cloward argue that if currently excluded political groups were to exercise their political muscle, our current social policies and priorities would reflect their input. They argue that Congress does pay attention to voter sentiment (e.g., the counting of telephone calls and mail in favor of or opposed to various proposed policies), and acts accordingly.

Finally, although the argument I put forth in this volume speaks to the power of various noneconomic factors in facilitating political change (i.e., money is not the golden panacea), funding the programs that we know are effective is vital to our future well-being as a nation. Marian Wright Edelman, founder of the Children's Defense Fund, writes of the importance of funding:

The Children's Defense Fund was conceived in the cauldron of Mississippi's summer project of 1964 and in the Head Start battles of 1965, where both the great need for and limits of local action were apparent. As a private civil rights lawyer, I learned that I could have only limited, albeit important, impact on meeting epidemic family and child needs in that poor state without coherent national policy and investment strategies to complement community empowerment strategies. I also learned that critical civil and political rights would not mean much to a hungry, homeless, illiterate child and family if they lacked the social and economic means to exercise them. (1992: 11)

In 1991, the National Conference of Catholic Bishops' Pastoral Letter noted: "The most important work to help our children is done quietly—in our homes and neighborhoods, our parishes and community organizations. No government can love a child and no policy can substitute for a family's care, but clearly families can be helped or hurt in their irreplaceable roles. Government can either support or undermine families as they cope with the moral, social, and economic stresses of caring for children" (in Edelman 1992: 80).

For those critics who argue that government involvement is detrimental to encouraging economic independence, Edelman reminds us:

Throughout our history, we have given government help to our people and then have forgotten that fact when it came time to celebrate our people's achievements. Two hundred years ago, Congress granted federal lands to the states to help maintain public schools. In 1862, President Lincoln signed the Morrill Land-Grant Act, granting land for colleges. The first food voucher and energy assistance programs came, not during the New Deal or the War on Poverty, but at the end of the Civil War, when Congress and President Lincoln created the Freedman's Bureau. Federal help for vaccinations, vocational education, and maternal health began, not with Kennedy, Johnson, and Carter, but under Madison, Wilson, and Harding, respectively. (1992: 90)

Part of the dilemma in providing funding for children's welfare programs is that many welfare benefits must first pass through the hands of their parents. If some do not wish to condone the "bad behavior" of poor children's parents (for example, their mothers not working in the paid labor force), then certainly programs can be supported that benefit children directly. Head Start, the school lunch program, and quality day care are a few such examples.

Once we find programs such as Head Start that make a large difference in children's lives in the long run—and as such are highly cost-effective (Ellwood 1989: 288)—we must fund these programs in such a way that they are available to all who qualify. This sort of program provides substantial assistance to the low-income working population, while increasing the incentive of welfare recipients to enter the workforce (Reischauer 1989: 40). For precisely these reasons, this type of program is most likely to attract a broad base of political support.

In order to address concerns regarding children's welfare and our country's future, perhaps enfranchised groups—adult voters—will choose to represent children's issues. There is moral injustice in our current course of society-wide child neglect, as well as serious socioeconomic costs associated with this neglect. Organizations such as the Children's Defense Fund are important political voices for children's interests, but meeting or not meeting children's needs involves issues that eventually affect each and every one of us.

Reference Matter

Bibliography

Abshire, D. M., and R. D. Nurnberger, eds. 1981. *The Growing Power of Congress*. New York: Sage.

AFLA. American Federation of Labor Archives. 1934. American Federation of Labor Annual Meeting Proceedings.

———. American Federation of Labor Archives. 1935. American Federation of Labor Annual Meeting Proceedings.

———. American Federation of Labor Archives. 1940. American Federation of Labor Annual Meeting Proceedings.

———. American Federation of Labor Archives. 1948. AFL-CIO Annual Meeting Proceedings.

———. American Federation of Labor Archives. 1950. AFL-CIO Annual Meeting Proceedings.

———. American Federation of Labor Archives. 1971. AFL-CIO Annual Meeting Proceedings.

———. American Federation of Labor Archives. 1983. AFL-CIO Annual Meeting Proceedings.

Albjerg, Victor L. 1952. "Political Realignments." *Current History* 23, no. 134 (Oct.): 239–45.

ALC. American Life Convention. 1935. Proceedings of the Thirteenth Annual Meeting of the American Life Convention, Chicago.

Altmeyer, Arthur J. 1937. "Statistical Requirements of the Social Security Board for Efficient Administration." *Journal of the American Statistical Association* 32 (Mar.): 15–18.

———. 1966. *The Formative Years of Social Security*. Madison: University of Wisconsin Press.

Amenta, Edwin, and Sunita Parikh. 1991. "Capitalists Did Not Want the Social Security Act: A Critique of the 'Capitalist Dominance' Thesis." *American Sociological Review* 56: 124–29.

Amenta, Edwin, and Theda Skocpol. 1988. "Redefining the New Deal: World War II and the Development of Social Provision in the United States." In M. Weir, A. Orloff, and T. Skocpol, eds., *The Politics of Social Policy in the United States*, pp. 81–122. Princeton, N.J.: Princeton University Press.

American Association of Retired Persons (AARP). 1986. "Aging America: Trends and Projections." Washington, D.C.: U.S. Congress Senate Special Committee on Aging, AARP, Federal Council on Aging, and Administration on Aging.

Ashworth, Donna. 1936. "The New Deal as I See It." *Current History* 44 (Apr.): 41–43.

Baldwin, Peter. 1990. *The Politics of Social Solidarity: Class Bases of the European Welfare State, 1875–1975.* Cambridge: Cambridge University Press.

Beard, Charles and Mary. 1939. *The Rise of American Civilization.* Vol. 3, *America in Midpassage.* New York: Macmillan.

Becker, Gary. 1983. "A Theory of Competition Among Pressure Groups for Political Influence." *Quarterly Journal of Economics* 98, no. 3: 371–400.

Beito, David T. 1989. *Taxpayers in Revolt: Tax Resistance During the Great Depression.* Chapel Hill: University of North Carolina Press.

Benac, Nancy. 1989a. "AARP Grew from an Idea for Insurance to the 2nd Largest Non-profit Organization." *San Antonio Light*, Sept. 17: J10.

———. 1989b. "Proposal Allowing Full Benefits to Child-care Workers Blasted." *San Antonio Light*, Sept. 17: A7.

Berkowitz, Edward D. 1991. *America's Welfare State: From Roosevelt to Reagan.* Baltimore: Johns Hopkins University Press.

Block, Fred. 1977. "The Ruling Class Does Not Rule: Notes on the Marxist Theory of the State." *Socialist Revolution* 7: 6–28.

———. 1987. *Revising State Theory.* Philadelphia: Temple University Press.

Block, Fred, Richard A. Cloward, Barbara Ehrenreich, and Frances Fox Piven. 1987. *The Mean Season: The Attack on The Welfare State.* New York: Pantheon.

Boskin, Michael J., ed. 1978. *The Crisis in Social Security: Problems and Prospects.* San Francisco: Institute for Contemporary Studies.

Brinkley, Alan. 1982. *Voices of Protest: Huey Long, Father Coughlin, and the Great Depression.* New York: Alfred A. Knopf.

Brittain, John A. 1971. "The Incidence of Social Security Payroll Taxes." *American Economic Review* Mar.: 110–25.

Brock, Horace W. 1982. "Social Security Inequity." *New York Times*, Aug. 30: 17.

Brunsson, Nils. 1985. *The Irrational Organization: Irrationality as a Basis for Organizational Action and Change.* New York: John Wiley & Sons.

Burawoy, Michael. 1990. "Marxism as Science: Historical Challenges and Theoretical Growth." *American Sociological Review* 55: 775–93.

Burch, Philip. 1973. "The NAM as an Interest Group." *Politics and Society* 4: 97–130.

Burns, Eveline M. 1936. "Financial Aspects of the Social Security Act." *American Economic Review* 26: 12–22.

Burstein, Paul. 1985. *Discrimination, Jobs, and Politics: The Struggle for Equal Employment Opportunity in the United States Since the New Deal.* Chicago: University of Chicago Press.

Caporaso, James A., ed. 1989. *The Elusive State: International and Comparative Perspectives.* New York: Sage.

Cates, Jerry. 1983. *Insuring Inequality: Administrative Leadership in Social Security, 1935–54.* Ann Arbor: University of Michigan Press.

Clague, E. 1937. "Statistical and Economic Problems in the Administration of Social Security." *American Statistical Association Journal* 32: 509–16.

Cohen, Wilbur J. 1957. *Retirement Policies Under Social Security: A Legislative History of Retirement Ages, the Retirement Test, and Disability Benefits.* Berkeley: University of California Press.

———. 1963. "Medical Care for the Aged." *Current History* 45 (Aug.): 118–19.

Conkin, Paul K. 1967. *FDR and the Origins of the Welfare State.* New York: Thomas Y. Crowell.

Connolly, W. E. 1969. *The Bias of Pluralism.* New York: Atherton.

CQA. 1972. *Congressional Quarterly Almanac.* Washington, D.C.: Congressional Quarterly Service.

———. 1983. *Congressional Quarterly Almanac.* Washington, D.C.: Congressional Quarterly Service.

CR. 1935. *Congressional Record,* vol. 79, 74th Cong., 1st sess. Washington, D.C.: GPO.

———. 1946. *Congressional Record,* vol. 119, 79th Cong., 1st sess. Washington, D.C.: GPO.

———. 1949. *Congressional Record,* vol. 177, 81st Cong., 1st sess. Washington, D.C.: GPO.

———. 1972. *Congressional Record,* vol. 118, 92d Cong., 2d sess. Washington, D.C.: GPO.

———. 1977. *Congressional Record,* vol. 123, 95th Cong., 2d sess. Washington, D.C.: GPO.

———. 1983. *Congressional Record,* vol. 129, 98th Cong., 2d sess. Washington, D.C.: GPO.

Cutright, Phillips. 1965. "Political Structure, Economic Development, and National Social Security Programs." *American Journal of Sociology* 70: 537–50.

Cyert, Richard M., and James G. March. 1963. *A Behavioral Theory of the Firm*. Englewood Cliffs, N.J.: Prentice-Hall.

Dahl, Robert. 1967. *Pluralist Democracy in the United States: Conflict and Consent*. Chicago: Rand McNally.

———. 1982. *Dilemmas of Pluralist Democracy: Autonomy vs. Control*. New Haven, Conn.: Yale University Press.

———. 1989. *Democracy and Its Critics*. New Haven, Conn.: Yale University Press.

Dain Bosworth, Inc. 1990. "Pension Plans Mean Choices for Baby Boomers." Company Newsletter, vol. 1, issue 4 (Jan.): 1.

David, Paul A. 1985. "Ciio and the Economics of QWERTY." *Economic History*, May: 332–37.

DeParle, Jason. 1993. "Complexity of a Fiscal Giant: A Primer on Social Security." *New York Times*, Feb. 11: A1 and A17.

Derthick, Martha. 1979. *Policymaking for Social Security*. Washington, D.C.: Brookings Institution.

———. 1990. *Agency Under Stress: The Social Security Administration in American Government*. Washington, D.C.: Brookings Institution.

Devine, Joel A. 1985. "State and State Expenditure." *American Sociological Review* 50: 150–65.

Dilley, Mary. 1938. "Social, Political, Economic, and Financial Implications of the Administration of the Old Age Reserve Account of the Social Security Act of 1935." Unpublished M.A. thesis, University of Arizona.

DiMaggio, Paul J., and Walter W. Powell. 1983. "The Iron Cage Revisited: Institutional Isomorphism and Collective Rationality in Organizational Fields." *American Sociological Review* 48: 147–60.

Domhoff, G. William. 1990. *The Power Elite and the State*. New York: Aldine de Gruyter.

Dore, Ronald P. 1973. *British Factory, Japanese Factory: The Origins of National Diversity in Industrial Relations*. Berkeley: University of California Press.

Edelman, Marian Wright. 1992. *The Measure of Our Success: A Letter to My Children and Yours*. Boston: Beacon Press.

Ellwood, David T. 1989. "Conclusion." *Welfare Policies for the 1990s*. Cambridge, Mass.: Harvard University Press.

Epstein, Abraham. 1933. "Experience Under State Old Age Pension Laws in 1932." *Monthly Labor Review* 37: 251–61.

———. 1935. "Social Security Under the New Deal." *Nation* 141: 261–63.

————. 1936. *Insecurity: A Challenge to America.* New York: Random House.

————. 1937. "Future Social Security: Needed Amendments." *New Republic* 89: 373–76.

Esping-Andersen, Gosta. 1978. "Social Class, Social Democracy, and the State: Party Policy and Party Decomposition in Denmark and Sweden." *Comparative Politics* 11: 42–58.

————. 1985. *Politics Against Markets: The Social Democratic Road to Power.* Princeton, N.J.: Princeton University Press.

————. 1990. *The Three Worlds of Welfare Capitalism.* Princeton, N.J.: Princeton University Press.

Evans, Peter, Dietrich Rueschemeyer, and Theda Skocpol. 1985. "On the Road to a More Adequate Understanding of the State." In Evans, Rueschemeyer, and Skocpol, eds., *Bringing the State Back In*, pp. 347–66. New York: Cambridge University Press.

Ferejohn, John A. 1974. *Pork Barrel Politics: Rivers and Harbors Legislation, 1947–1968.* Stanford, Calif.: Stanford University Press.

Ferrara, Peter J. 1980. *Social Security: The Inherent Contradiction.* San Francisco: Cato Institute.

Finegold, Kenneth, and Theda Skocpol. 1984. "State, Party, and Industry: From Business Recovery to the Wagner Act in America's New Deal." In Charles C. Bright and Susan F. Harding, eds., *Statemaking and Social Movements: Essays in History and Theory*, pp. 159–92. Ann Arbor: University of Michigan Press.

Fligstein, Neil. 1991. "The Structural Transformation of American Industry: An Institutional Account of the Causes of Diversification in the Largest Firms, 1919–79." In Walter W. Powell and Paul J. DiMaggio, eds., *The New Institutionalism in Organizational Analysis*, pp. 311–36. Chicago: University of Chicago Press.

Fligstein, Neil, and Doug McAdam. n.d. "A Political-Cultural Approach to the Problem of Strategic Action." Unpublished paper.

Folsom, Marion B. 1936. "Social Security Laws and Administration." *American Labor Legislation Review* 26: 165–73.

Gable, R. W. 1953. "NAM: Influential Lobby or Kiss of Death?" *Journal of Politics* 15: 254–73.

Galaskiewicz, J. 1979. "The Structure of Community Interorganizational Networks." *Social Forces* 57: 1346–64.

Gamson, William A. 1975. *The Strategy of Social Protest.* Homewood, Ill.: Dorsey.

Gold, David, Clarence Lo, and Erik Wright. 1975. "Recent Developments in Marxist Theories of the Capitalist State." *Monthly Review* 27: 29–43.

Gollin, James. 1981. *The Star-Spangled Retirement Dream.* New York: Scribner's.

Graebner, Norman A. 1956. "The Changing Nature of the Democratic Party." *Current History* 31, no. 180 (Aug.): 71.

———. 1960. "Eisenhower's Popular Leadership." *Current History* 39, no. 227 (July): 232.

Graebner, William. 1980. *A History of Retirement: The Meaning and Function of an American Institution, 1885–1978.* New Haven, Conn.: Yale University Press.

Gratton, Brian. 1986. *Urban Elders: Family, Work, and Welfare Among Boston's Aged, 1890–1950.* Philadelphia: Temple University Press.

Gruber, Katherine, ed. 1987. *Encyclopedia of Associations.* 21st ed. Vol. 1, parts 1–2. Detroit: Gale Research, Inc.

Haines, Herbert H. 1984. "Black Radicalization and the Funding of Civil Rights: 1957–1970." *Social Problems* 32: 31–43.

Hammond, Mary K. 1953. "The 1952 Election." *Current History* 24, no. 137 (Jan.): 26–31.

Heclo, Hugh. 1978. "Issue Networks and the Executive Establishment." In Anthony King, ed., *The New American Political System,* pp. 87–124. Washington, D.C.: American Enterprise Institute.

Hendricks, David. 1992. *San Antonio Express-News,* Apr. 1: 1-B.

Hewlett, Sylvia Ann. 1991. *When the Bough Breaks: The Cost of Neglecting Our Children.* New York: Basic Books.

Higley, John, Michael G. Burton, and G. Lowell Field. 1990. "In Defense of Elite Theory: A Reply to Cammack." *American Sociological Review* 55: 421–26.

Hooks, Gregory. 1993. "The Weakness of Strong Theories: The U.S. State's Dominance of the World War II Investment Process." *American Sociological Review* 58: 37–53.

House Document no. 92–80. 1971. "Report of the 1971 Advisory Council on Social Security," 92 (1).

Hunger Action Forum. 1990. Vol. 3, no. 7 (Aug.): 1.

HWMCH. 1946. *House Ways and Means Committee Hearings.* "Social Security." Washington, D.C.: GPO.

———. 1950. *House Ways and Means Committee Hearings.* "Social Security Revision." Washington, D.C.: GPO.

———. 1970. *House Ways and Means Committee Hearings.* "Social Security and Welfare Proposals." Washington, D.C.: GPO.

———. 1973. *House Ways and Means Committee Hearings.* "Payments to Social Security Trust Funds." Washington, D.C.: GPO.

———. 1976a. *House Ways and Means Committee Hearings.* "Background

Material on Social Security Coverage of Governmental Employees."
Washington, D.C.: GPO.

———. 1976b. *House Ways and Means Committee Hearings.* "Decoupling the Social Security Benefit Structure." Washington, D.C.: GPO.

———. 1977. *House Ways and Means Committee Hearings.* "Social Security Benefits for Students." Washington, D.C.: GPO.

Jones, Landon Y. 1980. *Great Expectations: America and the Baby Boom Generation.* New York: Coward, McCann & Geogehegan.

Katz, Michael B. 1986. *In the Shadow of the Poorhouse: A Social History of Welfare in America.* New York: Basic Books.

Kaufman, Herbert. 1981. *The Administrative Behavior of Federal Bureau Chiefs.* Washington, D.C.: Brookings Institution.

Kearl, Michael C., Crista Moore, and J. Scott Osberg. 1982. "Political Implications of the 'New Ageism.' " *International Journal of Aging and Human Development* 15, no. 3: 167–83.

Keynes, John Maynard. 1936. *General Theory of Employment, Interest, and Money.* New York: Harcourt, Brace.

Kingdon, John W. 1981. *Congressmen's Voting Decisions.* 2d ed. New York: Harper & Row.

———. 1984. *Agendas, Alternatives, and Public Policies.* Boston: Little, Brown.

Klobus-Edwards, P., J. N. Edwards, and A. D. Watts. 1984. Women, Work, and Social Participation. *Journal of Voluntary Action Research* 13: 7–22.

Knoke, David. 1983. "Organization Sponsorship and Influence Reputation of Social Influence Associations." *Social Forces* 61: 1065–87.

———. 1986. "Associations and Interest Groups." In *Annual Review of Sociology* 12:1–21. Palo Alto, Calif.: Annual Reviews, Inc.

———. 1988. "Incentives in Collective Action Organizations." *American Sociological Review* 53: 311–29.

Knoke, David, and Edward O. Laumann. 1983. "Issue Publics in National Policy Domains." Presented at the Annual Meeting of the American Sociological Association, Toronto, Canada, August.

Korpi, Walter. 1983. *The Democratic Class Struggle.* London: Routledge & Kegan Paul.

Latimer, Murray Webb. 1929. "Old Age Pensions in America." *American Labor Legislation Review* 19: 55–66.

Latimer, Murray Webb, and Karl Tuffel. 1940. *Trends in Industrial Pensions.* New York: Industrial Relations Counselors, Inc.

Laumann, Edward O., and David Knoke. 1987. *The Organizational State: Social Choice in National Policy Domains.* Madison: University of Wisconsin Press.

Light, Paul. 1985. *Artful Work: The Politics of Social Security Reform.* New York: Random House.

Lindblom, Charles E. 1959. "The Science of Muddling Through." *Public Administration Review* 19: 78–88.

———. 1980. *The Policy-Making Process.* 2d ed. Englewood Cliffs, N.J.: Prentice-Hall.

Lipset, Seymour Martin, Martin Trow, and James Coleman. 1956. *Union Democracy: The Inside Politics of the International Typographical Union.* New York: Free Press.

Lopez, Edward A. 1987. "Constitutional Background to the Social Security Act of 1935." *Social Security Bulletin* 50, no. 1: 5–11.

Lubove, Roy. 1963. "The New Deal and National Health." *Current History* 45, no. 264 (Aug.): 77–82.

———. 1986. *The Struggle for Social Security, 1900–1935.* 2d ed. Pittsburgh: University of Pittsburgh Press.

McAdam, Doug. 1982. *Political Process and the Development of Black Insurgency, 1930–1970.* Chicago: University of Chicago Press.

McConnell, John W. 1956. *Economic Needs of Older People.* New York: Twentieth Century Fund.

McNutt, Paul V. 1940. "If the Republicans Win." *American Mercury,* Mar.: 271–72, File Folder, "USCC," Chairman's Files, 1935–42, Record Group 47, National Archives, Washington, D.C.

McQuaid, Kim, 1979. "The Frustration of Corporate Revival in the Early New Deal." *The Historian* 41: 682–704.

Macionis, John J., and Nijole V. Benokraitis, eds. 1989. *Seeing Ourselves: Classic, Contemporary, and Cross-Cultural Readings in Sociology.* Englewood Cliffs, N.J.: Prentice-Hall.

March, James G., and Johan P. Olsen. 1984. "The New Institutionalism: Organizational Factors in Political Life." *American Political Science Review* 78: 734–49.

———. 1989. *Rediscovering Institutions: The Organizational Basis of Politics.* New York: Free Press.

Mayhew, David R. 1986. *Placing Parties in American Politics: Organization, Electoral Settings, and Government Activity in the Twentieth Century.* Princeton, N.J.: Princeton University Press.

Meyer, John W., and Brian Rowan. 1977. "Institutionalized Organizations: Formal Structure as Myth and Ceremony." *American Journal of Sociology* 83: 340–63.

Meyer, John W., and W. Richard Scott. 1983. *Organizational Environments: Ritual and Rationality.* Beverly Hills, Calif.: Sage.

Meyers, R. J. 1937. "Effect of the Social Security Act on the Life Insurance Needs of Labor." *Journal of Political Economy* 45: 681–86.

Mitchell, Donald W. 1950. "The Risks of Cold War." *Current History* 19, no. 107 (July): 5–9.

Mitchell, William Lloyd. 1964. *Social Security in America*. Washington, D.C.: Robert B. Luce.

Moe, Terry M. 1988. "Interests, Institutions, and Positive Theory: The Politics of the NLRB." In Karen Orren and Stephen Skowronek, eds., *Studies in American Political Development*, vol. 2. New Haven, Conn.: Yale University Press.

Murphy, Patricia. 1991. *Women and Politics: Domestic Relations Legislative Components*. Unpublished dissertation, University of New Hampshire.

Murray, Charles A. 1984. *Losing Ground: American Social Policy, 1950–1980*. New York: Basic Books.

Nash, Gerald D., Noel J. Pugach, and Richard F. Tomasson, eds. 1988. *Social Security: The First Half-Century*. Albuquerque: University of New Mexico Press.

NYT. 1992. *New York Times*. "Seniors and Juniors," Sept. 30: A24.

O'Connor, James. 1973. *The Fiscal Crisis of the State*. New York: St. Martin's Press.

Olson, Mancur, Jr. 1965. *The Logic of Collective Action*. Cambridge, Mass.: Harvard University Press.

———. 1982. *The Rise and Decline of Nations*. New Haven, Conn.: Yale University Press.

Oriol, William E. 1987. *Federal Public Policy on Aging Since 1960: An Annotated Bibliography*. Westport, Conn.: Greenwood Press.

Orloff, Ann Shola. 1988. "The Political Origins of America's Belated Welfare State." In M. Weir, A. Orloff, and T. Skocpol, eds., *The Politics of Social Policy in the United States*, pp. 37–80. Princeton, N.J.: Princeton University Press.

Orloff, Ann Shola, and Theda Skocpol. 1984. "Why Not Equal Protection? Explaining the Politics of Public Social Spending in Britain, 1900–1911, and the United States, 1880s–1920." *American Sociological Review* 49: 726–50.

Peacock, A. R., and J. Wiseman. 1961. *The Growth of Public Expenditure in the United Kingdom*. Princeton, N.J.: Princeton University Press.

Pear, Robert. 1987. "Bowen Wants to End Social Security's Limit on Earnings." *Arizona Daily Star*, Nov. 29: 6.

Perkins, Frances. 1946. *The Roosevelt I Knew*. New York: Viking Press.

Perlik, William F. 1950. "Pensions in Collective Bargaining." *Yale Law Journal*, Mar.: 683.

Perrow, Charles. 1986. *Complex Organizations: A Critical Essay*. New York: Random House.

Pfeffer, Jeffrey, 1982. *Organizations and Organization Theory*. Boston: Pitman.

Pfeffer, Jeffrey, and Gerald R. Salancik. 1978. *The External Control of Organizations: A Resource Dependence Perspective*. New York: Harper & Row.

Piven, Frances Fox, and Richard A. Cloward. 1971. *Regulating the Poor: The Functions of Public Welfare*. New York: Vintage.

———. 1982. *The New Class War: Reagan's Attack on the Welfare State*. New York: Pantheon.

———. 1988. *Why Americans Don't Vote*. New York: Pantheon.

Polsby, Nelson W. 1984. *Political Innovation in America: The Politics of Policy Initiation*. New Haven, Conn.: Yale University Press.

———. 1986. *Congress and the Presidency*. 4th ed. Englewood Cliffs, N.J.: Prentice-Hall.

Poulantzas, Nicos. 1978. *State, Power, Socialism*. London: New Left Books.

Pratt, H. 1976. *The Gray Lobby*. Chicago: University of Chicago Press.

Quadagno, Jill S. 1984. "Welfare Capitalism and the Social Security Act of 1935." *American Sociological Review* 49: 632–47.

———. 1985. "From Old Age Assistance to Supplemental Security Income: The Political Economy of Relief in the South." Paper presented at the Center for the Study of Industrial Societies, Project on the Future Directions of Federal Social Policy, University of Chicago, February.

———. 1988. *The Transformation of Old Age Security: Class and Politics in the American Welfare State*. Chicago: University of Chicago Press.

Reischauer, Robert D. 1989. "The Welfare Reform Legislation: Directions for the Future." In Phoebe H. Cottingham and David T. Ellwood, eds., *Welfare Policy for the 1990s*, pp. 10–40. Cambridge, Mass.: Harvard University Press.

Ritzer, George. 1993. The McDonaldization of Society: An Investigation into the Changing Character of Contemporary Social Life. Newbury Park, N.J.: Pine Forge Press.

Robertson, Ian. 1987. *Sociology*. 3d ed. New York: Worth.

Rossi, Alice S. 1993. "Intergenerational Relations: Gender, Norms, and Behavior." In Vern L. Bengtson and W. Andrew Achenbaum, eds., *The Changing Contract Across Generations*, pp. 190–211. New York: Aldine de Gruyter.

Rukeyser, Louis, and John Cooney. 1988. " 'Big Picture' of Labor Market Shows Strong Signs of Old Age: Demographics Bring Full Weight to Bear on the America of the 80s and 90s." *San Antonio Light*, Sept. 11: D1–D5.

Salisbury, Robert H. 1969. "An Exchange Theory of Interest Groups." *Midwest Journal of Political Science* 8: 1–32.

———. 1978. "Key Concepts of Citizenship: Perspectives and Dilemmas," U.S. Department of Health, Education, and Welfare, Office of Education, HEW Publication no. (OE) 78-07005.

———. 1984. "Interest Representation: The Dominance of Institutions." *American Political Science Review* 78: 64–76.

Salisbury, Robert H., John P. Heinz, Edward O. Laumann, and Robert L. Nelson. 1987. "Who Works with Whom? Interest Group Alliances and Opposition." *American Political Science Review* 81: 1217–34.

San Antonio Light. 1989a. "Magazines: Youth Movement," Parade Magazine, May 28: 16.

———. 1989b. "Link Seen Between U.S. Savings Drop, Cuts in IRA Deductions," AP story, Sept. 17: B7.

———. 1989c. "Senior," Oct. 30: E4.

Sayre, Wallace. 1936. "Political Ground-Swell." *Current History*, June: 53–60.

Schlesinger, Arthur M., Jr. 1959. *The Age of Roosevelt*, vol. 2, *The Coming of the New Deal*. Boston: Houghton Mifflin.

———. 1960. *The Age of Roosevelt*, vol. 3, *The Politics of Upheaval*. Boston: Houghton Mifflin.

Sherrill, Robert. 1982. "American Demagogues," review of Alan Brinkley's *Voices of Protest. New York Times Book Review*, July 11: 13.

Skocpol, Theda. 1980. "Political Response to Capitalist Crisis: Neo-Marxist Theories of the State and the Case of the New Deal." *Politics and Society* 10, no. 2: 155–201.

———, ed. 1984. *Vision and Method in Historical Sociology*. Cambridge, Mass.: Cambridge University Press.

———. 1992. *Protecting Soldiers and Mothers: The Political Origins of Social Policy in the United States*. Cambridge, Mass.: Harvard University Press.

Skocpol, Theda, and Edwin Amenta. 1985. "Did Capitalists Shape Social Security?" *American Sociological Review* 50: 572–75.

———. 1986. "States and Social Policies." *Annual Review of Sociology* 12: 131–57. Palo Alto, Calif.: Annual Reviews, Inc.

Skocpol, Theda, and Kenneth Finegold. 1982. "State Capacity and Economic Intervention in the Early New Deal." *Political Science Quarterly* 97: 255–78.

Skocpol, Theda, and John Ikenberry. 1983. "The Political Formation of the American Welfare State in Historical and Comparative Perspective." *Comparative Social Research* 6: 87–148.

Slichter, Sumner. 1949. "The Pressing Problem of Old-Age Security." *New York Times Magazine,* Oct. 16: 9.

SSA. 1975. *Annual Report of the Social Security Administration,* Washington, D.C.

———. Social Security Administration. 1989. *Social Security Bulletin, Annual Statistical Supplement.*

Social Security Bulletin. 1971–85. Annual Statistical Supplement.

SSB. 1986. *Social Security Bulletin.* "Social Security Programs in the United States," vol. 49, no. 1 (Jan.).

Starr, Mark. 1959. "Union Welfare Funds." *Current History* 36, no. 214 (June): 338.

Steinberg, Ronnie. 1982. *Wages and Hours: Labor and Reform in Twentieth-Century America.* New Brunswick, N.J.: Rutgers University Press.

Terkel, Studs. 1974. *Working.* New York: Random House.

Thurow, Lester C. 1980. *The Zero-Sum Society.* New York: Basic Books.

Tilly, Charles. 1975. *The Formation of National States in Western Europe.* Princeton, N.J.: Princeton University Press.

———. 1981. *As Sociology Meets History.* New York: Academic Press.

Tocqueville, Alexis de. 1951. *Democracy in America,* vol. 2. Phillips Bradley, ed. New York: Alfred A. Knopf.

Torres-Gil, Fernando M. 1993. "Interest Group Politics: Generational Changes in the Politics of Aging." In Vern L. Bengtson and W. Andrew Achenbaum, eds., *The Changing Contract Across Generations,* pp. 239–57. New York: Aldine de Gruyter.

Tufte, Edward. 1978. *Political Control of the Economy.* Princeton, N.J.: Princeton University Press.

USBC (United States Bureau of the Census). 1975. *Historical Statistics of the United States, Colonial Times to 1970.* Part 2. U.S. Department of Commerce, Bureau of the Census.

Useem, Michael. 1979. "The Social Organization of the American Business Elite and Participation of Corporation Directors in the Governance of American Institutions." *American Sociological Review* 44: 553–72.

———. 1984. *The Inner Circle: Large Corporations and the Rise of Business Political Activity in the U.S. and U.K.* New York: Oxford University Press.

USNA. United States National Archives. File Folder "011-011.1" Chairman's Files, 1935–42. Record Group 47. Washington, D.C.

———. File Folder "032.11," Chairman's Files, 1935–42. Record Group 47. Washington, D.C.

———. File Folder "Advisory Council Meeting of November 5–6, 1937," Chairman's Files, 1935–42. Record Group 47. Washington, D.C.

————. File Folder "Advisory Council through 1937," Chairman's Files, 1935–42. Record Group 47. Washington, D.C.

————. File Folder "Advisory Council 1938," Chairman's Files, 1935–42. Record Group 47. Washington, D.C.

————. File Folder "AFL-1940," Chairman's Files, 1935–42. Record Group 47. Washington, D.C.

————. File Folder "Altmeyer-011," Chairman's Files, 1935–42. Record Group 47. Washington, D.C.

————. File Folder "Amendment of the Social Security Act," Senate Finance Committee Report, March 16, 1939, Chairman's Files, 1935–42. Record Group 47. Washington, D.C.

————. File Folder "Amendments 1937," Memo to President Roosevelt from Altmeyer, dated Sept. 11, 1937, Chairman's Files, 1935–42. Record Group 47. Washington, D.C.

————. File Folder "Amendments through May 1937," Chairman's Files, 1935–42. Record Group 47. Washington, D.C.

————. File Folder "Amendments 1938," Chairman's Files, 1935–42. Record Group 47. Washington, D.C.

————. File Folder "Amendments 1939," Chairman's Files, 1935–42. Record Group 47. Washington, D.C.

————. File Folder "Amendments—Discussion of Title II," Chairman's Files, 1935–42. Record Group 47. Washington, D.C.

————. File Folder "American Federation of Labor," Chairman's Files, 1935–42. Record Group 47. Washington, D.C.

————. File Folder "BAC to Department of Commerce Board," Social Security Central Files, Master Files, 1935–47, Washington, D.C.

————. File Folder "Business Advisory Council," letter from Huse to Bane, dated June 17, 1936, Chairman's Files, 1935–42. Record Group 47. Washington, D.C.

————. File Folder "Business Advisory Council Membership—1936," Associated Press article entitled "Roper Selects 18 Men to Fill Advisory Posts," Chairman's Files, 1935–42. Record Group 47. Washington, D.C.

————. File Folder "Committee Attention," Senate Finance Committee—SS (General; A-B). Record Group 43. Washington, D.C.

————. File Folder "Correspondence of Dr. Greenspan," Records of Temporary Committees, Commissions, and Boards (National Commission on Social Security Reform). Record Group 220. Washington, D.C.

————. File Folder "Correspondence with Commission Members, February 10–June 21, 1982," Records of Temporary Committees, Commissions, and Boards (National Commission on Social Security Reform). Record Group 220. Washington, D.C.

————. File Folder "Correspondence with Commission Members, July 6–November 5, 1982," Records of Temporary Committees, Commissions, and Boards (National Commission on Social Security Reform). Record Group 220. Washington, D.C.

————. File Folder "Democratic National Committee," Chairman's Files, 1935–42. Record Group 47. Washington, D.C.

————. File Folder "Doughton, Robert L." Chairman's Files, 1935–42. Record Group 47. Washington, D.C.

————. File Folder "General—No Response Correspondence to Robert J. Myers," Records of Temporary Committees, Commissions, and Boards (National Commission on Social Security Reform). Record Group 220. Washington, D.C.

————. File Folder "Insurance Industry-057.1," Central Files, Record Group 47. Washington, D.C.

————. File Folder "LaFollette, Robert M.," Chairman's Files, 1935–42. Record Group 47. Washington, D.C.

————. File Folder "Legislation Affecting SSA-OASI," Chairman's Files, 1935–42. Record Group 47. Washington, D.C.

————. File Folder "NAM," Chairman's Files, 1935–42. Record Group 47. Washington, D.C.

————. File Folder "NAM," 1981, Records of Temporary Committees, Commissions, and Boards (National Commission on Social Security Reform). Record Group 220. Washington, D.C.

————. File Folder "Non-profit Form Telegram," Senator Walter F. George's Files. Record Group 43. Washington, D.C.

————. File Folder "OASI Misc. (May, 1949)," Senator Walter F. George's Files. Record Group 43. Washington, D.C.

————. File Folder "OASI Misc.—April, 1950," Senate Finance Committee. Record Group 43. Washington, D.C.

————. File Folder "OASI Misc., June 1950," Senate Finance Committee. Record Group 43. Washington, D.C.

————. File Folder "OASI Misc.—June–August, 1950," Senate Finance Committee. Record Group 43. Washington, D.C.

————. File Folder "Old-Age Insurance," Chairman's Files, 1935–42. Record Group 47. Washington, D.C.

————. File Folder "Pat Harrison," Letter from Altmeyer to Harrison, dated March 15, 1939, Legislative Archives Division, Washington, D.C.

———. File Folder "Protest, Opposition, and Criticism," Chairman's Files, 1935–42. Record Group 47. Washington, D.C.

———. File Folder "Report on Recommended Changes," Chairman's Files, 1935–42. Record Group 47. Washington, D.C.

———. File Folder "Senate Finance Committee—SS (April, 1950)," Senator Walter F. George's Files. Record Group 43. Washington, D.C.

———. File Folder "Social Security Revision," Senate Finance Committee Hearing, (81)S931-4-A and (81)S932-5, Jan. 17–20, 1950, Senate Finance Committee. Record Group 43. Washington, D.C.

———. File Folder, "Special SS Files—Private Pension Plans," Senate Finance Committee. Record Group 43. Washington, D.C.

———. File Folder "SS—OASI Misc.," Senator Walter F. George's Files. Record Group 43. Washington, D.C.

———. File Folder "SS—OASI Misc. (April, 1949)," Robert L. Doughton's Files, Record Group 233. Washington, D.C.

———. File Folder "SS—OASI Misc. (May, 1949)," Senator Walter F. George's Files. Record Group 43. Washington, D.C.

———. File Folder "SS—OASI Misc. (Oct., 1949)," Senator Walter F. George's Files. Record Group 43. Washington, D.C.

———. File Folder "SS—OASI Misc. (Dec., 1949)," Senator Walter F. George's Files. Record Group 43. Washington, D.C.

———. File Folder "SS (Misc. May–June 1950)," Senator Walter F. George's Files. Record Group 43. Washington, D.C.

———. File Folder "SS—Misc. (October, 1950)," Senator Walter F. George's Files. Record Group 43. Washington, D.C.

———. File Folder "USCC," Chairman's Files, 1935–42. Record Group 47. Washington, D.C.

Walker, Jack L. 1983. "The Origins and Maintenance of Interest Groups in America." *American Political Science Review* 77: 390–406.

Warren, Sidney. 1955. "The Threat of Internal Communism." *Current History* 29, no. 170 (Oct.): 208.

Weaver, Carolyn L. 1982. *The Crisis in Social Security: Economic and Political Origins.* Durham, N.C.: Duke Press Policy Studies.

———, ed. 1990. *Social Security's Looming Surpluses: Prospects and Implications,* Washington, D.C.: American Enterprise Institute Press.

Weir, Margaret, Ann Shola Orloff, and Theda Skocpol. 1988. "Understanding American Social Politics," in Weir, Orloff, and Skocpol, eds., *The Politics of Social Policy in the United States,* pp. 3–27. Princeton, N.J.: Princeton University Press.

Werne, Benjamin. 1936. "Highlights of the Law." *Current History,* Dec.: 27–30.

Wiebe, Robert H. 1967. *The Search for Order: 1877–1920.* New York: Hill & Wang.

Wilensky, Harold. 1975. *The Welfare State and Equality: Structural and Ideological Roots of Public Expenditures.* Berkeley: University of California Press.

Willis, H. Parker. 1934. "Business on the Dole." *Current History,* Oct.: 1–8.

Wilson, James Q. 1973. *Political Organizations.* New York: Basic Books.

———. 1989. *Bureaucracy: What Government Agencies Do and Why They Do It.* New York: Basic Books.

Witte, Edwin E. 1962. *The Development of the Social Security Act.* Madison: University of Wisconsin Press.

WQ. 1986. *Women's Quarterly,* Autumn: 43.

Wright, G. 1974. "The Political Economy of New Deal Spending: An Econometric Analysis." *Review of Economic Statistics* 56: 30–38.

Index

In this index an "f" after a number indicates a separate reference on the next page, and an "ff" indicates separate references on the next two pages. A continuous discussion over two or more pages is indicated by a span of page numbers, e.g., "57–59." *Passim* is used for a cluster of references in close but not consecutive sequence.

Department of Labor, 53; Secretary
of Labor, 45f, 61
dependency ratios, in 1940, 89; in
the South, 107; low, 120, 195, 202;
alteration of by bringing in new
categories of workers, 133; stabilization of, 147; baby boomers and,
150ff, 205. *See also* Rossi, Alice
dependents of retired workers, 87
Depression, *see* Great Depression
Derthick, Martha, 6f, 59f, 114, 128,
148, 153, 155
De Tocqueville, Alexis, *see* Tocqueville, Alexis de
Detroit industrialists, 67
Dewson, Mary, 46, 71, 82
disability, benefits, 85, 117; insurance, 9, 97, 99f, 120–31 *passim*,
157; and means-testing for needy
disabled, 101; disability "freeze,"
118; recipients' dependents and
elimination of age-50 limitation,
119; disability compared with old
age and dependency, 125; for
Federal Civil Service retirees, 146
doctors, 116
Dole, Robert, 177
domestic anarchy feared in 1930s,
194
domestic problems and foreign
affairs, 88, 122
Domhoff, G. William, 13
double-dipping, 145f, 172
Doughton, Robert L., 51f, 82, 128
drug abuse, 212
Duncan, Richard, 51
DuPont, 57
Durenberger, David F., 150, 190
dynamic-wage assumption, *see* rising-
wage assumption

Earned Income Tax Credit, 207
earnings records, 138
Eastern Europe, 103

Eastman Kodak, 60
Eaton, Charles, 1, 55, 58
economic buffers in politics, 185
economic climate, non-zero-sum,
100
economic rationality, 101, 131
economic tipping point, 27, 133, 153
Edelman, Marian Wright, 217
Ehrlichman, John D., 137
Eisenhower, Dwight D., 117–19
elderly: poverty of, 3, 134f, 142, 147,
151; advocate groups, 135f, 139f,
147f, 162, 204, 208; encouraged
to work, 190, 204f; socioeconomic variation among, 190f,
208f; elderly voters, 192; elderly
child-care workers, 204; as "greedy
geezers," 213. *See also* poverty;
specific advocate groups' names
election-year timing, 31f, 99, 118,
154; avoidance of, 82, 157, 169,
195
elites, 35; and interests, 24
employers: employer organizations,
27; employer pension plans, 42,
109; campaign against reelection
of Roosevelt and Social Security,
67; employers' costs of payroll
tax passed on to consumer, 74f;
resistance to early Social Security
program, 79. *See also* business and
industry
End Poverty in Civilization, 49
Endicott Johnson Corporation, 56
energy assistance programs, 217
England, 20, 105
Enoff, Louis, 205
entitlement to benefits, 190f, 203,
215
entitlements, considerations to scale
back, 206
equity: across generations, 150, 190,
209f, 215; across racial boundaries
and social classes, 209, 215

106; high labor turnover, 109; excess profits tax, 110; wage credits for veterans, 131, 157, 176, 183; Japanese internees, 140, 176, 183

zero-population growth, 138

zero-sum contexts, and maturing of Social Security, 32, 150, 162, 186, 204; welfare/warfare, 102f; importance of equity, 192; in the future, 206, 214

Library of Congress Cataloging-in-Publication Data

Tynes, Sheryl R. 1957–
    Turning points in Social Security : from "cruel hoax" to
"sacred entitlement" / Sheryl R. Tynes
    p. cm.
Includes bibliographical references and index.
ISBN 0-8047-2579-9 (cloth : alk. paper)
1. Social Security—United States—History.   I. Title.
HD7125.T96 1996
368.4'3'00973—dc20
95-18238 CIP

This book is printed on acid-free, recycled paper.

Original printing 1996
Last figure below indicates year of this printing:
05 04 03 02 01 00 99 98 97 96